D0040780

WORD PICTURES
IN THE
NEW TESTAMENT

BOOKS BY PROFESSOR A. T. ROBERTSON

The English New Testament as a Whole:
SYLLABUS FOR NEW TESTAMENT STUDY
THE STUDENT'S CHRONOLOGICAL NEW TESTAMENT
STUDIES IN THE NEW TESTAMENT
NEW TESTAMENT HISTORY (AIRPLANE VIEW)

The Greek New Testament:
WORD PICTURES IN THE NEW TESTAMENT (IN SIX VOLS.)
A SHORT GRAMMAR OF THE GREEK NEW TESTAMENT
A GRAMMAR OF THE GREEK NEW TESTAMENT IN THE LIGHT
  OF HISTORICAL RESEARCH
THE MINISTER AND HIS GREEK NEW TESTAMENT
AN INTRODUCTION TO THE TEXTUAL CRITICISM OF THE NEW
  TESTAMENT
STUDIES IN THE TEXT OF THE NEW TESTAMENT

The Gospels and Jesus:
A HARMONY OF THE GOSPELS FOR STUDENTS OF THE LIFE OF
  CHRIST
A COMMENTARY ON MATTHEW
STUDIES IN MARK'S GOSPEL
LUKE THE HISTORIAN IN THE LIGHT OF RESEARCH
A TRANSLATION OF LUKE'S GOSPEL
THE DIVINITY OF CHRIST IN THE GOSPEL OF JOHN
JOHN THE LOYAL (THE MINISTRY OF THE BAPTIST)
THE PHARISEES AND JESUS (STONE LECTURES FOR 1916)
EPOCHS IN THE LIFE OF JESUS
KEYWORDS IN THE TEACHING OF JESUS
THE TEACHING OF JESUS CONCERNING GOD THE FATHER
THE CHRIST OF THE LOGIA (PORTRAITS OF CHRIST IN Q AND
  THE GOSPELS)
THE MOTHER OF JESUS: HER PROBLEMS AND HER GLORY

Paul:
PAUL AND THE INTELLECTUALS (EPISTLE TO THE COLOSSIANS)
EPOCHS IN THE LIFE OF PAUL
PAUL THE INTERPRETER OF CHRIST
PAUL'S JOY IN CHRIST (EPISTLE TO THE PHILIPPIANS)
THE GLORY OF THE MINISTRY (II COR. 2:12-6:10)
THE NEW CITIZENSHIP

Other Studies in the New Testament:
SOME MINOR CHARACTERS IN THE NEW TESTAMENT
STUDIES IN THE EPISTLE OF JAMES
MAKING GOOD IN THE MINISTRY (SKETCH OF JOHN MARK)
TYPES OF PREACHERS IN THE NEW TESTAMENT

Biography:
LIFE AND LETTERS OF JOHN ALBERT BROADUS

WORD PICTURES
IN THE
NEW TESTAMENT

BY

ARCHIBALD THOMAS ROBERTSON
A. M., D. D., LL. D., Litt. D.

PROFESSOR OF NEW TESTAMENT INTERPRETATION
IN THE
SOUTHERN BAPTIST THEOLOGICAL SEMINARY
OF
LOUISVILLE, KENTUCKY

VOLUME II

THE GOSPEL ACCORDING TO LUKE

BROADMAN PRESS
NASHVILLE, TENNESSEE

PRINTED IN THE UNITED STATES OF AMERICA

BY WAY OF INTRODUCTION

There is not room here for a full discussion of all the interesting problems raised by Luke as the author of the Gospel and Acts. One can find them ably handled in the Introduction to Plummer's volume on Luke's Gospel in the *International and Critical Commentary*, in the Introduction to Ragg's volume on Luke's Gospel in the *Westminster Commentaries*, in the Introduction to Easton's *Gospel According to St. Luke*, Hayes' *Synoptic Gospels and the Book of Acts*, Ramsay's *Luke the Physician*, Harnack's *Date of the Acts and the Synoptic Gospels*, Foakes-Jackson and Kirsopp Lake's *Beginnings of Christianity*, Carpenter's *Christianity According to St. Luke*, Cadbury's *The Making of Luke-Acts*, McLachlan's *St. Luke: The Man and His Work*, Robertson's *Luke the Historian in the Light of Research*, to go no further. It is a fascinating subject that appeals to scholars of all shades of opinion.

THE SAME AUTHOR FOR GOSPEL AND ACTS

The author of Acts refers to the Gospel specifically as "the first treatise," *ton prōton logon*, (Acts 1:1) and both are addressed to Theophilus (Luke 1:3; Acts 1:1). He speaks of himself in both books as "me" (*kàmoi*, Luke 1:3) and *I made* (*epoiēsamēn*, Acts 1:1). He refers to himself with others as "we" and "us" as in Acts 16:10, the "we" sections of Acts. The unity of Acts is here assumed until the authorship of Acts is discussed in Volume III. The same style appears in Gospel and Acts, so that the presumption is strongly in support of the author's statement. It is quite possible that the formal Introduction to the Gospel (1:1-4) was intended to apply to the Acts also which has only an introductory clause. Plummer argues that to suppose that the author of Acts imitated the Gospel purposely is to suppose a literary miracle. Even Cadbury, who is not convinced of the Lucan authorship, says: "In my study of Luke and Acts, their unity is a fundamental and illuminating axiom." He adds: "They are not merely two independent writings from the same pen; they are a single continuous work. Acts is neither an appendix nor an afterthought. It is probably an integral part of the author's original plan and purpose."

The Author of Acts a Companion of Paul

The proof of this position belongs to the treatment of Acts, but a word is needed here. The use of "we" and "us" in Acts 16:10 and from 20:6 to the end of chapter 28 shows it beyond controversy if the same man wrote the "we" sections and the rest of the Acts. This proof Harnack has produced with painstaking detail in his *Date of the Acts and the Synoptic Gospels* and in his volume *The Acts of the Apostles* and in his *Luke the Physician*.

This Companion of Paul a Physician

The argument for this position lies in the use of medical terms throughout the Gospel and the Acts. Hobart in his *Medical Language of St. Luke* proves that the author of both Gospel and Acts shows a fondness for medical terms best explained by the fact that he was a physician. Like most enthusiasts he overdid it and some of his proof does not stand the actual test of sifting. Harnack and Hawkins in his *Horae Synopticae* have picked out the most pertinent items which will stand. Cadbury in his *Style and Literary Method of Luke* denies that Luke uses Greek medical words more frequently in proportion than Josephus, Philo, Plutarch, or Lucian. It is to miss the point about Luke merely to count words. It is mainly the interest in medical things shown in Luke and Acts. The proof that Luke is the author of the books does not turn on this fact. It is merely confirmatory. Paul calls Luke "the beloved physician" (*ho iatros ho agapētos*, Col. 4:14), "my beloved physician." Together they worked in the Island of Malta (Acts 28:8–10) where many were healed and Luke shared with Paul in the appreciation of the natives who "came and were healed (*etherapeuonto*) who also honoured us with many honours." The implication there is that Paul wrought miracles of healing (*iasato*), while Luke practised his medical art also. Other notes of the physician's interest will be indicated in the discussion of details like his omitting Mark's apparent discredit of physicians (Mark 5:26) by a milder and more general statement of a chronic case (Luke 8:43).

This Companion and Author Luke

All the Greek manuscripts credit the Gospel to Luke in the title. We should know that Luke wrote these two books if there was no evidence from early writers. Irenaeus definitely ascribes the Gospel to Luke as does Clement of Alexandria, Tertullian, the Muratorian Fragment. Plummer holds that the authorship of the four great Epistles of Paul (I and II Corinthians, Galatians, Romans) which even Baur accepted, is scarcely more certain than the Lukan authorship of the Gospel. Even Renan says: "There is no very strong reason for supposing that Luke was not the author of the Gospel which bears his name."

A Sketch of Luke

His name is not a common one, and is probably a shortened form of *Lukios* and *Lukanos*. Some of the manuscripts of the Gospel actually have as the title *Kata Lukanon*. Dean Plumptre suggests that the Latin poet Lucanus was named after Luke who probably was the family physician when he was born. That is conjecture as well as the notion of Hayes that, since the brothers Gallio and Seneca were uncles of Lucanus they were influenced by Luke to be friendly toward Paul both in Corinth and in Rome. It is probable that Luke was a Greek, certainly a Gentile, possibly a freedman. So this man who wrote more than one-fourth of the New Testament was not a Jew. It is not certain whether his home was in Antioch or in Philippi. It is also uncertain whether he was already converted when Paul met him at Troas. The Codex Bezae has a "we" passage after Acts 11:27 which, if genuine, would bring Luke in contact with Paul before Troas. Hayes thinks that he was a slave boy in the family of Theophilus at Antioch, several conjectures in one. We do not know that Theophilus lived at Antioch. It may have been Rome. But, whether one of Paul's converts or not, he was a loyal friend to Paul. If he lived at Antioch, he could have studied medicine there and the great medical temple of Aesculapius was at Aegae, not far away. As a Greek physician, Luke was a university man and in touch with the science of his day. Greek medicine is the beginning of the science of medicine as it is known today. Tradition calls him a painter, but of that we know nothing. Certainly he was a humanist and a man of culture and broad sympathies and personal charm. He was the first genuine scientist who faced the problem of Christ and of Christianity. It must be said of him that he wrote his books with open mind and not as a credulous enthusiast.

THE DATE OF THE GOSPEL

There are two outstanding facts to mark off the date of this Gospel by Luke. It was later than the Gospel of Mark since Luke makes abundant use of it. It was before the Acts of the Apostles since he definitely refers to it in Acts 1:1.

Unfortunately the precise date of both *termini* is uncertain. There are still some scholars who hold that the author of the Acts shows knowledge of the *Antiquities* of Josephus and so is after A.D. 85, a mistaken position, in my opinion, but a point to be discussed when Acts is reached. Still others more plausibly hold that the Acts was written after the destruction of Jerusalem and that the Gospel of Luke has a definite allusion to that event (Luke 21:20f.), which is interpreted as a prophecy *post eventum* instead of a prediction by Christ a generation beforehand. Many who accept this view hold to authorship of both Acts and Gospel by Luke. I have long held the view, now so ably defended by Harnack, that the Acts of the Apostles closes as it does for the simple and obvious reason that Paul was still a prisoner in Rome. Whether Luke meant the Acts to be used in the trial in Rome, which may or may not have come to pass, is not the point. Some argue that Luke contemplated a third book which would cover the events of the trial and Paul's later career. There is no proof of that view. The outstanding fact is that the book closes with Paul already a prisoner for two years in Rome. If the Acts was written about A.D. 63, as I believe to be the case, then obviously the Gospel comes earlier. How much before we do not know. It so happens that Paul was a prisoner a little over two years in Caesarea. That period gave Luke abundant opportunity for the kind of research of which he speaks in Luke 1:1-4. In Palestine he could have access to persons familiar with the earthly life and teachings of Jesus and to whatever documents were already produced concerning such matters. Luke may have produced the Gospel towards the close of the stay of Paul in Caesarea or during the early part of the first Roman imprisonment, somewhere between A.D. 59 and 62. The other testimony concerns the date of Mark's Gospel which has already been discussed in volume I. There is no real difficulty in the way of the early date of Mark's Gospel.

All the facts that are known admit, even argue for a date by
A.D. 60. If Mark wrote his Gospel in Rome, as is possible,
it would certainly be before A.D. 64, the date of the burning
of Rome by Nero. There are scholars, however, who argue
for a much earlier date for his gospel, even as early as A.D.
50. The various aspects of the Synoptic problem are ably
discussed by Hawkins in his *Horae Synopticae*, by Sanday
and others in *Oxford Studies in the Synoptic Problem*, by
Streeter in his *The Four Gospels*, by Hayes in his *The Synoptic Gospels and the Book of Acts*, by Harnack in his *Date of
the Acts and the Synoptic Gospels*, by Stanton in his *The
Gospels as Historical Documents*, and by many others. My
own views are given at length in my *Studies in Mark's
Gospel* and in *Luke the Historian in the Light of Research*.

THE SOURCES OF THE GOSPEL

In his Preface or Prologue (1:1-4) the author tells us that
he had two kinds of sources, oral and written, and that they
were many, how many we have no way of telling. It is now
generally accepted that we know two of his written sources,
Mark's Gospel and Q or the Logia of Jesus (written by
Matthew, Papias says). Mark is still preserved and it is
not difficult for any one by the use of a harmony of the Gospels to note how Luke made use of Mark, incorporating
what he chose, adapting it in various ways, not using what
did not suit his purposes. The other source we only know
in the non-Markan portions of Matthew and Luke, that is
the material common to both, but not in Mark. This also
can be noted by any one in a harmony. Only it is probable
that this source was more extensive than just the portions
used by both Matthew and Luke. It is probable that both
Matthew and Luke each used portions of the Logia not used
by the other. But there is a large portion of Luke's Gospel
which is different from Mark and Matthew. Some scholars
call this source L. There is little doubt that Luke had an-

other document for the material peculiar to him, but it is also probable that he had several others. He spoke of "many." This applies especially to chapters 9 to 21. But Luke expressly says that he had received help from "eye-witnesses and ministers of the word," in oral form this means. It is, then, probable that Luke made numerous notes of such data and used them along with the written sources at his command. This remark applies particularly to chapters 1 and 2 which have a very distinct Semitic (Aramaic) colouring due to the sources used. It is possible, of course, that Mary the mother of Jesus may have written a statement concerning these important matters or that Luke may have had converse with her or with one of her circle. Ramsay, in his volume, *Was Christ Born at Bethlehem?* shows the likelihood of Luke's contact with Mary or her circle during these two years at Caesarea. Luke handles the data acquired with care and skill as he claims in his Prologue and as the result shows. The outcome is what Renan called the most beautiful book in the world.

The Character of the Book

Literary charm is here beyond dispute. It is a book that only a man with genuine culture and literary genius could write. It has all the simple grace of Mark and Matthew plus an indefinable quality not in these wonderful books. There is a delicate finish of detail and proportion of parts that give the balance and poise that come only from full knowledge of the subject, the chief element in a good style according to Dr. James Stalker. This scientific physician, this man of the schools, this converted Gentile, this devoted friend of Paul, comes to the study of the life of Christ with a trained intellect, with an historian's method of research, with a physician's care in diagnosis and discrimination, with a charm of style all his own, with reverence for and loyalty to Jesus Christ as Lord and Saviour. One could not afford

to give up either of the Four Gospels. They each supplement the other in a wonderful way. John's Gospel is the
greatest book in all the world, reaching the highest heights
of all. But if we had only Luke's Gospel, we should have
an adequate portrait of Jesus Christ as Son of God and Son
of Man. If Mark's is the Gospel for the Romans and
Matthew's for the Jews, the Gospel of Luke is for the Gentile world. He shows the sympathy of Jesus for the poor
and the outcast. Luke understands women and children
and so is the universal Gospel of mankind in all phases and
conditions. It is often called the Gospel of womanhood, of
infancy, of prayer, of praise. We have in Luke the first
Christian hymns. With Luke we catch some glimpses of
the child Jesus for which we are grateful. Luke was a friend
and follower of Paul, and verbal parallels with Paul's Epistles
do occur, but there is no Pauline propaganda in the Gospel
as Moffatt clearly shows (*Intr. to Lit. of the N.T.*, p. 281).
The Prologue is in literary *Koiné* and deserves comparison
with those in any Greek and Latin writers. His style is
versatile and is often coloured by his source. He was a great
reader of the Septuagint as is shown by occasional Hebraisms
evidently due to reading that translation Greek. He has
graciousness and a sense of humour as McLachlan and Ragg
show. Every really great man has a saving sense of humour
as Jesus himself had. Ramsay dares to call Luke, as shown
by the Gospel and Acts, the greatest of all historians not
even excepting Thucydides. Ramsay has done much to
restore Luke to his rightful place in the estimation of modern
scholars. Some German critics used to cite Luke 2:1–7 as a
passage containing more historical blunders than any similar passage in any historian. The story of how papyri and
inscriptions have fully justified Luke in every statement
here made is carefully worked out by Ramsay in his various
books, especially in *The Bearing of Recent Discovery on the
Trustworthiness of the New Testament*. The main feature

of this proof appears also in my *Luke the Historian in the Light of Research*.   So many items, where Luke once stood alone, have been confirmed by recent discoveries that the burden of proof now rests on those who challenge Luke in those cases where he still stands alone.

CONTENTS

THE GOSPEL ACCORDING TO LUKE

THE GOSPEL
ACCORDING TO LUKE

CHAPTER I

1. *Forasmuch as (epeidēper).* Here alone in the N.T., though common in literary Attic. Appears in the papyri. A triple compound (*epei* = since, *dē* = admittedly true, *per* = intensive particle to emphasize importance). *Many (polloi).* How many no one knows, but certainly more than two or three. We know that Luke used the Logia of Jesus written by Matthew in Aramaic (Papias) and Mark's Gospel. Undoubtedly he had other written sources. *Have taken in hand (epecheirēsan).* A literal translation of *epicheireō* (from *cheir*, hand and *epi*, upon). Both Hippocrates and Galen use this word in their introduction to their medical works. Here only in the N.T., though a common literary word. Common in the papyri for undertaking with no idea of failure or blame. Luke does not mean to cast reflection on those who preceded him. The apocryphal gospels were all much later and are not in his mind. Luke had secured fuller information and planned a book on a larger scale and did surpass them with the result that they all perished save Mark's Gospel and what Matthew and Luke possess of the Logia of Jesus. There was still room for Luke's book. That motive influences every author and thus progress is made. *To draw up, a narrative (anataxasthai diēgēsin).* Ingressive aorist middle infinitive. This verb *anataxasthai* has been found only in Plutarch's *Moral.* 968 CD about an elephant "rehearsing" by moonlight certain tricks it had been taught (Moulton and Milligan, *Vocabulary*). That was from memory going regularly through the thing again. But the idea in the word is plain enough. The word is composed of *tassō*, a common verb for arranging things in proper order and *ana*, again. Luke means to say that those before him had made attempts

to rehearse in orderly fashion various matters about Christ. "The expression points to a connected series of narratives in some order (*taxis*), topical or chronological rather than to isolated narratives" (Bruce). "They had produced something more than mere notes or anecdotes" (Plummer). *Diēgēsis* means leading or carrying a thing through, not a mere incident. Galen applies this word some seventy-five times to the writing of Hippocrates. *Which have been fulfilled* (*tōn peplērophorēmenōn*). Perfect passive participle from *plērophoreō* and that from *plērēs* (full) and *pherō* (to bring). Hence to bring or make full. The verb is rare outside of the LXX and the N.T. Papyri examples occur for finishing off a legal matter or a financial matter in full. Deissmann (*Light from the Ancient East*, pp. 86f.) gives examples from the papyri and inscriptions for completing a task or being convinced or satisfied in mind. The same ambiguity occurs here. When used of persons in the N.T. the meaning is to be convinced, or fully persuaded (Rom. 4:21; 14:5; Heb. 6:11; 10:22). When used of things it has the notion of completing or finishing (II Tim. 4:5, 17). Luke is here speaking of "matters" (*pragmatōn*). Luke may refer to the matters connected with Christ's life which have been brought to a close among us or accomplished. Bruce argues plausibly that he means fulness of knowledge "concerning the things which have become widely known among us Christians." In Col. 2:2 we have "fulness of understanding" (*tēs plērophorias tēs suneseōs*). In modern Greek the verb means to inform. The careful language of Luke here really pays a tribute to those who had preceded him in their narratives concerning Christ.

2. *Even as* (*kathōs*). This particle was condemned by the Atticists though occurring occasionally from Aristotle on. It is in the papyri. Luke asserts that the previous narratives had their sound basis. *Delivered unto us* (*paredōsan hēmin*). Second aorist active indicative of *paradidōmi*. Luke received

this tradition along with those who are mentioned above (the many). That is he was not one of the "eyewitnesses." He was a secondary, not a primary, witness of the events. Tradition has come to have a meaning of unreliability with us, but that is not the idea here. Luke means to say that the handing down was dependable, not mere wives' fables. Those who drew up the narratives had as sources of knowledge those who handed down the data. Here we have both written and oral sources. Luke had access to both kinds. *Which from the beginning were eyewitnesses and ministers of the word* (*hoi ap' archēs autoptai kai hupēretai genomenoi tou logou*). "Who" is better than "which" for the article here. The word for *eyewitnesses* (*autoptai*) is an old Greek word and appears in the papyri also. It means seeing with one's own eyes. It occurs here only in the N.T. We have the very word in the medical term *autopsy*. Greek medical writers often had the word. It is a different word from *epoptai* (eyewitness) in II Pet. 1:16, a word used of those who beheld heavenly mysteries. The word for "ministers" (*hupēretai*), under rowers or servants we have had already in Matt. 5:25; 26:58; Mark 14:54, 65, which see. We shall see it again in Luke 4:20 of the attendant in the synagogue. In the sense of a preacher of the gospel as here, it occurs also in Acts 26:16. Here "the word" means the gospel message, as in Acts 6:4; 8:4, etc. *From the beginning* apparently refers to the beginning of the ministry of Jesus as was true of the apostles (Acts 1:22) and of the early apostolic preaching (Acts 10:37–43). The Gospel of Mark follows this plan. The Gospel of Luke goes behind this in chapters 1 and 2 as does Matthew in chapters 1 and 2. But Luke is not here referring to himself. The matters about the childhood of Jesus Christ would not form part of the traditional preaching for obvious reasons.

3. *It seemed good to me also* (*edoxe kamoi*). A natural conclusion and justification of Luke's decision to write his

narrative. They had ample reason to draw up their narratives. Luke has more reason to do so because of his fuller knowledge and wider scope. *Having traced the course of all things (parēkolouthēkoti pāsin).* The perfect active participle of a common verb of the ancient Greek. Literally it means to follow along a thing in mind, to trace carefully. Both meanings occur abundantly in the ancient Greek. Cadbury (Appendix C to *Beginnings of Christianity,* Vol. II, pp. 489ff.) objects to the translation "having traced" here as implying research which the word does not here mean. Milligan (*Vocabulary*) is somewhat impressed by this argument. See my discussion of the point in Chapter XVI of *Studies in the Text of the N.T.* (The Implications in Luke's Preface) where the point is made that Luke here claims fulness of knowledge before he began to write his book. He had the traditions of the eyewitnesses and ministers of the word and the narratives previously drawn up. Whether he was a personal contemporary with any or all of these events we do not know and it is not particularly pertinent. He had *mentally* followed along by the side of these events. Galen used this verb for the investigation of symptoms. Luke got himself ready to write before he began by full and accurate knowledge of the subject. *Akribōs* (accurately) means going into minute details, from *akron,* the topmost point. And he did it *from the first (anōthen).* He seems to refer to the matters in Chapters 1:5 to 2:52, the Gospel of the Infancy. *In order (kathexēs).* Chronological order in the main following Mark's general outline. But in 9:51 to 18:10 the order is often topical. He has made careful investigation and his work deserves serious consideration. *Most excellent Theophilus (kratiste Theophile).* The name means god-lover or god-beloved. He may have been a believer already. He was probably a Gentile. Ramsay holds that "most excellent" was a title like "Your Excellency" and shows that he held office, perhaps a Knight. So of Felix (Acts 23:26) and Festus

(Acts 26:25). The adjective does not occur in the dedication in Acts 1:1.

4. *Mightest know* (*epignōis*). Second aorist active sub-junctive of *epiginōskō*. Full knowledge (*epi-*), in addition to what he already has. *The certainty* (*tēn asphaleian*). Make no slip (*sphallō*, to totter or fall, and *a* privative). Luke promises a reliable narrative. "Theophilus shall know that the faith which he has embraced has an impregnable histor-ical foundation" (Plummer). *The things* (*logōn*). Literally "words," the details of the words in the instruction. *Wast instructed* (*katēchēthēs*). First aorist passive indicative. Not in O.T. and rare in ancient Greek. Occurs in the papyri. The word *ēcheō* is our word echo (cf. I Thess. 1:8 for *exēchētai*, has sounded forth). *Katēcheō* is to sound down, to din, to instruct, to give oral instruction. Cf. I Cor. 14:9; Acts 21:21, 24; 18:25; Gal. 6:6. Those men doing the teaching were called *catechists* and those receiving it were called *catechu-mens*. Whether Theophilus was still a catechumen is not known. This Preface by Luke is in splendid literary *Koiné* and is not surpassed by those in any Greek writer (Herodo-tus, Thucydides, Polybius). It is entirely possible that Luke was familiar with this habit of Greek historians to write prefaces since he was a man of culture.

5. *There was* (*egeneto*). Not the usual *ēn* for "was," but there arose or came into notice. With this verse the literary *Koiné* of verses 1 to 4 disappears. To the end of chapter 2 we have the most Hebraistic (Aramaic) passage in Luke's writings, due evidently to the use of documents or notes of oral tradition. Plummer notes a series of such documents ending with 1:80, 2:40, 2:52. If the mother of Jesus was still alive, Luke could have seen her. She may have written in Aramaic an account of these great events. Natural re-serve would keep her from telling too much and from too early publicity. Luke, as a physician, would take special interest in her birth report. The supernatural aspects dis-

turb only those who do not admit the real Incarnation of Jesus Christ and who are unable to believe that God is superior to nature and that the coming of the Son of God to earth justifies such miraculous manifestations of divine power. Luke tells his story from the standpoint of Mary as Matthew gives his from the standpoint of Joseph. The two supplement each other. We have here the earliest documentary evidence of the origins of Christianity that has come down to us (Plummer). *Herod, King of Judea* (*Hērōidou basileōs tēs Ioudaias*). This note of time locates the events before the death of Herod the Great (as he was called later), appointed King of Judea by the Roman Senate B.C. 40 at the suggestion of Octavius and Antony. He died B.C. 4. *Of the course of Abijah* (*ex ephēmerias Abia*). Not in old Greek, but in LXX and modern Greek. Papyri have a verb derived from it, *ephēmereō*. Daily service (Neh. 13:30; I Chron. 25:8) and then a course of priests who were on duty for a week (I Chron. 23:6; 28:13). There were 24 such courses and that of Abijah was the eighth (I Chron. 24:10; II Chron. 8:14). Only four of these courses (Jedaiah, Immer, Pashur, Harim) returned from Babylon, but these four were divided into twenty-four with the old names. Each of these courses did duty for eight days, sabbath to sabbath, twice a year. On sabbaths the whole course did duty. At the feast of tabernacles all twenty-four courses were present. *Of the daughters of Aaron* (*ek tōn thugaterōn Aarōn*). "To be a priest and married to a priest's daughter was a double distinction" (Plummer). Like a preacher married to a preacher's daughter.

6. *Righteous before God* (*dikaioi enantion tou theou*). Old Testament conception and idiom. Cf. 2:25 about Simeon. Expanded in Old Testament language. Picture of "noblest product of Old Testament education" (Ragg) is Zacharias and Elisabeth, Mary and Joseph, Simeon and Anna who were "privileged to see with clear eyes the dawn of the New Testament revelation."

7. *Because that* (*kathoti*). Good Attic word, according to what. Only in Luke and Acts in the N.T. In the papyri. *Well stricken in years* (*probebēkotes en tais hēmerais autōn*). Wycliff has it right: "Had gone far in their days." Perfect active participle. See also verse 18.

8. *While he executed the priest's office* (*en tōi hierateuein auton*). A favourite idiom in Luke, *en* with the articular infinitive and the accusative of general reference where the genitive absolute could have been used or a temporal conjunction and finite verb. It is proper Greek, but occurs often in the LXX, which Luke read, particularly in imitation of the Hebrew infinitive construct. The word *hierateuō* does not appear in the ancient Greek, but in the LXX and this one example in Luke. It is on the Rosetta Stone and the early inscriptions so that the word was simply applied by the LXX translators from current usage.

9. *His lot was* (*elache*). Literally, *he obtained the lot*. Second aorist active indicative of *lagchanō*, to obtain by lot, a very old verb from Homer on. It is used either with the genitive as here, or the accusative as in Acts 1:17; II Pet. 1:1. Papyri show examples with the accusative. It was only once in a lifetime that a priest obtained the lot of going (*eiselthōn*, here nominative aorist active participle agreeing with the subject of *elache*) into the sanctuary (*ton naon*, not *to hieron*, the outer courts) and burning incense on the golden altar. "It was the great moment of Zacharias's life, and his heart was no doubt alert for the supernatural" (Ragg). The fortunate lot was "a white stone" to which Rev. 2:17 may refer. *Burn incense* (*tou thumiasai*). Here only in the N.T. Occurs on inscriptions. Hobart finds it used by medical writers for fumigating herbs. "Ascending the steps to the Holy Place, the priests spread the coals on the golden altar, and arranged the incense, and the chief operating priest was then left alone within the Holy Place to await the signal of the president to burn the incense. It was prob-

ably at this time that the angel appeared to Zacharias"
(Vincent).

10. *Were praying without* (*ēn proseuchomenon exō*). Periphrastic imperfect indicative picturing the posture of the
people while the clouds of incense rose on the inside of the
sanctuary.

11. *Appeared* (*ōphthē*). First aorist passive indicative.
It is the form used by Paul of the resurrection appearances
of Jesus (I Cor. 15:5–8). There is no use in trying to explain
away the reality of the angel. We must choose between ad-
mitting an objective appearance and a myth (Plummer).

13. *Is heard* (*eisēkousthē*). First aorist passive indicative.
A sort of timeless aorist, "was heard" when made, and so
"is heard" now. Probably the prayer was for a son in spite
of the great age of Elisabeth, though the Messianic redemption is possible also. *John* (*Iōanēn*). The word means that
God is gracious. The mention of the name should have
helped Zacharias to believe. The message of the angel
(verses 13 to 17) takes on a metrical form when turned into
Hebrew (Ragg) and it is a prose poem in Greek and English
like 1:30–33, 35–37, 42–45, 46–55, 68–70; 2:10–12, 14, 29–32,
34–35. Certainly Luke has preserved the earliest Christian
hymns in their oldest sources. He is the first critic of the
sources of the Gospels and a scholarly one.

14. *Gladness* (*agalliasis*). Only in the LXX and N.T.
so far as known. A word for extreme exultation. *Rejoice*
(*charēsontai*). Second future passive indicative. The coming of a prophet will indeed be an occasion for rejoicing.

15. *Strong drink* (*sikera*). A Hebrew word transliterated
into Greek, an intoxicating drink. Here only in the N.T.
John was to be a personal "dry" or Nazarite (Num. 6:3).
Shall not drink (*ou mē piēi*). Strong prohibition, double
negative and second aorist subjunctive. *The Holy Ghost*
(*pneumatos hagiou*). The Holy Spirit in contrast to the
physical excitement of strong drink (Plummer). Luke uses

this phrase 53 times, 12 in the Gospel, Mark and John 4 each, Matthew 5 times. *Even from his mother's womb* (*eti ek koilias mētros autou*). A manifest Hebraism. Cf. verse 41.

17. *Before his face* (*enōpion autou*). Not in the ancient Greek, but common in the papyri as in LXX and N.T. It is a vernacular *Koiné* word, adverb used as preposition from adjective *enōpios*, and that from *ho en ōpi ōn* (the one who is in sight). *Autou* here seems to be "the Lord their God" in verse 16 since the Messiah has not yet been mentioned, though he was to be actually the Forerunner of the Messiah. *In the spirit and power of Elijah* (*en pneumati kai dunamei Ēleiā*). See Isa. 40:1–11; Mal. 3:1–5. John will deny that he is actually Elijah in person, as they expected (John 1:21), but Jesus will call him Elijah in spirit (Mark 9:12 = Matt. 17:12). *Hearts of fathers* (*kardias paterōn*). Paternal love had died out. This is one of the first results of conversion, the revival of love in the home. *Wisdom* (*phronēsei*). Not *sophia*, but a word for practical intelligence. *Prepared* (*kateskeuasmenon*). Perfect passive participle, state of readiness for Christ. This John did. This is a marvellous forecast of the character and career of John the Baptist, one that should have caught the faith of Zacharias.

18. *Whereby* (*kata ti*). According to what. It was too good to be true and Zacharias demanded proof and gives the reason (for, *gar*) for his doubt. He had prayed for this blessing and was now sceptical like the disciples in the house of Mary about the return of Peter (Acts 12:14f.).

19. *Gabriel* (*Gabriēl*). The Man of God (Dan. 8:6; 9:21). The other angel whose name is given in Scripture is Michael (Dan. 10:13, 21; Jude 9; Rev. 12:7). The description of himself is a rebuke to the doubt of Zacharias.

20. *Thou shalt be silent* (*esēi siōpōn*). Volitive future periphrastic. *Not able to speak* (*mē dunamenos lalēsai*). Negative repetition of the same statement. His dumbness will continue "until" (*achri hēs hēmeras*) the events come to

pass "because" (*anth' hōn*). The words were to become
reality in due season (*kairon*, not *chronos*, time).

21. *Were waiting* (*ēn prosdokōn*). Periphrastic imperfect
again. An old Greek verb for expecting. Appears in papyri
and inscriptions. It denotes mental direction whether hope
or fear. *They marvelled* (*ethaumazon*). Imperfect tense,
were wondering. The Talmud says that the priest remained
only a brief time in the sanctuary. *While he tarried* (*en tōi
chronizein*). See verse 8 for the same idiom.

22. *Perceived* (*epegnōsan*). Second aorist indicative.
Clearly knew because he was not able to pronounce the
benediction from the steps (Num. 6:24–26). *Continued
making signs* (*ēn dianeuōn*). Periphrastic imperfect again.
He nodded and beckoned back and forth (*dia*, between).
Further proof of a vision that caused his dumbness.

23. *Ministration* (*leitourgias*). Our word liturgy. A
common word in ancient Greek for public service, work for
the people (*leōs ergon*). It is common in the papyri for the
service of the Egyptian priesthood as we see it in the LXX
of Hebrew priests (see also Heb. 8:6; 9:21; II Cor. 9:12;
Phil. 2:17, 30).

24. *Conceived* (*sunelaben*). Luke uses this word eleven
times and it occurs only five other times in the N.T. It is
a very old and common Greek word. He alone in the N.T.
has it for conceiving offspring (1:24, 31, 36; 2:21) though
James 1:15 uses it of lust producing sin. Hobart (*Medical
Language of Luke*, p. 91) observes that Luke has almost as
many words for pregnancy and barrenness as Hippocrates
(*en gastri echein*, 21:23; *egkuos*, 2:5; *steira*, 1:7; *ateknos*, 20:28).
Hid (*periekruben*). Only here in the N.T., but in late *Koinē*
writers. Usually considered second aorist active indicative
from *perikruptō*, though it may be the imperfect indicative
of a late form *perikrubō*. If it is aorist it is the constative
aorist. The preposition *peri* makes it mean completely (on
all sides) hid.

25. *My reproach* (*oneidos mou*). Keenly felt by a Jewish wife because the husband wanted an heir and because of the hope of the Messiah, and because of the mother's longing for a child.

26. *Was sent* (*apestalē*). Second aorist passive indicative of *apostellō* from which *apostle* comes. The angel Gabriel is God's messenger to Mary as to Zacharias (1:19).

27. *Betrothed* (*emnēsteumenēn*). Perfect passive participle. Betrothal usually lasted a year and unfaithfulness on the part of the bride was punished with death (Deut. 23:24f.).

28. *Highly favoured* (*kecharitōmenē*). Perfect passive participle of *charitoō* and means endowed with grace (*charis*), enriched with grace as in Eph. 1:6, *non ut mater gratiae, sed ut filia gratiae* (Bengel). The Vulgate *gratiae plena* "is right, if it means 'full of grace *which thou hast received*'; wrong, if it means 'full of grace *which thou hast to bestow*'" (Plummer). The oldest MSS. do not have "Blessed art thou among women" here, but in verse 42.

29. *Cast in her mind* (*dielogizeto*). Imperfect indicative. Note aorist *dietarachthē*. Common verb for reckoning up different reasons. She was both upset and puzzled.

30. *Favour* (*charin*). Grace. Same root as *chairō* (rejoice) and *charitoō* in verse 28. To find favour is a common O.T. phrase. *Charis* is a very ancient and common word with a variety of applied meanings. They all come from the notion of sweetness, charm, loveliness, joy, delight, like words of grace, Luke 4:22, growing grace, Eph. 4:29, with grace, Col. 4:6. The notion of kindness is in it also, especially of God towards men as here. It is a favourite word for Christianity, the Gospel of the grace of God (Acts 20:24) in contrast with law or works (John 1:16). Gratitude is expressed also (Luke 6:32), especially to God (Rom. 6:17). *With God* (*para tōi theōi*). Beside God.

31. *Conceive in thy womb* (*sullēmpsēi en gastri*). Adding *en gastri* to the verb of 1:24. Same idiom in Isa. 7:14 of

Immanuel. *Jesus* (*Iēsoun*). As to Joseph in Matt. 1:21, but without the explanation of the meaning. See on Matthew.

32. *The Son of the Most High* (*huios Hupsistou*). There is no article in the Greek, but the use of Most High in verse 35 clearly of God as here. In Luke 6:35 we find "sons of the Most High" (*huioi Hupsistou*) so that we cannot insist on deity here, though that is possible. The language of II Sam. 7:14 and Isa. 9:7 is combined here.

33. *Shall be no end* (*ouk estai telos*). Luke reports the perpetuity of this Davidic kingdom over the house of Jacob with no Pauline interpretation of the spiritual Israel though that was the true meaning as Luke knew. Joseph was of the house of David (Luke 1:27) and Mary also apparently (Luke 2:5).

35. *Shall overshadow thee* (*episkiasei*). A figure of a cloud coming upon her. Common in ancient Greek in the sense of obscuring and with accusative as of Peter's shadow in Acts 5:15. But we have seen it used of the shining bright cloud at the Transfiguration of Jesus (Matt. 17:5 = Mark 9:7 = Luke 9:34). Here it is like the Shekinah glory which suggests it (Ex. 40:38) where the cloud of glory represents the presence and power of God. *Holy, the Son of God* (*Hagion huios theou*). Here again the absence of the article makes it possible for it to mean "Son of God." See Matt. 5:9. But this title, like the Son of Man (*Ho huios tou anthrōpou*) was a recognized designation of the Messiah. Jesus did not often call himself Son of God (Matt. 27:43), but it is assumed in his frequent use of the Father, the Son (Matt. 11:27; Luke 10:21; John 5:19ff.). It is the title used by the Father at the baptism (Luke 3:22) and on the Mount of Transfiguration (Luke 9:35). The wonder of Mary would increase at these words. The Miraculous Conception or Virgin Birth of Jesus is thus plainly set forth in Luke as in Matthew. The fact that Luke was a physician gives added interest to his report.

36. *Kinswoman* (*suggenis*). Not necessarily cousin, but simply relative.

37. *No word* (*ouk rhēma*). *Rhēma* brings out the single item rather than the whole content (*logos*). So in verse 38.

39. *Arose* (*anastāsa*). Luke is very fond of this word, sixty times against twenty-two in the rest of the N.T. *Into the hill country* (*eis tēn orinēn*). Luke uses this adjective twice in this context (here and 1:65) instead of *to oros*, the mountains. It is an old word and is in the LXX, but nowhere else in the N.T. The name of the city where Zacharias lived is not given unless Judah here means Juttah (Josh. 15:55). Hebron was the chief city of this part of Judea.

40. *Saluted* (*ēspasato*). Her first glance at Elisabeth showed the truth of the angel's message. The two mothers had a bond of sympathy.

41. *Leaped* (*eskirtēsen*). A common enough incident with unborn children (Gen. 25:22), but Elisabeth was filled with the Holy Spirit to understand what had happened to Mary.

42. *With a loud cry* (*kraugēi megalēi*). A moment of ecstatic excitement. *Blessed art thou* (*eulogēmenē*). Perfect passive participle. A Hebraistic equivalent for the superlative.

43. *The mother of my Lord* (*hē mētēr tou Kuriou mou*). See Psa. 110:1. Only by the help of the Holy Spirit could Elisabeth know that Mary was to be the mother of the Messiah.

45. *For* (*hoti*). It is not certain whether *hoti* here is "that" or "because." It makes good sense either way. See also 7:16. This is the first beatitude in the New Testament and it is similar to the last one in the Gospels spoken to Thomas to discourage his doubt (John 20:29). Elisabeth wishes Mary to have full faith in the prophecy of the angel. This song of Elisabeth is as real poetry as is that of Mary (1:47–55) and Zacharias (1:68–70). All three spoke under the power of the Holy Spirit. These are the first New Testa-

ment hymns and they are very beautiful. Plummer notes four strophes in Mary's Magnificat (46–48, 49 and 50, 51–53, 54 and 55). Every idea here occurs in the Old Testament, showing that Mary's mind was full of the spiritual message of God's word.

46. *Doth magnify* (*megalunei*). Latin, *magnificat*. Harnack argues that this is also the song of Elisabeth because a few Latin MSS. have it so, but Mary is correct. She draws her material from the O.T. and sings in the noblest strain.

47. *Hath rejoiced* (*ēgalliasen*). This is aorist active indicative. Greek tenses do not correspond to those in English. The verb *agalliaō* is a Hellenistic word from the old Greek *agallō*. It means to exult. See the substantive *agalliasis* in Luke 1:14, 44. Mary is not excited like Elisabeth, but breathes a spirit of composed rapture. *My spirit* (*to pneuma mou*). One need not press unduly the difference between "soul" (*psuchē*) in verse 46 and "spirit" here. Bruce calls them synonyms in parallel clauses. Vincent argues that the soul is the principle of individuality while the spirit is the point of contact between God and man. It is doubtful, however, if the trichotomous theory of man (body, soul, and spirit) is to be insisted on. It is certain that we have an inner spiritual nature for which various words are used in Mark 12:30. Even the distinction between intellect, emotions, and will is challenged by some psychologists. *God my Saviour* (*tōi theōi tōi sotēri mou*). Article with each substantive. God is called Saviour in the O.T. (Deut. 32:15, Psa. 24:5; 95:1).

48. *The low estate* (*tēn tapeinōsin*). The bride of a carpenter and yet to be the mother of the Messiah. Literal sense here as in 1:52. *Shall call me blessed* (*makariousin me*). So-called Attic future of an old verb, to felicitate. Elisabeth had already given her a beatitude (*makaria*, 1:45). Another occurs in 11:27. But this is a very different thing from the

worship of Mary (Mariolatry) by Roman Catholics. See my *The Mother of Jesus: Her Problems and Her Glory.*

50. *Fear* (*phoboumenois*). Dative of the present middle participle. Here it is reverential fear as in Acts 10:2; Col. 3:22. The bad sense of dread appears in Matt. 21:46 Mark 6:20, Luke 12:4.

51. *Showed strength* (*epoiēsen kratos*). "Made might" (Wycliff). A Hebrew conception as in Psa. 118:15. Plummer notes six aorist indicatives in this sentence (51–63), neither corresponding to our English idiom, which translates here by "hath" each time. *Imagination* (*dianoiāi*). Intellectual insight, moral understanding.

52. *Princes* (*dunastas*). Our word dynasty is from this word. It comes from *dunamai*, to be able.

54. *Hath holpen* (*antelabeto*). Second aorist middle indicative. A very common verb. It means to lay hold of with a view to help or succour. *Servant* (*paidos*). Here it means "servant," not "son" or "child," its usual meaning.

58. *Had magnified* (*emegalunen*). Aorist active indicative. Same verb as in verse 46. *Rejoiced with her* (*sunechairon autēi*). Imperfect tense and pictures the continual joy of the neighbours, accented also by *sun-* (cf. Phil. 2:18) in its mutual aspect.

59. *Would have called* (*ekaloun*). Conative imperfect, tried to call.

62. *Made signs* (*eneneuon*). Imperfect tense, repeated action as usual when making signs. In 1:22 the verb used of Zacharias is *dianeuōn*. *What he would have him called* (*to ti an theloi kaleisthai auto*). Note article *to* with the indirect question, accusative of general reference. The optative with *an* is here because it was used in the direct question (cf. Acts 17:18), and is simply retained in the indirect. *What would he wish him to be called?* (*if he could speak*), a conclusion of the fourth-class condition.

63. *Tablet* (*pinakidion*). Diminutive of *pinakis*. In Aris-

totle and the papyri for writing tablet, probably covered with wax. Sometimes it was a little table, like Shakespeare's "the table of my memory" (Hamlet, i. 5). It was used also of a physician's note-book. *Wrote, saying (egrapsen legōn)*. Hebrew way of speaking (II Kings 10:6).

64. *Immediately (parachrēma)*. Nineteen times in the N.T., seventeen in Luke. *Opened (aneōichthē)*. First aorist passive indicative with double augment. The verb suits "mouth," but not "tongue" *(glōssa)*. It is thus a zeugma with tongue. Loosed or some such verb to be supplied.

65. *Fear (phobos)*. Not terror, but religious awe because of contact with the supernatural as in the case of Zacharias (1:12). Were noised abroad *(dielaleito)*. Imperfect passive. Occurs in Polybius. In the N.T. only here and Luke 6:11. It was continuous talk back and forth between *(dia)* the people.

66. *What then (ti ara)*. With all these supernatural happenings they predicted the marvellous career of this child. Note *Ti, what*, not *Tis, who*. Cf. Acts 12:18. *They laid them up (ethento*, second aorist middle indicative) as Mary did (2:19). *The hand of the Lord (cheir Kuriou)*. Luke's explanation in addition to the supernatural events. The expression occurs only in Luke's writing (Acts 11:21, 13:11).

67. *Prophesied (eprophēteusen)*. Under the guidance of the Holy Spirit. This *Benedictus (Eulogētos, Blessed)* of Zacharias (68 to 79) may be what is referred to in verse 64 "he began to speak blessing God" *(eulogōn)*. Nearly every phrase here is found in the O.T. (Psalms and Prophets). He, like Mary, was full of the Holy Spirit and had caught the Messianic message in its highest meaning.

68. *Hath visited (epeskepsato)*. An old Greek word with a Hebraic colouring to look into with a view to help. The papyri have plenty of examples of the verb in the sense of inspecting, examining. *Redemption (lutrōsin)* here originally

referred to political redemption, but with a moral and spiritual basis (verses 75, 77).

69. *Horn of salvation (keras sōtērias).* A common metaphor in the O.T. (I Sam. 2:10; II Sam. 23:3, etc.). It represents strength like the horns of bulls. Cf. Psa. 132:17.

70. *Since the world began (ap' aiōnos).* Better "from of old" (Weymouth, American Revision).

73. *The oath which he sware (horkon hon ōmosen).* Antecedent attracted to case of the relative. The oath appears in Gen. 22:16–18. The oppression of the Gentiles seems to be in the mind of Zacharias. It is not certain how clearly he grasped the idea of the spiritual Israel as Paul saw it in Galatians and Romans.

74. *Delivered (rhusthentas).* First aorist passive participle of an old verb, *rhuomai.* The accusative case appears, where the dative could have been used to agree with *hēmin,* because of the infinitive *latreuein* (verse 74) *to serve* (from *latros,* for hire). But Plato uses the word of service for God so that the bad sense does not always exist.

75. *In holiness and righteousness (en hosiotēti kai dikaiosunēi).* Not a usual combination (Eph. 4:24; Tit. 1:8; I Thess. 2:10). The Godward and the manward aspects of conduct (Bruce). *Hosios,* the eternal principles of right, *dikaios,* the rule of conduct before men.

76. *Yea and thou (kai su de).* Direct address to the child with forecast of his life (cf. 1:13–17). *Prophet (prophētēs).* The word here directly applied to the child. Jesus will later call John a prophet and more than a prophet. *The Lord (Kuriou).* Jehovah as in 1:16.

77. *Knowledge of salvation (gnōsin sōtērias).* "This is the aim and end of the work of the Forerunner" (Plummer).

78. *Tender mercy (splagchna eleous).* Bowels of mercy literally (I Peter. 3:8; James 3:11). Revised margin has it, hearts of mercy. *The dayspring from on high (anatolē ex hupsous).* Literally, rising from on high, like the rising sun

or stars (Isa. 60:19). The word is used also of a sprouting plant or branch (Jer. 23:5; Zech. 6:12), but that does not suit here. *Shall visit* (*epeskepsetai*), correct text, cf. 1:68.

79. *To shine upon* (*epiphānai*). First aorist active infinitive of *epiphainō* (liquid verb). An old verb to give light, to shine upon, like the sun or stars. See also Acts 27:20; Tit. 2:11; 3:4. *The shadow of death* (*skiāi thanatou*). See Psa. 107:10, where darkness and shadow of death are combined as here. Cf. also Isa. 9:1. See on Matt. 4:16. *To guide* (*tou kateuthūnai*). Genitive of the articular infinitive of purpose. The light will enable them in the dark to see how to walk in a straight path that leads to "the way of peace." We are still on that road, but so many stumble for lack of light, men and nations.

80. *Grew* (*ēuxane*). Imperfect active, was growing. *Waxed strong* (*ekrataiouto*). Imperfect again. The child kept growing in strength of body and spirit. *His shewing* (*anadeixeōs autou*). Here alone in the N.T. It occurs in Plutarch and Polybius. The verb appears in a sacrificial sense. The boy, as he grew, may have gone up to the passover and may have seen the boy Jesus (Luke 2:42–52), but he would not know that he was to be the Messiah. So these two boys of destiny grew on with the years, the one in the desert hills near Hebron after Zacharias and Elisabeth died, the other, the young Carpenter up in Nazareth, each waiting for "his shewing unto Israel."

CHAPTER II

1. *Decree from Caesar Augustus* (*dogma para Kaisaros Augoustou*). Old and common word from *dokeō*, to think, form an opinion. No such decree was given by Greek or Roman historians and it was for long assumed by many scholars that Luke was in error. But papyri and inscriptions have confirmed Luke on every point in these crucial verses 2:1–7. See W. M. Ramsay's books (*Was Christ Born at Bethelehem? Luke the Physician. The Bearing of Recent Discovery on the Trustworthiness of the N.T.*). *The World* (*tēn oikoumenēn*). Literally, *the inhabited* (*land, gēn*). Inhabited by the Greeks, then by the Romans, then the whole world (Roman world, the world ruled by Rome). So Acts 11:28; 17:6. *Should be enrolled* (*apographesthai*). It was a census, not a taxing, though taxing generally followed and was based on the census. This word is very old and common. It means to write or copy off for the public records, to register.

2. *The first enrolment* (*apographē prōtē*). A definite allusion by Luke to a series of censuses instituted by Augustus, the second of which is mentioned by him in Acts 5:37. This second one is described by Josephus and it was supposed by some that Luke confused the two. But Ramsay has shown that a periodical fourteen-year census in Egypt is given in dated papyri back to A.D. 20. The one in Acts 5:37 would then be A.D. 6. This is in the time of Augustus. The first would then be B.C. 8 in Egypt. If it was delayed a couple of years in Palestine by Herod the Great for obvious reasons, that would make the birth of Christ about B.C. 6 which agrees with the other known data. *When Quirinius* (*Kurēniou*). Genitive absolute. Here again Luke has been at-

tacked on the ground that Quirinius was only governor of
Syria once and that was A.D. 6 as shown by Josephus (*Ant.*
XVIII. I. 1). But Ramsay has proven by inscriptions that
Quirinius was twice in Syria and that Luke is correct here
also. See summary of the facts in my *Luke the Historian in
the Light of Research*, pp. 118–29.

3. *Each to his own city* (*hekastos eis tēn heautou polin*). A
number of papyri in Egypt have the heading enrolment by
household (*apographē kat' oikian*). Here again Luke is
vindicated. Each man went to the town where his family
register was kept.

5. *To enrol himself with Mary* (*apograpsasthai sun Ma-
riam*). Direct middle. "With Mary" is naturally taken
with the infinitive as here. If so, that means that Mary's
family register was in Bethlehem also and that she also be-
longed to the house of David. It is possible to connect
"with Mary" far back with "went up" (*anebē*) in verse 4,
but it is unnatural to do so. There is no real reason for
doubting that Mary herself was a descendant of David and
that is the obvious way to understand Luke's genealogy of
Jesus in Luke 3:23–38). The Syriac Sinaitic expressly says
that both Joseph and Mary were of the house and city of
David. *Betrothed* (*emnēsteumenēn*). Same verb as in 1:27,
but here it really means "married" or "espoused" as Matt.
1:24f. shows. Otherwise she could not have travelled with
Joseph. *Great with child* (*enkuōi*). Only here in N.T.
Common Greek word.

6. *That she should be delivered* (*tou tekein autēn*). For the
bearing the child as to her. A neat use of the articular infinitive, second aorist active, with the accusative of general
reference. From *tiktō*, common verb.

7. *Her firstborn* (*ton prōtotokon*). The expression naturally means that she afterwards had other children and we
read of brothers and sisters of Jesus. There is not a particle of evidence for the notion that Mary refused to bear

other children because she was the mother of the Messiah. *Wrapped in swaddling clothes (esparganōsen).* From *sparganon*, a swathing band. Only here and verse 12 in the N.T., but in Euripides, Aristotle, Hippocrates, Plutarch. Frequent in medical works. *In a manger (en phatnēi).* In a crib in a stall whether in a cave (Justin Martyr) or connected with the inn we do not know. The cattle may have been out on the hills or the donkeys used in travelling may have been feeding in this stall or another near. *In the inn (en tōi katalumati).* A lodging-house or khan, poor enough at best, but there was not even room in this public place because of the crowds for the census. See the word also in Luke 22:11 and Mark 14:14 with the sense of guest-room (cf. I Kings 1:13). It is the Hellenistic equivalent for *katagōgeion* and appears also in one papyrus. See Ex. 4:24. There would sometimes be an inner court, a range or arches, an open gallery round the four sides. On one side of the square, outside the wall, would be stables for the asses and camels, buffaloes and goats. Each man had to carry his own food and bedding.

8. *Abiding in the field (agraulountes).* From *agros*, field and *aulē*, court. The shepherds were making the field their court. Plutarch and Strabo use the word. *Keeping watch (phulassontes phulakas).* Cognate accusative. They were bivouacking by night and it was plainly mild weather. In these very pastures David had fought the lion and the bear to protect the sheep (I Sam. 17:34f.). The plural here probably means that they watched by turns. The flock may have been meant for the temple sacrifices. There is no way to tell.

9. *Stood by them (epestē autois).* Ingressive aorist active indicative. Stepped by their side. The same word in Acts 12:7 of the angel there. Paul uses it in the sense of standing by in Acts 22:20. It is a common old Greek word, *ephistēmi. Were sore afraid (ephobēthēsan phobon megan).*

First aorist passive indicative with cognate accusative (the passive sense gone), they feared a great fear.

10. *I bring you good tidings of great joy* (*euaggelizomai hūmin charan megalēn*). Wycliff, "I evangelize to you a great joy." The active verb *euaggelizō* occurs only in late Greek writers, LXX, a few papyri examples, and the N.T. The middle (deponent) appears from Aristophanes on. Luke and Paul employ both substantive *euaggelion* and verb *euaggelizō* very frequently. It is to Paul's influence that we owe their frequency and popularity in the language of Christendom (George Milligan, *The Epistles to the Thessalonians*, p. 143). The other Gospels do not have the verb save Matt. 11:5 and that in a quotation (Isa. 61:1).

11. *Is born* (*etechthē*). First aorist passive indicative from *tiktō*. Was born. *Saviour* (*sōtēr*). This great word is common in Luke and Paul and seldom elsewhere in the N.T. (Bruce). The people under Rome's rule came to call the emperor "Saviour" and Christians took the word and used it of Christ. See inscriptions (Deissmann, *Light from the Ancient East*, p. 344). *Christ the Lord* (*Christos Kurios*). This combination occurs nowhere else in the N.T. and it is not clear what it really means. Luke is very fond of *Kurios* (*Lord*) where the other Gospels have Jesus. It may mean "Christ the Lord," "Anointed Lord," "Messiah, Lord," "The Messiah, the Lord," "An Anointed One, a Lord," or "Lord Messiah." It occurs once in the LXX (Lam. 4:20) and is in Ps. of Sol. 17:36. Ragg suggests that our phrase "the Lord Jesus Christ" is really involved in "A Saviour (Jesus) which is Christ the Lord." See on Matt. 1:1 for Christ and Matt. 21:3 for Lord.

13. *Host* (*stratias*). A military term for a band of soldiers common in the ancient Greek. Bengel says: "Here the army announces peace." *Praising* (*ainountōn*). Construction according to sense (plural, though *stratias* is singular).

14. *Among men in whom he is well pleased* (*en anthrōpois*

eudokias). The Textus Receptus (Authorized Version also
has *eudokia*, but the genitive *eudokias* is undoubtedly correct, supported by the oldest and best uncials. (Aleph, A
B D W). C has a lacuna here. Plummer justly notes how
in this angelic hymn Glory and Peace correspond, in the
highest and on earth, to God and among men of goodwill.
It would be possible to connect "on earth" with "the highest" and also to have a triple division. There has been much
objection raised to the genitive *eudokias*, the correct text.
But it makes perfectly good sense and better sense. As a
matter of fact real peace on earth exists only among those
who are the subjects of God's goodwill, who are character-
ized by goodwill toward God and man. This word *eudokia*
we have already had in Matt. 11:26. It does not occur in the
ancient Greek. The word is confined to Jewish and Christian writings, though the papyri furnish instances of *eudokē-
sis*. Wycliff has it "to men of goodwill."

15. *Said to one another* (*elaloun pros allēlous*). Imperfect
tense, inchoative, "began to speak," each to the other. It
suggests also repetition, they kept saying, *Now* (*dē*). A
particle of urgency. *This thing* (*to rhēma touto*). A Hebraistic and vernacular use of *rhēma* (something said) as something done. See on Luke 1:65. The ancient Greek used
logos in this same way.

16. *With haste* (*speusantes*). Aorist active participle of
simultaneous action. *Found* (*aneuran*). Second aorist active indicative of a common Greek verb *aneuriskō*, but only
in Luke in the N.T. The compound *ana* suggests a search
before finding.

17. *Made known* (*egnōrisan*). To others (verse 18) besides
Joseph and Mary. The verb is common from Aeschylus on,
from the root of *ginōskō* (to know). It is both transitive and
intransitive in the N.T.

19. *Kept* (*suneterei*). Imperfect active. She kept on keeping together (*sun-*) all these things. They were meat and

drink to her.   She was not astonished, but filled with holy
awe.   The verb occurs from Aristotle on.   She could not
forget.   But did not Mary keep also a Baby Book?   And may
not Luke have seen it?   *Pondering (sunballousa)*.   An old
Greek word.   Placing together for comparison.   Mary would
go over each detail in the words of Gabriel and of the shepherds and compare the sayings with the facts so far developed
and brood over it all with a mother's high hopes and joy.

21.   *His name was called Jesus (kai eklēthē to onoma autou
Iēsous)*.   The *kai* is left untranslated or has the sense of
"then" in the apodosis.   The naming was a part of the cere-
mony of circumcision as is shown also in the case of John the
Baptist (Luke 1:59–66).

22.   *The days of their purification (hai hēmerai tou katharis-
mou autōn)*.   The old manuscripts have "their" (*autōn*) instead of "her" (*autēs*) of the later documents.   But it is not
clear whether "their" refers to Mary and Joseph as is true
of "they brought" or to Mary and the child.   The mother
was Levitically unclean for forty days after the birth of a son
(Lev. 12:1–8).   *To present him to the Lord (parastēsai tōi
Kuriōi)*.   Every first-born son was thus redeemed by the
sacrifice (Ex. 13:2–12) as a memorial of the sparing of the
Israelitish families (Num. 18:15f.).   The cost was about two
dollars and a half in our money.

23.   *In the law of the Lord (en nomōi Kuriou)*.   No articles,
but definite by preposition and genitive.   Vincent notes that
"law" occurs in this chapter five times.   Paul (Gal. 4:4) will
urge that Jesus "was made under the law" as Luke here explains.   The law did not require that the child be brought to
Jerusalem.   The purification concerned the mother, the
presentation the son.

24.   *A pair of turtledoves, or two young pigeons (Zeugos
trugonōn ē duo nossous peristerōn)*.   The offspring of the poor,
costing about sixteen cents, while a lamb would cost nearly
two dollars.   The "young of pigeons" is the literal meaning.

25. *Devout (eulabēs).* Used only by Luke (Acts 2:5; 8:2; 22:12) in the N.T. Common in ancient Greek from Plato on. It means taking hold well or carefully (*eu* and *labein*) and so reverently, circumspectly. *Looking for the consolation of Israel (prosdechomenos paraklēsin tou Israel).* Old Greek verb to admit to one's presence (Luke 15:2) and then to expect as here and of Anna in verse 38. *Paraklēsin* here means the Messianic hope (Isa. 11:10; 40:1), calling to one's side for cheer. *Upon him (ep' auton).* This is the explanation of his lively Messianic hope. It was due to the Holy Spirit. Simeon and Anna are representatives of real piety in this time of spiritual dearth and deadness.

26. *It had been revealed unto him (ēn autōi kechrēmatismenon).* Periphrastic past perfect passive indicative. Common Greek verb. First to transact business from *chrēma* and that from *chraomai,* to use, make use of; then to do business with public officials, to give advice (judges, rulers, kings), then to get the advice of the Delphic and other oracles (Diodorus, Plutarch). The LXX and Josephus use it of God's commands. A Fayum papyrus of 257 B.C. has the substantive *chrēmastismos* for a divine response (cf. Rom. 11:4). See Deissmann, *Light From the Ancient East,* p. 153. *Before (prin ē).* Classic Greek idiom after a negative to have subjunctive as here (only example in the N.T.) or the optative after past tense as in Acts 25:16 (subjunctive changed to optative in indirect discourse). Elsewhere in the N.T. the infinitive follows *prin* as in Matt. 1:18.

27. *When the parents brought in the child Jesus (en tōi eisagagein tous goneis to paidion Iēsoun).* A neat Greek and Hebrew idiom difficult to render into English, very common in the LXX; *In the bringing the Child Jesus as to the parents.* The articular infinitive and two accusatives (one the object, the other accusative of general reference). *After the custom of the law (kata to eithismenon tou nomou).* Here the perfect passive participle *eithismenon,* neuter singular from *ethizō*

(common Greek verb, to accustom) is used as a virtual substantive like *to ethos* in 1:8.   Luke alone in the N.T. uses either word save *ethos* in John 19:40, though *eiōtha* from *ethō*, occurs also in Matt. 27:15; Mark 10:1.

28. *Then he* (*kai autos*).   *Kai* as in 2:21.   *Autos*, emphatic subject, he after the parents.   *Arms* (*agkalas*).   Old Greek word, here only in the N.T.   It means the curve or inner angle of the arm.

29. *Now lettest thou* (*nun apolueis*).   Present active indicative, *Thou art letting*.   The *Nunc Dimittis*, adoration and praise.   It is full of rapture and vivid intensity (Plummer) like the best of the Psalms.   The verb *apoluō* was common for the manumission of slaves and Simeon here calls himself "thy slave (*doulon sou*), Lord (*Despota*, our despot)."   See II Pet. 2:1.

31. *Of all the peoples* (*pantōn tōn laōn*).   Not merely Jews. Another illustration of the universality of Luke's Gospel seen already in 1:70 in the hymn of Zacharias.   The second strophe of the song according to Plummer showing what the Messiah will be to the world after having shown what the Messiah is to Simeon.

32. *Revelation to the Gentiles* (*apokalupsin ethnōn*).   Objective genitive.   The Messiah is to be light (*phōs*) for the Gentiles in darkness (1:70) and glory (*doxa*) for Israel (cf. Rom. 9:1–5; Isa. 49:6).   The word *ethnos* originally meant just a crowd or company, then a race or nation, then the nations other than Israel (the people, *ho laos*) or the people of God.   The word Gentile is Latin from *gens*, a tribe or nation. But the world-wide mission of the Messiah comes out clearly in these early chapters in Luke.

33. *His father and his mother* (*ho patēr autou kai hē mētēr*). Luke had already used "parents" in 2:27.   He by no means intends to deny the Virgin Birth of Jesus so plainly stated in 1:34–38.   He merely employs here the language of ordinary custom.   The late MSS. wrongly read "and Joseph" instead

of "his father." *Were marvelling* (*ēn thaumazontes*). The masculine gender includes the feminine when both are referred to. But *ēn* is singular, not *ēsan*, the normal imperfect plural in this periphrastic imperfect. This is due to the wide space between copula and participle. The copula *ēn* agrees in number with *ho patēr* while the participle coming last agrees with both *ho pater kai hē mētēr* (cf. Matt. 17:3; 22:40). If one wonders why they marvelled at Simeon's words after what they had heard from Gabriel, Elisabeth, and the Shepherds, he should bear in mind that every parent is astonished and pleased at the fine things others see in the child. It is a mark of unusual insight for others to see so much that is obvious to the parent. Simeon's prophecy had gone beyond the angel's outline and it was surprising that he should know anything about the child's destiny.

34. *Is set for the falling and the rising up of many in Israel* (*Keitai eis ptōsin kai anastasin pollōn en tōi Israēl*). Present indicative of the old defective verb appearing only in present and imperfect in the N.T. Sometimes it is used as the passive of *tithēmi* as here. The falling of some and the rising up of others is what is meant. He will be a stumbling-block to some (Isa. 8:14; Matt. 21:42, 44; Rom. 9:33; I Pet. 2:16f.) who love darkness rather than light (John 3:19), he will be the cause of rising for others (Rom. 6:4, 9; Eph. 2:6). "Judas despairs, Peter repents: one robber blasphemes, the other confesses" (Plummer). Jesus is the magnet of the ages. He draws some, he repels others. This is true of all epoch-making men to some extent. *Spoken against* (*antilegomenon*). Present passive participle, continuous action. It is going on today. Nietzsche regarded Jesus Christ as the curse of the race because he spared the weak.

35. *A sword* (*rhomphaia*). A large sword, properly a long Thracian javelin. It occurs in the LXX of Goliath's sword (I Sam. 17:51). How little Mary understood the meaning of Simeon's words that seemed so out of place in the midst

of the glorious things already spoken, a sharp thorn in their roses, a veritable bitter-sweet. But one day Mary will stand by the Cross of Christ with this Thracian javelin clean through her soul, *stabat Mater Dolorosa* (John 19:25). It is only a parenthesis here, and a passing cloud perhaps passed over Mary's heart already puzzled with rapture and ecstasy. *May be revealed* (*apokaluphthōsin*). Unveiled. First aorist passive subjunctive after *hopōs an* and expresses God's purpose in the mission of the Messiah. He is to test men's thoughts (*dialogismoi*) and purposes. They will be compelled to take a stand for Christ or against him. That is true today.

36. *One Anna a prophetess* (*Hanna prophētis*). The word *prophētis* occurs in the N.T. only here and Rev. 2:20. In old Greek writers it means a woman who interprets oracles. The long parenthesis into verse 37 tells of her great age. Montefiore makes it 106 as she was 15 when married, married 7 years, a widow 84.

37. *Which departed not* (*hē ouk aphistato*). Imperfect indicative middle. She kept on not leaving. The Spirit kept her in the temple as he led Simon to the temple (Plummer). The case of "the temple" (*tou hierou*) is ablative. *Night and day* (*nukta kai hēmeran*). Accusative of duration of time, all night and all day. She never missed a service in the temple.

38. *Coming up* (*epistāsa*). Second aorist active participle. The word often has the notion of coming suddenly or bursting in as of Martha in Luke 10:40. But here it probably means coming up and standing by and so hearing Simeon's wonderful words so that her words form a kind of footnote to his. *Gave thanks* (*anthōmologeito*). Imperfect middle of a verb (*anthomologeō*) in common use in Greek writers and in the LXX though here alone in the N.T. It had the idea of a mutual agreement or of saying something before one (*anti*). Anna was evidently deeply moved and repeated her thanks-

giving and kept speaking (*elalei*, imperfect again) "to all them that were looking for (*prosdechomenois*, as in 1:35 of Simeon) the redemption of Jerusalem (*lutrōsin Ierousalēm*)." There was evidently a group of such spirits that gathered in the temple either men around her and Simeon or whom she met from time to time. There was thus a nucleus of old saints in Jerusalem prepared for the coming of the Messiah when he at last appears as the Messiah in Jerusalem (John 2 and 3). These probably all passed away. But they had a happy hour of hope and joy. The late MSS. have "in Jerusalem" but "of Jerusalem" is correct. What they meant by the "redemption of Jerusalem" is not clear, whether political or spiritual or both. Simeon was looking for the consolation of Israel (2:25) and Zacharias (1:68) sang of redemption for Israel (Isa. 40:2).

39. *To their own city Nazareth* (*eis polin heautōn Nazaret*). See on Matt. 2:23 about Nazareth. Luke tells nothing of the flight to Egypt and the reason for the return to Nazareth instead of Bethlehem, the place of the birth of Jesus as told in Matt. 2:13–23. But then neither Gospel gives all the details of this period. Luke has also nothing about the visit of the wise men (Matt. 2:1–12) as Matthew tells nothing of the shepherds and of Simeon and Anna (Luke 2:8–28). The two Gospels supplement each other.

40. *The child grew* (*ēuxane*). Imperfect indicative of a very ancient verb (*auxanō*). This child grew and waxed strong (*ekrataiouto*, imperfect middle), a hearty vigorous little boy (*paidion*). Both verbs Luke used in 1:80 of the growth of John the Baptist as a child. Then he used also *pneumati*, in spirit. Here in addition to the bodily development Luke has "filled with wisdom" (*plēroumenon sophiāi*). Present passive participle, showing that the process of filling with wisdom kept pace with the bodily growth. If it were only always true with others! We need not be troubled over this growth in wisdom on the part of Jesus any more than over

his bodily growth. "The intellectual, moral, and spiritual growth of the Child, like the physical, was real. His was a perfect humanity developing perfectly, unimpeded by hereditary or acquired defects. It was the first instance of such a growth in history. For the first time a human infant was realizing the ideal of humanity" (Plummer). *The grace of God* (*charis theou*). In full measure.

41. *Every year* (*kat' etos*). This idiom only here in the N.T., a common Greek construction. Every male was originally expected to appear at the passover, pentecost, and tabernacles (Ex. 23:14–17; 34:23; Deut. 16:16). But the Dispersion rendered that impossible. But pious Palestinian Jews made a point of going at least to the passover. Mary went with Joseph as a pious habit, though not required by law to go.

42. *Twelve years old* (*etōn dōdeka*). Predicate genitive. Luke does not say that Jesus had not been to Jerusalem before, but at twelve a Jewish boy became a "son of the law" and began to observe the ordinances, putting on the phy-lacteries as a reminder. *They went up* (*anabainontōn autōn*). Genitive absolute with present active participle, a loose construction here, for the incident narrated took place *after* they had gone up, not *while* they were gong up. "On their usual going up" (Plummer).

43. *When they had fulfilled the days* (*teleiōsantōn tas hēmeras*). Genitive absolute again, but aorist participle (effective aorist). "The days" may mean the full seven days (Ex. 12:15f.; Lev. 23:6–8; Deut. 16:3), or the two chief days after which many pilgrims left for home. *As they were returning* (*en tōi hupostrephein antous*). The articular infinitive with *en*, a construction that Luke often uses (1:21; 2:27). *The boy, Jesus* (*Iēsous ho pais*). More exactly, "Jesus the boy." In verse 40 it was "the child" (*to paidion*), here it is "the boy" (*ho pais*, no longer the diminutive form). It was not disobedience on the part of "the boy" that made him remain

behind, but intense interest in the services of the temple;
"involuntary preoccupation" (Bruce) held him fast.

44. *In the company* (*en tēi sunodiāi*). The caravan going
together on the road or way (*sun, hodos*), a journey in company, then by metonymy the company itself. A common
Greek word (Plutarch, Strabo, etc.). The women usually
went ahead and the men followed. Joseph may have thought
Jesus was with Mary and Mary that he was with Joseph.
"The Nazareth caravan was so long that it took a whole day
to look through it" (Plummer). *They sought for him* (*anezē-
toun auton*). Imperfect active. Common Greek verb. Note
force of *ana*. They searched up and down, back and forth, a
thorough search and prolonged, but in vain.

45. *Seeking for him* (*anazētountes auton*). Present participle of the same verb. This was all that was worth while
now, finding the lost boy.

46. *After three days* (*meta hēmeras treis*). One day out,
one day back, and on the third day finding him. *In the
temple* (*en tōi hierōi*). Probably on the terrace where members of the Sanhedrin gave public instruction on sabbaths
and feast-days, so probably while the feast was still going on.
The rabbis probably sat on benches in a circle. The listen-
ers on the ground, among whom was Jesus the boy in a rapture of interest. *Both hearing them and asking them questions*
(*kai akouonta autōn kai eperōtōnta autous*). Paul sat at the
feet of Gamaliel (Acts 22:3). Picture this eager boy alive
with interest. It was his one opportunity in a theological
school outside of the synagogue to hear the great rabbis ex-
pound the problems of life. This was the most unusual of
all children, to be sure, in intellectual grasp and power.
But it is a mistake to think that children of twelve do not
think profoundly concerning the issues of life. What father
or mother has ever been able to answer a child's questions?

47. *Were amazed* (*existanto*). Imperfect indicative middle,
descriptive of their continued and repeated astonishment.

Common verb *existēmi* meaning that they stood out of
themselves as if their eyes were bulging out. The boy had
a holy thirst for knowledge (Plummer), and he used a boy's
way of learning. *At his understanding (epi tēi sunesei).*
Based on (*epi*), the grasp and comprehension from *suniēmi*,
comparing and combining things. Cf. Mark. 12:33. *His
answers (tais apokrisesin autou).* It is not difficult to ask
hard questions, but this boy had astounding answers to
their questions, revealing his amazing intellectual and
spiritual growth.

48. *They were astonished (exeplagēsan).* Second aorist
passive indicative of an old Greek word (*ekplēssō*), to strike
out, drive out by a blow. Joseph and Mary "were struck
out" by what they saw and heard. Even they had not
fully realized the power in this wonderful boy. Parents
often fail to perceive the wealth of nature in their children.

49. *Son (teknon).* Child, literally. It was natural for
Mary to be the first to speak. *Why (Ti).* The mother's
reproach of the boy is followed by a confession of negligence
on her part and of Joseph (*sorrowing, odunōmenoi*). *Thy
father (ho pater sou).* No contradiction in this. Alford says:
"Up to this time Joseph had been so called by the holy
child himself, but from this time never." *Sought (ezētoumen).*
Imperfect tense describing the long drawn out search for
three days. *How is it that (Ti hoti).* The first words of
Jesus preserved to us. This crisp Greek idiom without
copula expresses the boy's amazement that his parents
should not know that there was only one possible place in
Jerusalem for him. *I must be (dei einai me).* Messianic
consciousness of the necessity laid on him. Jesus often uses
dei (must) about his work. Of all the golden dreams of any
boy of twelve here is the greatest. *In my Father's house
(en tois tou patros mou).* Not "about my Father's business,"
but "in my Father's house" (cf. Gen. 41:51). Common
Greek idiom. And note "my," not "our." When the boy

first became conscious of his peculiar relation to the Father in heaven we do not know. But he has it now at twelve and it will grow within him through the years ahead in Nazareth.

50. *They understood not* (*ou sunēkan*). First aorist active indicative (one of the k aorists). Even Mary with all her previous preparation and brooding was not equal to the dawning of the Messianic consciousness in her boy. "My Father is God," Jesus had virtually said, "and I must be in His house." Bruce observes that a new era has come when Jesus calls God "Father," not *Despotes*. "Even we do not yet fully understand" (Bruce) what Jesus the boy here said.

51. *He was subject unto them* (*ēn hupotassomenos autois*). Periphrastic imperfect passive. He continued subject unto them, this wondrous boy who really knew more than parents and rabbis, this gentle, obedient, affectionate boy. The next eighteen years at Nazareth (Luke 3:23) he remained growing into manhood and becoming the carpenter of Nazareth (Mark 6:3) in succession to Joseph (Matt. 13:55) who is mentioned here for the last time. Who can tell the wistful days when Jesus waited at Nazareth for the Father to call him to his Messianic task? *Kept* (*dietērei*). Imperfect active. Ancient Greek word (*diatēreō*), but only here and Acts 15:29 in the N.T. though in Gen. 37:11. She kept thoroughly (*dia*) all these recent sayings (or things, *rhēmata*). In 2:19 *sunetērei* is the word used of Mary after the shepherds left. These she kept pondering and comparing all the things. Surely she has a full heart now. Could she foresee how destiny would take Jesus out beyond her mother's reach?

52. *Advanced in wisdom and stature* (*proekopten tēi sophiāi kai hēlikiāi*). Imperfect active, he kept cutting his way forward as through a forest or jungle as pioneers did. He kept growing in stature (*hēlikia* may mean age, as in 12:25,

but stature here) and in wisdom (more than mere knowledge). His physical, intellectual, moral, spiritual development was perfect. "At each stage he was perfect for that
stage" (Plummer). *In favour (chariti)*. Or grace. This is
ideal manhood to have the favour of God and men.

CHAPTER III

1. *Now in the fifteenth year* (*en etei de pentekaidekatōi*). Tiberius Caesar was ruler in the provinces two years before Augustus Caesar died. Luke makes a six-fold attempt here to indicate the time when John the Baptist began his ministry. John revived the function of the prophet (*Ecce Homo*, p. 2) and it was a momentous event after centuries of prophetic silence. Luke begins with the Roman Emperor, then mentions Pontius Pilate Procurator of Judea, Herod Antipas, Tetrarch of Galilee (and Perea), Philip, Tetrarch of Iturea and Trachonitis, Lysanias, Tetrarch of Abilene (all with the genitive absolute construction) and concludes with the high-priesthood of Annas and Caiaphas (son-in-law and successor of Annas). The ancients did not have our modern system of chronology, the names of rulers as here being the common way. Objection has been made to the mention of Lysanias here because Josephus (*Ant.* XXVII. 1) tells of a Lysanias who was King of Abila up to B.C. 36 as the one referred to by Luke with the wrong date. But an inscription has been found on the site of Abilene with mention of "Lysanias the tetrarch" and at the time to which Luke refers (see my *Luke the Historian in the Light of Research*, pp. 167f.). So Luke is vindicated again by the rocks.

2. *The Word of God came unto John* (*egeneto rhēma theou epi Iōanēn*). The great epoch marked by *egeneto* rather than *ēn*. *Rhēma theou* is some particular utterance of God (Plummer), common in LXX, here alone in the N.T. Then John is introduced as the son of Zacharias according to Chapter I. Matthew describes him as the Baptist, Mark as the Baptizer. No other Gospel mentions Zacharias. Mark begins his Gospel here, but Matthew and Luke have

two Infancy Chapters before. Luke alone tells of the coming of the word to John. All three Synoptics locate him "in the wilderness" (*en tēi erēmōi*) as here, Mark 1:4; Matt. 3:1 (adding "of Judea").

3. *All the region round about Jordan* (*pāsan perichōron tou Iordanou*). The wilderness was John's abode (1:80) so that he began preaching where he was. It was the plain (Gen. 13:10f.) or valley of the Jordan, El Ghor, as far north as Succoth (II Chron. 4:17). Sometimes he was on the eastern bank of the Jordan (John 10:40), though usually on the west side. His baptizing kept him near the river. *The baptism of repentance unto remission of sins* (*baptisma metanoias eis aphesin hamartiōn*). The same phrase as in Mark 1:4, which see for discussion of these important words. The word remission (*aphesis*) "occurs in Luke more frequently than in all the other New Testament writers combined" (Vincent). In medical writers it is used for the relaxing of disease.

4. *As it is written* (*hōs gegraptai*). The regular formula for quotation, perfect passive indicative of *graphō*. *Isaiah the prophet* (*Ēsaiou tou prophētou*). The same phrase in Mark 1:2 (correct text) and Matt. 3:3. Mark, as we have seen, adds a quotation from Mal. 3:1 and Luke gives verses 4 and 5 of Isa. 40 not in Matthew or Mark (Luke 3:5 and 6). See Matt. 3:3 and Mark 1:3 for discussion of Luke 4:4.

5. *Valley* (*pharagx*). Here only in the N.T., though in the LXX and ancient Greek. It is a ravine or valley hedged in by precipices. *Shall be filled* (*plērōthēsetai*). Future passive indicative of *plēroō*. In 1845 when the Sultan visited Brusa the inhabitants were called out to clear the roads of rocks and to fill up the hollows. Oriental monarchs often did this very thing. A royal courier would go ahead to issue the call. So the Messiah sends his herald (John) before him to prepare the way for him. Isaiah described the preparation for the Lord's triumphal march and John used it with great

force. *Hill* (*bounos*). Called a Cyrenaic word by Herodotus, but later Greek writers use it as does the LXX. *Brought low* (*tapeinōthēsetai*). Future passive indicative of *tapeinoō*. Literal meaning here of a verb common in the metaphorical sense. *Crooked* (*skolia*). Common word, curved, opposite of *orthos* or *euthus*, straight.

6. *All flesh* (*pāsa sarx*). Used in the N.T. of the human race alone, though in the LXX brutes are included. *The salvation of God* (*to sotērion tou theou*). The saving act of God. This phrase aptly describes Luke's Gospel which has in mind the message of Christ for all men. It is the universal Gospel.

7. *To the multitude that went out* (*tois exporeuomenois ochlois*). Plural, *Multitudes*. The present participle also notes the repetition of the crowds as does *elegen* (imperfect), he used to say. Matt. 3:7 to 10 singles out the message of John to the Pharisees and Sadducees, which see for discussion of details. Luke gives a summary of his preaching to the crowds with special replies to these inquiries: the multitudes, 10 and 11, the publicans 12 and 13, the soldiers 14. *To be baptized of him* (*baptisthēnai hup' autou*). This is the purpose of their coming. Matt. 3:7 has simply "to his baptism." John's metaphors are from the wilderness (vipers, fruits, axe, slave boy loosing sandals, fire, fan, thrashing-floor, garner, chaff, stones). *Who warned you?* (*tis hepedeixen humin;*). The verb is like our "suggest" by proof to eye, ear, or brain (Luke 6:47; 12:5; Acts 9:16; 20:35; Matt. 3:7). Nowhere else in the N.T. though common ancient word (*hupodeiknumi*, show under, point out, give a tip or private hint).

10. *Asked* (*epērotōn*). Imperfect tense, repeatedly asked. *What then must we do?* (*ti oun poiēsōmen;*). Deliberative aorist subjunctive. More exactly, *What then are we to do, What then shall we do?* Same construction in verses 12 and 14. The *oun* refers to the severe things already said by John (Luke 3:7-9).

11. *Coats* (*chitōnas*). The inner and less necessary undergarment. The outer indispensable *himation* is not mentioned. Note the specific and different message to each class. John puts his finger on the weaknesses of the people right before him.

12. *Also publicans* (*kai telōnai*). We have had the word already in Matthew (5:46; 9:10; 11:19; 18:17; 21:31f.) and Mark (11:15f.). It is sometimes coupled with harlots and other sinners, the outcasts of society. The word is made up from *telos*, tax, and *ōneomai*, to buy, and is an old one. The renter or collector of taxes was not popular anywhere, but least of all when a Jew collected taxes for the Romans and did it by terrible graft and extortions. *Extort* (*prassete*). The verb means only to do or practice, but early the tax-collectors learned how to "do" the public as regular "bloodsuckers." Lucian links them with crows and sycophants.

14. *Soldiers also* (*kai strateuomenoi*). Men on service, *militantes* rather than *milites* (Plummer). So Paul in II Tim. 2:4. An old word like *stratiōtēs*, soldier. Some of these soldiers acted as police to help the publicans. But they were often rough and cruel. *Do violence to no man* (*mēdena diaseisēte*). Here only in the N.T., but in the LXX and common in ancient Greek. It means to shake (seismic disturbance, earthquake) thoroughly (*dia*) and so thoroughly to terrify, to extort money or property by intimidating (3 Macc. 7:21). The Latin employs *concutere*, so. It was a process of blackmail to which Socrates refers (Xenophon, *Memorabilia*, ii. 9, 1). This was a constant temptation to soldiers. Might does not make right with Jesus. *Neither exact anything wrongfully* (*mēde sukophantēsēte*). In Athens those whose business it was to inform against any one whom they might find exporting figs out of Attica were called fig-showers or sycophants (*sukophantai*). From *sukon*, fig, and *phainō*, show. Some modern scholars reject this explanation since no actual examples of the word meaning merely

a fig-shower have been found. But without this view it is
all conjectural. From the time of Aristophanes on it was
used for any malignant informer or calumniator. These
soldiers were tempted to obtain money by informing against
the rich, blackmail again. So the word comes to mean to
accuse falsely. The sycophants came to be a regular class
of informers or slanderers in Athens. Socrates is quoted by
Xenophon as actually advising Crito to employ one in self-
defence, like the modern way of using one gunman against
another. Demosthenes pictures a sycophant as one who
"glides about the market like a scorpion, with his venomous
sting all ready, spying out whom he may surprise with misfortune and ruin and from whom he can most easily extort
money, by threatening him with an action dangerous in its
consequences" (quoted by Vincent). The word occurs only
in Luke in the N.T., here and in Luke 19:8 in the confession
of Zaccheus. It occurs in the LXX and often in the old
Greek. *Be content with your wages (arkeisthe tois opsōniois
humōn)*. Discontent with wages was a complaint of mercen-
ary soldiers. This word for wages was originally anything
cooked (*opson*, cooked food), and bought (from *ōneomai*, to
buy). Hence, "rations," "pay," wages. *Opsarion*, diminutive of *opson*, was anything eaten with bread like broiled fish.
So *opsōnion* comes to mean whatever is bought to be eaten
with bread and then a soldier's pay or allowance (Polybius,
and other late Greek writers) as in I Cor. 9:7. Paul uses
the singular of a preacher's pay (II Cor. 11:8) and the plural
of the wages of sin (Rom. 6:23) = death (death is the diet
of sin).

15. *Were in expectation (prosdokōntos)*. Genitive absolute
of this striking verb already seen in 1:21. *Reasoned (dialogi-
zomenōn)*. Genitive absolute again. John's preaching about
the Messiah and the kingdom of God stirred the people
deeply and set them to wondering. *Whether haply he were
the Christ (mēpote autos eiē ho Christos)*. Optative *eiē* in in-

direct question changed from the indicative in the direct (Robertson, *Grammar*, p. 1031). John wrought no miracles and was not in David's line and yet he moved people so mightily that they began to suspect that he himself (*autos*) was the Messiah. The Sanhedrin will one day send a formal committee to ask him this direct question (John 1:19).

16. *He that is mightier than I* (*ho ischuroteros mou*). Like Mark 1:7, "the one mightier than I." Ablative case (*mou*) of comparison. John would not turn aside for the flattery of the crowd. He was able to take his own measure in comparison with the Messiah and was loyal to him (see my *John the Loyal*). Compare Luke 3:16 with Mark 1:7f. and Matt. 3:11f. for discussion of details. Luke has "fire" here after "baptize with the Holy Ghost" as Matt. 3:11, which see. This bold Messianic picture in the Synoptic Gospels shows that John saw the Messiah's coming as a judgment upon the world like fire and the fan of the thrashing-floor, and with unquenchable fire for the chaff (Luke 3:17 = Matt. 3:12). But he had the spiritual conception also, the baptism in the Holy Spirit which will characterize the Messiah's Mission and so will far transcend the water baptism which marked the ministry of John.

18. *Many other exhortations* (*polla men oun kai hetera*). Literally, many and different things did John *evangelize*, *euaggelizeto*, to the people. Luke has given a bare sample of the wonderful messages of the Baptist. Few as his words preserved are they give a definite and powerful conception of his preaching.

19. *Reproved* (*elegchomenos*). Present passive participle of *elegchō*, an old verb meaning in Homer to treat with contempt, then to convict (Matt. 18:15), to expose (Eph. 5:11), to reprove as here. The substantive *elegchos* means proof (Heb. 11:1) and *elegmos*, censure (II Tim. 3:16). Josephus (*Ant.* XVIII. V. 4) shows how repulsive this marriage was to Jewish feeling. *Evil things* (*ponērōn*). Incorporated into

the relative sentence. The word is from *ponos, poneō*, toil, work, and gives the active side of evil, possibly with the notion of work itself as evil or at least an annoyance. The "evil eye" (*ophthalmos ponēros* in Mark 7:22) was a "mischief working eye" (Vincent). In Matt. 6:23 it is a diseased eye. So Satan is "the evil one" (Matt. 5:37; 6:13, etc.). It is a very common adjective in the N.T. as in the older Greek. *Had done (epoiēsen).* Aorist active indicative, not past perfect, merely a summary constative aorist, *he did.*

20. *Added (prosethēken).* First aorist active indicative (kappa aorist). Common verb (*prostithēmi*) in all Greek. In N.T. chiefly in Luke and Acts. Hippocrates used it of applying wet sponges to the head and Galen of applying a decoction of acorns. There is no evidence that Luke has a medical turn to the word here. The absence of the conjunction *hoti (that)* before the next verb *katekleisen (shut up)* is asyndeton. This verb literally means *shut down*, possibly with a reference to closing down the door of the dungeon, though it makes sense as a perfective use of the preposition, like our "shut up" without a strict regard to the idea of "down." It is an old and common verb, though here and Acts 26:10 only in the N.T. See Matt. 14:3 for further statement about the prison.

21. *When all the people were baptised (en tōi baptisthēnai hapanta ton laon).* The use of the articular aorist infinitive here with *en* bothers some grammarians and commentators. There is no element of time in the aorist infinitive. It is simply punctiliar action, literally "in the being baptized as to all the people." Luke does not say that all the people were baptized before Jesus came or were baptized at the same time. It is merely a general statement that Jesus was baptized in connexion with or at the time of the baptizing of the people as a whole. *Jesus also having been baptized (kai Iēsou baptisthentos).* Genitive absolute con-

struction, first aorist passive participle. In Luke's sentence the baptism of Jesus is merely introductory to the descent of the Holy Spirit and the voice of the Father. For the narrative of the baptism see Mark 1:9 and Matt. 3:13–16. *And praying* (*kai proseuchomenou*). Alone in Luke who so often mentions the praying of Jesus. Present participle and so naturally meaning that the heaven was opened while Jesus was praying though not necessarily in answer to his prayer. *The heaven was opened* (*aneōichthēnai ton ouranon*). First aorist passive infinitive with double augment, whereas the infinitive is not supposed to have any augment. The regular form would be *anoichthēnai* as in D (Codex Bezae). So the augment appears in the future indicative *kateaxei* (Matt. 12:20) and the second aorist passive subjunctive *kateagōsin* (John 19:31). Such unusual forms appear in the *Koiné*. This infinitive here with the accusative of general reference is the subject of *egeneto* (it came to pass). Matt. 3:16 uses the same verb, but Mark 1:10 has *schizomenous*, rent asunder.

22. *Descended* (*katabēnai*). Same construction as the preceding infinitive. *The Holy Ghost* (*to pneuma to hagion*). The Holy Spirit. Mark 1:10 has merely the Spirit (*to pneuma*) while Matt. 3:16 has the Spirit of God (*pneuma theou*). *In a bodily form* (*sōmatikōi eidei*). Alone in Luke who has also "as a dove" (*hōs peristeran*) like Matthew and Mark. This probably means that the Baptist saw the vision that looked like a dove. Nothing is gained by denying the fact or possibility of the vision that looked like a dove. God manifests his power as he will. The symbolism of the dove for the Holy Spirit is intelligible. We are not to understand that this was the beginning of the Incarnation of Christ as the Cerinthian Gnostics held. But this fresh influx of the Holy Spirit may have deepened the Messianic consciousness of Jesus and certainly revealed him to the Baptist as God's Son. *And a voice came out of heaven* (*kai phōnēn ex ouranou ge*

nesthai). Same construction of infinitive with accusative of general reference. The voice of the Father to the Son is given here as in Mark 1:11, which see, and Matt. 3:17 for discussion of the variation there. The Trinity here manifest themselves at the baptism of Jesus which constitutes the formal entrance of Jesus upon his Messianic ministry. He enters upon it with the Father's blessing and approval and with the power of the Holy Spirit upon him. The deity of Christ here appears in plain form in the Synoptic Gospels. The consciousness of Christ is as clear on this point here as in the Gospel of John where the Baptist describes him after his baptism as the Son of God (John 1:34).

23. *Jesus Himself* (*autos Iēsous*). Emphatic intensive pronoun calling attention to the personality of Jesus at this juncture. When he entered upon his Messianic work. *When he began to teach* (*archomenos*). The words "to teach" are not in the Greek text. The Authorized Version "began to be about thirty years of age," is an impossible translation. The Revised Version rightly supplies "to teach" (*didaskein*) after the present participle *archomenos*. Either the infinitive or the participle can follow *archomai*, usually the infinitive in the *Koiné*. It is not necessary to supply anything (Acts 1:22). *Was about thirty years of age* (*en hōsei etōn triakonta*). Tyndale has it right "Jesus was about thirty yere of age when he beganne." Luke does not commit himself definitely to precisely thirty years as the age of Christ. The Levites entered upon full service at that age, but that proves nothing about Jesus. God's prophets enter upon their task when the word of God comes to them. Jesus may have been a few months under or over thirty or a year or two less or more. *Being Son (as was supposed) of Joseph, the son of Heli* (*ōn huios hōs enomizeto Iōsēph tou Helei*). For the discussion of the genealogy of Jesus see on Matt. 1:1–17. The two genealogies differ very widely and many theories have been proposed about them. At

once one notices that Luke begins with Jesus and goes
back to Adam, the Son of God, while Matthew begins with
Abraham and comes to "Joseph the husband of Mary of
whom was born Jesus who is called Christ" (1:16). Matthew
employs the word "begot" each time, while Luke has the
article *tou* repeating *huiou* (Son) except before Joseph. They
agree in the mention of Joseph, but Matthew says that
"Jacob begat Joseph" while Luke calls "Joseph the son of
Heli." There are other differences, but this one makes one
pause. Joseph, of course, did not have two fathers. If we
understand Luke to be giving the real genealogy of Jesus
through Mary, the matter is simple enough. The two genealogies differ from Joseph to David except in the cases of
Zorobabel and Salathiel. Luke evidently means to suggest
something unusual in his genealogy by the use of the phrase
"as was supposed" (*hōs enomizeto*). His own narrative in
Luke 1:26–38 has shown that Joseph was not the actual
father of Jesus. Plummer objects that, if Luke is giving the
genealogy of Jesus through Mary, *huios* must be used in
two senses here (son as was supposed of Joseph, and grand-
son through Mary of Heli). But that is not an unheard of
thing. In neither list does Matthew or Luke give a complete
genealogy. Just as Matthew uses "begat" for descent, so
does Luke employ "son" in the same way for descendant.
It was natural for Matthew, writing for Jews, to give the
legal genealogy through Joseph, though he took pains to
show in 1:16 and in 1:18–25 that Joseph was not the actual
father of Jesus. It was equally natural for Luke, a Greek
himself and writing for the whole world, to give the actual
genealogy of Jesus through Mary. It is in harmony with
Pauline universality (Plummer) that Luke carries the genealogy back to Adam and does not stop with Abraham. It
is not clear why Luke adds "the Son of God" after Adam
(3:38). Certainly he does not mean that Jesus is the Son of
God only in the sense that Adam is. Possibly he wishes to

dispose of the heathen myths about the origin of man and to show that God is the Creator of the whole human race, Father of all men in that sense. No mere animal origin of man is in harmony with this conception.

CHAPTER IV

1. *Full of the Holy Spirit (plērēs pneumatos hagiou).* An evident allusion to the descent of the Holy Spirit on Jesus at his baptism (Luke 3:21f.). The distinctness of the Persons in the Trinity is shown there, but with evident unity. One recalls also Luke's account of the overshadowing of Mary by the Holy Spirit (1:35). Matt. 4:1 says that "Jesus was led of the Spirit" while Mark 1:12 states that the Spirit driveth him forth" which see for discussion. "Jesus had been endowed with supernatural power; and He was tempted to make use of it in furthering his own interests without regard to the Father's will" (Plummer). *Was led by the Spirit (ēgeto en toi pneumati).* Imperfect passive, continuously led. *En* may be the instrumental use as often, for Matt. 4:1 has here *hupo* of direct agency. But Matthew has the aorist passive *anēchthē* which may be ingressive as he has *eis tēn erēmon* (into the wilderness) while Luke has *en tōi erēmōi* (in the wilderness). At any rate Luke affirms that Jesus was now continuously under the guidance of the Holy Spirit. Hence in this same sentence he mentions the Spirit twice. *During the forty days (hēmerās tesserakonta).* Accusative of duration of time, to be connected with "led" not with "tempted." He was led in the Spirit during these forty days (cf. Deut. 8:2, forty years). The words are amphibolous also in Mark 1:13. Matt. 4:2 seems to imply that the three recorded temptations came at the close of the fasting for forty days. That can be true and yet what Luke states be true also. These three may be merely specimens and so "representative of the struggle which continued throughout the whole period" (Plummer).

2. *Being tempted (peirazomenos).* Present passive par-

ticiple and naturally parallel with the imperfect passive *ēgeto* (was led) in verse 1. This is another instance of poor verse division which should have come at the end of the sentence. See on Matt. 4:1 and Mark 1:13 for the words "tempt" and "devil." The devil challenged the Son of man though also the Son of God. It was a contest between Jesus, full of the Holy Spirit, and the slanderer of men. The devil had won with Adam and Eve. He has hopes of triumph over Jesus. The story of this conflict is given only in Matt. 4:1–11 and Luke 4:1–13. There is a mere mention of it in Mark 1:12f. So then here is a specimen of the Logia of Jesus (Q), a non-Markan portion of Matthew and Luke, the earliest document about Christ. The narrative could come ultimately only from Christ himself. It is noteworthy that it bears all the marks of the high conception of Jesus as the Son of God found in the Gospel of John and in Paul and Hebrews, the rest of the New Testament in fact, for Mark, Matthew, Luke, Acts, Peter, and Jude follow in this same strain. The point is that modern criticism has revealed the Messianic consciousness of Jesus as God's Son at his Baptism and in his Temptations at the very beginning of his ministry and in the oldest known documents about Christ (The Logia, Mark's Gospel). *He did eat nothing (ouk ephagen ouden).* Second aorist (constative) active indicative of the defective verb *esthiō.* Mark does not give the fast. Matt. 4:2 has the aorist active participle *nēsteusas* which usually means a religious fast for purposes of devotion. That idea is not excluded by Luke's words. The entrance of Jesus upon his Messianic ministry was a fit time for this solemn and intense consecration. This mental and spiritual strain would naturally take away the appetite and there was probably nothing at hand to eat. The weakness from the absence of food gave the devil his special opportunity to tempt Jesus which he promptly seized. *When they were completed (suntelestheisōn autōn).* Genitive absolute with the first aorist passive participle feminine plural because *hemerōn* (days) is feminine. According to Luke the hunger (*epeinasen*, became hungry, ingressive aorist active indicative) came at the close of the forty days as in Matt. 4:2.

3. *The Son of God* (*huios tou theou*). No article as in Matt. 4:3. So refers to the relationship as Son of God rather than to the office of Messiah. Manifest reference to the words of the Father in Luke 3:22. Condition of the first class as in Matthew. The devil assumes that Jesus is Son of God. *This stone* (*tōi lithōi toutōi*). Perhaps pointing to a particular round stone that looked in shape and size like a loaf of bread. Stanley (*Sinai and Palestine*, p. 154) on Mt. Carmel found crystallizations of stones called "Elijah's melons." The hunger of Jesus opened the way for the diabolic suggestion designed to inspire doubt in Jesus toward his Father. Matthew has "these stones." Bread (*artos*). Better "loaf." For discussion of this first temptation see on Matt. 4:3f. Jesus felt the force of each of the temptations without yielding at all to the sin involved. See discussion on Matthew also for reality of the devil and the objective and subjective elements in the temptations. Jesus quotes Deut. 8:3 in reply to the devil.

5. *The world* (*tēs oikoumenēs*). The inhabited world. In Matt. 4:8 it is *tou kosmou*. *In a moment of time* (*en stigmēi chronou*). Only in Luke and the word *stigmē* nowhere else in the N.T. (from *stizō*, to prick, or puncture), a point or dot. In Demosthenes, Aristotle, Plutarch. Like our "second" of time or tick of the clock. This panorama of all the kingdoms of the world and the glory of them in a moment of time was mental, a great feat of the imagination (a mental satanic "movie" performance), but this fact in no way discredits the idea of the actual visible appearance of Satan also. This second temptation in Luke is the third in Matthew's order. Luke's order is geographical (wilderness, mountain, Jerusalem). Matthew's is climacteric (hunger,

nervous dread, ambition). There is a climax in Luke's order
also (sense, man, God). There is no way to tell the actual
order.

6. *All this authority (tēn exousian tautēn hapasan).* Matt.
4:9 has "all these things." Luke's report is more specific. *And the glory of them (kai tēn doxan autōn).* Matt.
4:8 has this in the statement of what the devil did, not what
he said. *For it hath been delivered unto me (hoti emoi parade-
dotai).* Perfect passive indicative. Satan here claims possession of world power and Jesus does not deny it. It may
be due to man's sin and by God's permission. Jesus calls
Satan "the ruler of this world" (John 12:31, 14:30, 16:11).
To whomsoever I will (hoi an thelō). Present subjunctive
with *an* in an indefinite relative sentence. This audacious
claim, if allowed, makes one wonder whether some of the
world rulers are not, consciously or unconsciously, agents of
the devil. In several American cities there has been proven
a definite compact between the police and the underworld of
crime. But the tone of Satan here is one of superiority to
Jesus in world power. He offers him a share in it on one
condition.

7. *Wilt worship before me (proskunēseis enōpion emou).*
Matt. 4:9 has it more bluntly "worship me." That is
what it really comes to, though in Luke the matter is more
delicately put. It is a condition of the third class (*ean* and
the subjunctive). Luke has it "thou therefore if" (*su oun
ean*), in a very emphatic and subtle way. It is the ingressive
aorist (*proskunēseis*), just bow the knee once up here in my
presence. The temptation was for Jesus to admit Satan's
authority by this act of prostration (fall down and worship),
a recognition of authority rather than of personal merit.
It shall all be thine (estai sou pāsa). Satan offers to turn over
all the keys of world power to Jesus. It was a tremendous
grand-stand play, but Jesus saw at once that in that case
he would be the agent of Satan in the rule of the world by

bargain and graft instead of the Son of God by nature and world ruler by conquest over Satan. The heart of Satan's program is here laid bare. Jesus here rejected the Jewish idea of the Messiah as an earthly ruler merely. "He rejects Satan as an ally, and thereby has him as an implacable enemy" (Plummer.)

8. *Thou shalt worship* (*proskunēseis*). Satan used this verb to Jesus who turns it against him by the quotation from Deut. 6:13. Jesus clearly perceived that one could not worship both Satan and God. He had to choose whom he would serve. Luke does not give the words, "Get thee hence, Satan" (Matt. 4:10), for he has another temptation to narrate.

9. Led him (*ēgagen*). Aorist active indicative of *agō*. Matt. 4:5 has *paralambanei* (dramatic present). *The wing of the temple* (*to pterugion tou hierou*). See on Matt. 4:5. It is not easy to determine precisely what it was. *From hence* (*enteuthen*). This Luke adds to the words in Matthew, which see. *To guard thee* (*tou diaphulaxai se*). Not in Matt. 4:6 quoted by Satan from Psa. 91:11 and 12. Satan does not misquote this Psalm, but he misapplies it and makes it mean presumptuous reliance on God. This compound verb is very old, but occurs here alone in the N.T. and that from the LXX. Luke repeats *hoti* (recitative *hoti* after *gegraptai*, is written) after this part of the quotation.

12. *It is said* (*eirētai*). Perfect passive indicative, stands said, a favourite way of quoting Scripture in the N.T. In Matt. 4:7 we have the usual "it is written" (*gegraptai*). Here Jesus quotes Deut. 6:16. Each time he uses Deuteronomy against the devil. The LXX is quoted. It is the volitive future indicative with *ouk*, a common prohibition. Jesus points out to the devil that testing God is not trusting God (Plummer).

13. *Every temptation* (*panta peirasmon*). These three kinds exhaust the avenues of approach (the appetites, the nerves,

the ambitions). Satan tried them all. They formed a cycle (Vincent). Hence "he was in all points tempted like as we are" (Heb. 4:15). "The enemy tried all his weapons, and was at all points defeated" (Plummer). Probably all during the forty days the devil tempted him, but three are representatives of all. *For a season (achri kairou).* Until a good opportunity should return, the language means. We are thus to infer that the devil returned to his attack from time to time. In the Garden of Gethsemane he tempted Jesus more severely than here. He was here trying to thwart the purpose of Jesus to go on with his Messianic plans, to trip him at the start. In Gethsemane the devil tried to make Jesus draw back from the culmination of the Cross with all its agony and horror. The devil attacked Jesus by the aid of Peter (Mark 8:33), through the Pharisees (John 8:40ff.), besides Gethsemane (Luke 22:42, 53).

14. *Returned (hupestrepsen).* Luke does not fill in the gap between the temptations in the wilderness of Judea and the Galilean Ministry. He follows the outline of Mark. It is John's Gospel alone that tells of the year of obscurity (Stalker) in various parts of the Holy Land. *In the power of the Spirit (en tēi dunamei tou pneumatos).* Luke in these two verses (14 and 15) gives a description of the Galilean Ministry with three marked characteristics (Plummer): the power of the spirit, rapid spread of Christ's fame, use of the Jewish synagogues. Luke often notes the power of the Holy Spirit in the work of Christ. Our word dynamite is this same word *dunamis* (power). *A fame (phēmē).* An old Greek word found in the N.T. only here and Matt. 9:26. It is from *phēmi,* to say. Talk ran rapidly in every direction. It assumes the previous ministry as told by John.

15. *And he taught (kai autos edidasken).* Luke is fond of this mode of transition so that it is not certain that he means to emphasize "he himself" as distinct from the rumour about him. It is the imperfect tense, descriptive of the habit of

Jesus. The synagogues were an open door to Jesus before the hostility of the Pharisees was aroused. *Being glorified* (*doxazomenos*). Present passive participle, durative action like the imperfect *edidasken*. General admiration of Jesus everywhere. He was the wonder teacher of his time. Even the rabbis had not yet learned how to ridicule and oppose Jesus.

16. *Where he had been brought up* (*hou ēn tethrammenos*). Past perfect passive periphrastic indicative, a state of completion in past time, from *trephō*, a common Greek verb. This visit is before that recorded in Mark 6:1-6 = Matt. 13:54-58 which was just before the third tour of Galilee. Here Jesus comes back after a year of public ministry elsewhere and with a wide reputation (Luke 4:15). Luke may have in mind 2:51, but for some time now Nazareth had not been his home and that fact may be implied by the past perfect tense. *As his custom was* (*kata to eiōthos autōi*). Second perfect active neuter singular participle of an old *ethō* (Homer), to be accustomed. Literally according to what was customary to him (*autōi*, dative case). This is one of the flashlights on the early life of Jesus. He had the habit of going to public worship in the synagogue as a boy, a habit that he kept up when a grown man. If the child does not form the habit of going to church, the man is almost certain not to have it. We have already had in Matthew and Mark frequent instances of the word synagogue which played such a large part in Jewish life after the restoration from Babylon. *Stood up* (*anestē*). Second aorist active indicative and intransitive. Very common verb. It was the custom for the reader to stand except when the Book of Esther was read at the feast of Purim when he might sit. It is not here stated that Jesus had been in the habit of standing up to read here or elsewhere. It was his habit to go to the synagogue for worship. Since he entered upon his Messianic work his habit was to teach in the synagogues (Luke 4:15). This was

apparently the first time that he had done so in Nazareth. He may have been asked to read as Paul was in Antioch in Pisidia (Acts 13:15). The ruler of the synagogue for that day may have invited Jesus to read and speak because of his now great reputation as a teacher. Jesus could have stood up voluntarily and appropriately because of his interest in his home town. *To read (anagnōnai).* Second aorist active infinitive of *anaginōskō,* to recognize again the written characters and so to read and then to read aloud. It appears first in Pindar in the sense of read and always so in the N.T. This public reading aloud with occasional comments may explain the parenthesis in Matt. 24:15 (Let him that readeth understand).

17. *Was delivered (epedothē).* First aorist passive indicative of *epididōmi,* to give over to, a common verb. At the proper stage of the service "the attendant" or "minister" (*hupēretēs,* under rower) or "beadle" took out a roll of the law from the ark, unwrapped it, and gave it to some one to read. On sabbath days some seven persons were asked to read small portions of the law. This was the first lesson or *Parashah.* This was followed by a reading from the prophets and a discourse, the second lesson or *Haphtarah.* This last is what Jesus did. *The book of the prophet Isaiah (biblion tou prophētou Esaiou).* Literally, " a roll of the prophet Isaiah." Apparently Isaiah was handed to Jesus without his asking for it. But certainly Jesus cared more for the prophets than for the ceremonial law. It was a congenial service that he was asked to perform. Jesus used Deuteronomy in his temptations and now Isaiah for this sermon. The Syriac Sinaitic manuscript has it that Jesus stood up after the attendant handed him the roll. *Opened (anoixas).* Really it was *unrolled (anaptuxas)* as Aleph D have it. But the more general term *anoixas* (from *anoigō,* common verb) is probably genuine. *Anaptussō* does not occur in the N.T. outside of this passage if genuine. *Found the place (heuren ton topon).*

Second aorist active indicative. He continued to unroll
(rolling up the other side) till he found the passage desired.
It may have been a fixed lesson for the day or it may have
been his own choosing. At any rate it was a marvellously
appropriate passage (Isa. 61:1 and 2 with one clause omitted
and some words from 58:6). It is a free quotation from the
Septuagint. *Where it was written* (*hou ēn gegrammenon*).
Periphrastic pluperfect passive again as in 4:16.

18. *Anointed me* (*echrisen me*). First aorist active indicative of the verb *chriō* from which *Christ* (*Christos*) is derived,
the Anointed One. Isaiah is picturing the Jubilee year and
the release of captives and the return from the Babylonian
exile with the hope of the Messiah through it all. Jesus here
applies this Messianic language to himself. "The Spirit of
the Lord is upon me" as was shown at the baptism (Luke
3:21) where he was also "anointed" for his mission by the
Father's voice (3:22). *To the poor* (*ptōchois*). Jesus singles
this out also as one of the items to tell John the Baptist in
prison (Luke 7:22). Our word *Gospel* is a translation of the
Greek *Euaggelion*, and it is for the poor. *He hath sent me*
(*apestalken me*). Change of tense to perfect active indicative.
He is now on that mission here. Jesus is God's *Apostle* to
men (John 17:3, Whom thou didst send). *Proclaim* (*kē-
ruxai*). As a herald like Noah (II Pet. 2:5). *To the captives*
(*aichmalōtois*). Prisoners of war will be released (*aichmē*,
a spear point, and *halōtos*, from *haliskomai*, to be captured).
Captured by the spear point. Common word, but here only
in the N.T. *Set at liberty* (*aposteilai*). First aorist active
infinitive of *apostellō*. Same verb as *apestalken*, above.
Brought in here from Isa. 58:6. Plummer suggests that Luke
inserts it here from memory. But Jesus could easily have
turned back the roll and read it so. *Them that are bruised*
(*tethrausmenous*). Perfect passive participle of *thrauō*, an
old verb, but here only in the N.T. It means to break in
pieces, broken in heart and often in body as well. One loves

to think that Jesus felt it to be his mission to mend broken hearts like pieces of broken earthenware, real rescue-mission work. Jesus mends them and sets them free from their limitations.

19. *The acceptable year of the Lord (eniauton Kuriou dekton)*. He does not mean that his ministry is to be only one year in length as Clement of Alexandria and Origen argued. That is to turn figures into fact. The Messianic age has come, Jesus means to say. On the first day of the year of Jubilee the priests with sound of trumpet proclaimed the blessings of that year (Lev. 25:8–17). This great passage justly pictures Christ's conception of his mission and message.

20. *He closed the book (ptuxas to biblion)*. Aorist active participle of *ptussō*. Rolled up the roll and gave it back to the attendant who had given it to him and who put it away again in its case. *Sat down (ekathisen)*. Took his seat there as a sign that he was going to speak instead of going back to his former seat. This was the usual Jewish attitude for public speaking and teaching (Luke 5:3; Matt. 5:1; Mark 4:1; Acts 16:13). *Were fastened on him (ēsan atenizontes autōi)*. Periphrastic imperfect active and so a vivid description. Literally, the eyes of all in the synagogue were gazing fixedly upon him. The verb *atenizō* occurs in Aristotle and the Septuagint. It is from the adjective *atenēs* and that from *teinō*, to stretch, and copulative or intensive *a*, not *a* privative. The word occurs in the N.T. here and in 22:56, ten times in Acts, and in II Cor. 3:7, 13. Paul uses it of the steady eager gaze of the people at Moses when he came down from the mountain when he had been communing with God. There was something in the look of Jesus here that held the people spellbound for the moment, apart from the great reputation with which he came to them. In small measure every effective speaker knows what it is to meet the **eager** expectations of an audience.

21. *And he began to say (ērxato de legein)*. Aorist ingressive active indicative and present infinitive. He began speaking. The moment of hushed expectancy was passed. These may or may not be the first words uttered here by Jesus. Often the first sentence is the crucial one in winning an audience. Certainly this is an arresting opening sentence. *Hath been fulfilled (peplērōtai)*. Perfect passive indicative, *stands fulfilled*. "Today this scripture (Isa. 61:1, 2, just read) stands fulfilled in your ears." It was a most amazing statement and the people of Nazareth were quick to see the Messianic claim involved. Jesus could only mean that the real year of Jubilee had come, that the Messianic prophecy of Isaiah had come true today, and that in him they saw the Messiah of prophecy. There are critics today who deny that Jesus claimed to be the Messiah. To be able to do that, they must reject the Gospel of John and all such passages as this one. And it is no apocalyptic eschatological Messiah whom Jesus here sets forth, but the one who forgives sin and binds up the broken-hearted. The words were too good to be true and to be spoken here at Nazareth by one of their own townsmen!

22. *Bare him witness (emarturoun)*. Imperfect active, perhaps inchoative. They all began to bear witness that the rumours were not exaggerations (4:14) as they had supposed, but had foundation in fact if this discourse or its start was a fair sample of his teaching. The verb *martureō* is a very old and common one. It is frequent in Acts, Paul's Epistles, and the Johannine books. The substantive *martur* is seen in our English *martyr*, one who witnesses even by his death to his faith in Christ. *And wondered (kai ethaumazon)*. Imperfect active also, perhaps inchoative also. They began to marvel as he proceeded with his address. This verb is an old one and common in the Gospels for the attitude of the people towards Jesus. *At the words of grace (epi tois logois tēs charitos)*. See on Luke 1:30, 2:52 for this wonderful word

charis so full of meaning and so often in the N.T. The genitive case (case of genus or kind) here means that the words that came out of the mouth of Jesus in a steady stream (present tense, *ekporeuomenois*) were marked by fascination and charm. They were "winning words" as the context makes plain, though they were also "gracious" in the Pauline sense of "grace." There is no necessary antithesis in the ideas of graceful and gracious in these words of Jesus. *Is not this Joseph's son?* (*Ouchi huios estin Iōsēph houtos;*). Witness and wonder gave way to bewilderment as they began to explain to themselves the situation. The use of *ouchi* intensive form of *ouk* in a question expects the answer "yes." Jesus passed in Nazareth as the son of Joseph as Luke presents him in 3:23. He does not stop here to correct this misconception because the truth has been already amply presented in 1:28–38, 2:49. This popular conception of Jesus as the son of Joseph appears also in John 1:45. The puzzle of the people was due to their previous knowledge of Jesus as the carpenter (Mark 6:3; the carpenter's son, Matt. 13:55). For him now to appear as the Messiah in Nazareth where he had lived and laboured as the carpenter was a phenomenon impossible to credit on sober reflection. So the mood of wonder and praise quickly turned with whispers and nods and even scowls to doubt and hostility, a rapid and radical transformation of emotion in the audience.

23. *Doubtless* (*pantos*). Adverb. Literally, at any rate, certainly, assuredly. Cf. Acts 21:22, 28:4. *This parable* (*tēn parabolēn tautēn*). See discussion on Matt. 13. Here the word has a special application to a crisp proverb which involves a comparison. The word physician is the point of comparison. Luke the physician alone gives this saying of Jesus. The proverb means that the physician was expected to take his own medicine and to heal himself. The word *parabolē* in the N.T. is confined to the Synoptic Gospels except Heb. 9:9, 11:19. This use for a proverb occurs also

in Luke 5:36, 6:39. This proverb in various forms appears not only among the Jews, but in Euripides and Aeschylus among the Greeks, and in Cicero's *Letters*. Hobart quotes the same idea from Galen, and the Chinese used to demand it of their physicians. The point of the parable seems to be that the people were expecting him to make good his claim to the Messiahship by doing here in Nazareth what they had heard of his doing in Capernaum and elsewhere. "Establish your claims by direct evidence" (Easton). This same appeal (Vincent) was addressed to Christ on the Cross (Matt. 27:40, 42). There is a tone of sarcasm towards Jesus in both cases. *Heard done* (*ēkousamen genomena*). The use of this second aorist middle participle *genomena* after *ēkousamen* is a neat Greek idiom. It is punctiliar action in indirect discourse after this verb of sensation or emotion (Robertson, *Grammar*, pp. 1040–42, 1122–24). *Do also here* (*poiēson kai hōde*). Ingressive aorist active imperative. Do it here in thy own country and town and do it now. Jesus applies the proverb to himself as an interpretation of their real attitude towards himself.

24. *And he said* (*eipen de*). Also in 1:13. The interjection of these words here by Luke may indicate a break in his address, though there is no other indication of an interval here. Perhaps they only serve to introduce solemnly the new proverb like the words *Verily I say unto you* (*amēn legō humin*). This proverb about the prophet having no honour in his own country Jesus had already applied to himself according to John 4:44. Both Mark 6:4 and Matt. 13:57 give it in a slightly altered form on the last visit of Jesus to Nazareth. The devil had tempted Jesus to make a display of his power to the people by letting them see him floating down from the pinnacle of the temple (Luke 4:9–11).

25. *Three years and six months* (*etē tria kai mēnas hex*). Accusative of duration of time without *epi* (doubtful). The same period is given in James 5:17, the popular Jewish way

of speaking. In I Kings 18:1 the rain is said to have come in the third year. But the famine probably lasted still longer.

26. *Unto Zarephath* (*eis Sarepta*). The modern village Surafend on the coast road between Tyre and Sidon. *Unto a woman that was a widow* (*pros gunaika chēran*). Literally, unto a woman a widow (like our vernacular widow woman). This is an illustration of the proverb from the life of Elijah (I Kings 17:8 and 9). This woman was in the land of Sidon or Phoenicia, a heathen, where Jesus himself will go later.

27. *In the time of Elisha the prophet* (*epi Elisaiou tou prophētou*). This use of *epi* with the genitive for "in the time of" is a good Greek idiom. The second illustration of the proverb is from the time of Elisha and is another heathen, *Naaman the Syrian* (*Naiman ho Syros*). He was the lone leper that was cleansed by Elisha (II Kings 5:1, 14).

28. *They were all filled with wrath* (*eplēsthēsan pantes thumou*). First aorist passive indicative of the common verb *pimplēmi* followed by the genitive case. The people of Nazareth at once caught on and saw the point of these two Old Testament illustrations of how God in two cases blessed the heathen instead of the Jewish people. The implication was evident. Nazareth was no better than Capernaum if as good. He was under no special obligation to do unusual things in Nazareth because he had been reared there. Town pride was insulted and it at once exploded in a burst of rage.

29. *They rose up and cast him forth* (*anastantes exebalon*). Second aorist ingressive active participle and second aorist effective active indicative. A movement towards lynching Jesus. *Unto the brow of the hill* (*hēos ophruos tou orous*). Eyebrow (*ophrus*), in Homer, then any jutting prominence. Only here in the N.T. Hippocrates speaks of the eyebrow hanging over. *Was built* (*ōikodomēto*). Past perfect indicative, stood built. *That they might throw him down headlong* (*hōste katakrēmnisai auton*). Neat Greek idiom with *hōste*

for intended result, "so as to cast him down the precipice."
The infinitive alone can convey the same meaning (Matt.
2:2; 20:28; Luke 2:23). *Krēmnos* is an overhanging bank
or precipice from *kremannumi*, to hang. *Kata* is down. The
verb occurs in Xenophon, Demosthenes, LXX, Josephus.
Here only in the N.T. At the southwest corner of the town
of Nazareth such a cliff today exists overhanging the Maro-
nite convent. Murder was in the hearts of the people. By
pushing him over they hoped to escape technical guilt.

30. *He went his way* (*eporeueto*). Imperfect tense, he
was going on his way.

31. *Came down* (*katēlthen*). Mark 1:21 has the historical
present, *they go into* (*eisporeuontai*). Capernaum (Tell
Hum) is now the headquarters of the Galilean ministry,
since Nazareth has rejected Jesus. Luke 4:31–37 is parallel
with Mark 1:21–28 which he manifestly uses. It is the first
of Christ's miracles which they give. *Was teaching them* (*ēn
didaskōn autous*). Periphrastic imperfect. Mark has *edidasken* first and then *ēn didaskōn*. "Them" here means the
people present in the synagogue on the sabbath, construction
according to sense as in Mark 1:22.

32. Rest of the sentence as in Mark, which see, except
that Luke omits "and not as their scribes" and uses *hoti ēn*
instead of *hōs echōn*.

33. *Which had* (*echōn*). Mark has *en*. *A spirit of an unclean demon* (*pneuma daimoniou akathartou*). Mark has
"unclean spirit." Luke's phrase here is unique in this
combination. Plummer notes that Matthew has *daimonion*
ten times and *akatharton* twice as an epithet of *pneuma;*
Mark has *daimonion* thirteen times and *akatharton* eleven
times as an epithet of *pneuma*. Luke's Gospel uses *daimonion* twenty-two times and *akatharton* as an epithet, once of
daimonion as here and once of *pneuma*. In Mark the man
is in (*en*) the power of the unclean spirit, while here the man
"has" a spirit of an unclean demon. *With a loud voice*

(*phōnēi megalēi*). Not in Mark. Really a scream caused by the sudden contact of the demon with Jesus.

34. *Ah!* (*Ea*). An interjection frequent in the Attic poets, but rare in prose. Apparently second person singular imperative of *eaō*, to permit. It is expressive of wonder, fear, indignation. Here it amounts to a diabolical screech. For the rest of the verse see discussion on Mark 1:24 and Matt. 8:29. The muzzle (*phimos*) occurs literally in I Cor. 9:9, I Tim. 5:18, and metaphorically here and Mark 1:25, 4:39, Matt. 22:12.

35. *Had thrown him down in the midst* (*rhipsan auton eis to meson*). First aorist (effective) participle of *rhiptō*, an old verb with violent meaning, to fling, throw, hurl off or down. *Having done him no hurt* (*mēden blapsan auton*). Luke as a physician carefully notes this important detail not in Mark. *Blaptō*, to injure, or hurt, occurs in the N.T. only here and in Mark 16:18, though a very common verb in the old Greek.

36. *Amazement came* (*egeneto thambos*). Mark has *ethambēthēsan*. *They spake together one with another* (*sunelaloun pros allēlous*). Imperfect indicative active and the reciprocal pronoun. Mark has simply the infinitive *sunzētein* (question). *For* (*hoti*). We have here an ambiguous *hoti* as in 1:45, which can be either the relative "that" or the casual *hoti* "because" or "for," as the Revised Version has it. Either makes good sense. Luke adds here *dunamei* (*with power*) to Mark's "authority" (*exousian*). *And they come out* (*exerchontai*). So Luke where Mark has "and they obey him" (*kai upakouousin autōi*).

37. *Went forth a rumour* (*exeporeueto ēchos*). Imperfect middle, kept on going forth. Our very word *echo* in this word. Late Greek form for *ēchō* in the old Greek. Used for the roar of the waves on the shore. So in Luke 21:25. Vivid picture of the resounding influence of this day's work in the synagogue, in Capernaum.

38. *He rose up* (*anastas*). Second aorist active participle of *anistēmi*, a common verb. B. Weiss adds here "from the teacher's seat." Either from his seat or merely leaving the synagogue. This incident of the healing of Peter's mother-in-law is given in Mark 1:29–34 and Matt. 8:14–17, which see for details. *Into the house of Simon* (*eis tēn oikian Simōnos*). "Peter's house" (Matt. 8:14). "The house of Simon and Andrew" (Mark 1:29). Paul's reference to Peter's wife (I Cor. 9:5) is pertinent. They lived together in Capernaum. This house came also to be the Capernaum home of Jesus. *Simon's wife's mother* (*penthera tou Simōnos*). The word *penthera* for mother-in-law is old and well established in usage. Besides the parallel passages (Mark 1:30; Matt. 8:14; Luke 4:38) it occurs in the N.T. only in Luke 12:53. The corresponding word *pentheros*, father-in-law, occurs in John 18:13 alone in the N.T. *Was holden with a great fever* (*ēn sunechomenē puretōi megalōi*). Periphrastic imperfect passive, the analytical tense accenting the continuous fever, perhaps chronic and certainly severe. Luke employs this verb nine times and only three others in the N.T. (Matt. 4:24 passive with diseases here; II Cor. 5:14 active; Phil. 1:23 passive). In Acts 28:8 the passive "with dysentery" is like the construction here and is a common one in Greek medical writers as in Greek literature generally. Luke uses the passive with "fear," Luke 8:37, the active for holding the hands over the ears (Acts 7:57) and for pressing one or holding together (Luke 8:45; 19:43; 22:63), the direct middle for holding oneself to preaching (Acts 18:5). It is followed here by the instrumental case. Hobart (*Medical Language of Luke*, p. 3) quotes Galen as dividing fevers into "great" (*megaloi*) and "small" (*smikroi*).

39. *He stood over her* (*epistas epanō autēs*). Second aorist active participle. Only in Luke. Surely we are not to take Luke to mean that Jesus here took the exorcist's position

and was rebuking a malignant personality. The attitude of Jesus is precisely that of any kindly sympathetic physician. Mark 1:31 and Matt. 8:15 mention the touch of her hand rather than the tender look over her head. *Rebuked* (*epitimēsen*). Only in Luke. Jesus bade the fever leave her as he spoke to the wind and the waves and Luke uses this same verb (8:24). *Rose up and ministered* (*anastāsa diēkonei*). Second aorist active participle as in verse 38, but inchoative imperfect tense *diēkonei*, from *diakoneō* (note augment of compound verb). She rose up immediately, though a long high fever usually leaves one very weak. The cure was instantaneous and complete. She began to minister at once and kept it up.

40. *When the sun was setting* (*dunontos tou hēliou*). Genitive absolute and present participle (*dunō*, late form of *duō*) picturing the sunset scene. Even Mark 1:32 has here the aorist indicative *edusen* (punctiliar active). It was not only cooler, but it was the end of the sabbath when it was not regarded as work (Vincent) to carry a sick person (John 5:10). And also by now the news of the cure of the demoniac of Peter's mother-in-law had spread all over the town. *Had* (*eichon*). Imperfect tense including all the chronic cases. *With divers diseases* (*nosois poikilais*). Instrumental case. For "divers" say "many coloured" or "variegated." See on Matt. 4:24; Mark 1:34. *Brought* (*ēgagon*). Constative summary second aorist active indicative like Matt. 8:16, *prosenegkan*, where Mark 1:32 has the imperfect *epheron*, brought one after another. *He laid his hands on every one of them and healed them* (*ho de heni hekastōi autōn tas cheiras epititheis etherapeuen autous*). Note the present active participle *epititheis* and the imperfect active *etherapeuen*, picturing the healing one by one with the tender touch upon each one. Luke alone gives this graphic detail which was more than a mere ceremonial laying on of hands. Clearly the cures of Jesus reached the physical, mental, and spiritual planes of

human nature. He is Lord of life and acted here as Master
of each case as it came.

41. *Came out* (*exērcheto*, singular, or *exērchonto*, plural). Imperfect tense, repetition, from one after another. *Thou art
the Son of God* (*Su ei ho huios tou theou*). More definite
statement of the deity of Jesus than the witness of the demoniac in the synagogue (Luke 4:34 = Mark 1:24), like the
words of the Father (Luke 3:22) and more so than the condition of the devil (Luke 4:3, 9). In the Canterbury Revision "devils" should always be "demons" (*daimonia*) as
here. *Suffered them not to speak* (*ouk eia auta lalein*). Imperfect third singular active of *eaō*, very old and common
verb with syllabic augment *ei*. The tense accents the continued refusal of Jesus to receive testimony to his person
and work from demons. Cf. Matt. 8:4 to the lepers. *Because they knew* (*hoti ēideisan*). Causal, not declarative,
hoti. Past perfect of the second perfect *oida*. *That he was
the Christ* (*ton Christon auton einai*). Infinitive in indirect
assertion with the accusative of general reference. *Ton
Christon* = *the Anointed*, the Messiah.

42. *When it was day* (*genomenēs hēmeras*). Genitive absolute with aorist middle participle. Mark 1:35 notes it was
"a great while before day" (which see for discussion) when
Jesus rose up to go after a restless night. No doubt, because of the excitement of the previous sabbath in Capernaum. He went out to pray (Mark 1:35). *Sought after
him* (*epezētoun auton*). Imperfect active indicative. The
multitudes kept at it until "they came unto him" (*ēlthon
heōs autou*, aorist active indicative). They accomplished
their purpose, *heōs autou*, right up to him. *Would have
stayed him* (*kateichon auton*). Better, *They tried to hinder
him*. The conative imperfect active of *katechō*, an old and
common verb. It means either to hold fast (Luke 8:15), to
take, get possession of (Luke 14:9) or to hold back, to re-
tain, to restrain (Philem. 13; Rom. 1:18; 7:6; II Thess. 2:6;

Luke 4:42). In this passage it is followed by the ablative case. *That he should not go from them (tou mē poreuesthai ap' autōn).* Literally, "from going away from them." The use of *mē* (not) after *kateichon* is the neat Greek idiom of the redundant negative after a verb of hindering like the French *ne* (Robertson, *Grammar*, p. 1171).

43. *I must (me dei).* Jesus felt the urge to go with the work of evangelism "to the other cities also," to all, not to a favoured few. *For therefore was I sent (hoti epi touto apestalēn).* "A phrase of Johannine ring" (Ragg). Second aorist passive indicative of *apostellō*. Christ is the great Apostle of God to men.

44. *Was preaching (ēn kērussōn).* Periphrastic imperfect active, describing his first tour of Galilee in accord with the purpose just stated. One must fill in details, though Mark 1:39 and Matt. 8:23–25 tell of the mass of work done on this campaign.

CHAPTER V

1. *Pressed upon him* (*epikeisthai*). Luke in this paragraph
(5:1–11; Mark 1:16–20; Matt. 4:18–22) does not follow the
chronology of Mark as he usually does. It seems reasonably
clear that the renewed call of the four fishermen came before
the first tour of Galilee in Luke 4:42–44. It is here assumed
that Luke is describing in his own way the incident given in
Mark and Matthew above. Luke singles out Simon in a
graphic way. This verb *epikeisthai* is an old one and means to
lie upon, rest upon as of a stone on the tomb (John 11:38) or
of fish on the burning coals (John 21:9). So it is used of a
tempest (Acts 27:20) and of the urgent demands for Christ's
crucifixion (Luke 23:23). Here it vividly pictures the eager
crowds around Jesus. *En tōi epikeisthai* is a favourite idiom
with Luke as we have already seen, *en* with the articular
infinitive in the locative case. *That* (*kai*). *Kai* does not
technically mean the declarative conjunction "that," but
it is a fair rendering of the somewhat awkward idiom of Luke
to a certain extent imitating the Hebrew use of *wav*. *Was
standing* (*ēn hestōs*). Periphrastic second past perfect of
histēmi which here is equal to a practical imperfect. *By the
lake* (*para tēn limnēn*). The use of the accusative with *para*,
alongside, after a verb of rest used to be called the pregnant
use, came and was standing. But that is no longer necessary,
for the accusative as the case of extension is the oldest of the
cases and in later Greek regains many of the earlier uses of
the other cases employed for more precise distinctions. See
the same idiom in verse 2. We need not here stress the
notion of extension. "With characteristic accuracy Luke
never calls it a sea, while the others never call it a lake"
(Plummer).

2. *Two boats (ploia duo)*. Some MSS. have *ploiaria*, little boats, but *ploia* was used of boats of various sizes, even of ships like *nēes*. *The fishermen (hoi haleeis)*. It is an old Homeric word that has come back to common use in the *Koiné*. It means "sea-folk" from *hals*, sea. *Were washing (eplunon)*. Imperfect active, though some MSS. have aorist *eplunan*. Vincent comments on Luke's use of five verbs for washing: this one for cleaning, *apomassō* for wiping the dust from one's feet (10:11), *ekmassō* of the sinful woman wiping Christ's feet with her hair (7:38, 44), *apolouō* of washing away sins (symbolically, of course) as in Acts 22:16, and *louō* of washing the body of Dorcas (Acts 9:37) and the stripes of the prisoners (Acts 16:33). On "nets" see on Matt. 4:20, Mark 1:18.

3. *To put out a little (epanagagein oligon)*. Second aorist infinitive of the double compound verb *ep-an-agō*, found in Xenophon and late Greek writers generally. Only twice in the N.T. In Matt. 21:18 in the sense of leading back or returning and here in the sense of leading a ship up upon the sea, to put out to sea, a nautical term. *Taught (edikasken)*. Imperfect active, picturing Jesus teaching from the boat in which he was seated and so safe from the jam of the crowd. "Christ uses Peter's boat as a pulpit whence to throw the net of the Gospel over His hearers" (Plummer).

4. *Had left speaking (epausato lalōn)*. He ceased speaking (aorist middle indicative and present active participle, regular Greek idiom). *Put out into the deep (epanagage eis to bathos)*. The same double compound verb as in verse 3, only here second aorist active imperative second person singular. *Let down (chalasate)*. Peter was master of the craft and so he was addressed first. First aorist active imperative second person plural. Here the whole crew are addressed. The verb is the regular nautical term for lowering cargo or boats (Acts 27:17, 30). But it was used for lowering anything from a higher place (Mark 2:4; Acts 9:25; II Cor.

11:33). *For a catch* (*eis agran*). This purpose was the startling thing that stirred up Simon.

5. *Master* (*epistata*). Used only by Luke in the N.T. and always in addresses to Christ (8:24, 45; 9:33, 49; 17:13). Common in the older writers for superintendent or overseer (one standing over another). This word recognizes Christ's authority. *We toiled* (*kopiasantes*). This verb is from *kopos* (*work, toil*) and occurs from Aristophanes on. It used to be said that the notion of weariness in toil appears only in the LXX and the N.T. But Deissmann (*Light from the Ancient East*, pp. 312f.) cites examples from inscriptions on tombstones quite in harmony with the use in the N.T. Peter's protest calls attention also to the whole night of fruitless toil. *But at thy word* (*epi de tōi rhēmati sou*). On the base of *epi*. Acquiescence to show his obedience to Christ as "Master," but with no confidence whatsoever in the wisdom of this particular command. Besides, fishing in this lake was Peter's business and he really claimed superior knowledge on this occasion to that of Jesus.

6. *They inclosed* (*sunekleisan*). Effective aorist active indicative with perfective compound *sun*. *They shut together*. *Were breaking* (*dierēsseto*). Imperfect passive singular (*diktua* being neuter plural). This is the late form of the old verb *diarēgnumi*. The nets were actually tearing in two (*dia-*) and so they would lose all the fish.

7. *They beckoned* (*kateneusan*). Possibly they were too far away for a call to be understood. Simon alone had been ordered to put out into the deep. So they used signs. *Unto their partners* (*tois metechois*). This word *metochos*, from *metechō*, to have with, means participation with one in common blessings (Heb. 3:1, 14; 6:4; 12:8). While *koinōnos* (verse 10 here of James and John also) has the notion of personal fellowship, partnership. Both terms are here employed of the two pairs of brothers who have a business company under Simon's lead. *Help them* (*sullabesthai*). Second aorist

middle infinitive. Take hold together with and so to help.
Paul uses it in Phil. 4:3. It is an old word that was sometimes employed for seizing a prisoner (Luke 22:54) and for
conception (*con-capio*) by a woman (Luke 1:24). *So that
they began to sink* (*hōste buthizesthai auta*). Consecutive use
of *hōste* and the infinitive (present tense, inchoative use,
beginning to sink). An old verb from *buthos*. In the N.T.
only here and I Tim. 6:9.

8. *Fell down at Jesus' knees* (*prosepesen tois gonasin Iēsou*).
Just like Peter, from extreme self-confidence and pride
(verse 5) to abject humilation. But his impulse here was
right and sincere. His confession was true. He was a sinful
man.

9. *For he was amazed* (*thambos gar perieschen*). Literally,
For a wonder held him round. Aorist active indicative. It
held Peter fast and all the rest.

10. *Thou shalt catch men* (*esēi zōgrōn*). Periphrastic future
indicative, emphasizing the linear idea. The old verb
Zōgreō means to catch alive, not to kill. So then Peter is to
be a catcher of men, not of fish, and to catch them alive and
for life, not dead and for death. The great Pentecost will
one day prove that Christ's prophecy will come true. Much
must happen before that great day. But Jesus foresees the
possibilities in Simon and he joyfully undertakes the task
of making a fisher of men out of this poor fisher of fish.

11. *They left all, and followed him* (*aphentes panta ēkolou-
thēsan*). Then and there. They had already become his
disciples. Now they leave their business for active service
of Christ. The conduct of this group of business men should
make other business men to pause and see if Jesus is calling
them to do likewise.

12. *Behold* (*kai idou*). Quite a Hebraistic idiom, this use
of *kai* after *egeneto* (almost like *hoti*) with *idou* (interjection)
and no verb. *Full of leprosy* (*plērēs lepras*). Mark 1:40 and
Matt. 8:2 have simply "a leper" which see. Evidently a

bad case full of sores and far advanced as Luke the physician notes. The law (Lev. 13:12f.) curiously treated advanced cases as less unclean than the earlier stages. *Fell on his face* (*pesōn epi prosōpon*). Second aorist active participle of *piptō*, common verb. Mark 1:40 has "kneeling" (*gonupetōn*) and Matt. 8:40 "worshipped" (*prosekunei*). All three attitudes were possible one after the other. All three Synoptics quote the identical language of the leper and the identical answer of Jesus. His condition of the third class turned on the "will" (*theleis*) of Jesus who at once asserts his will (*thelō*) and cleanses him. All three likewise mention the touch (*hēpsato*, verse 13) of Christ's hand on the unclean leper and the instantaneous cure.

14. *To tell no man* (*mēdeni eipein*). This is an indirect command after the verb "charged" (*parēggeilen*). But Luke changes (*constructio variata*) to the direct quotation, a common idiom in Greek and often in Luke (Acts 1:4f.). Here in the direct form he follows Mark 1:43 and Matt. 8:4. See discussion there about the direction to go to the priest to receive a certificate showing his cleansing, like our release from quarantine (Lev. 13:39; 14:2–32). *For a testimony unto them* (*eis marturion autois*). The use of *autois* (them) here is "according to sense," as we say, for it has no antecedent in the context, just to people in general. But this identical phrase with absence of direct reference occurs in Mark and Matthew, pretty good proof of the use of one by the other. Both Matt. 8:4 and Luke 5:14 follow Mark 1:44.

15. *So much the more* (*mallon*). Mark 1:45 has only "much" (*polla*, many), but Mark tells more about the effect of this disobedience. *Went abroad* (*diērcheto*). Imperfect tense. The fame of Jesus kept going. *Came together* (*sunērchonto*). Imperfect tense again. The more the report spread, the more the crowds came.

16. *But he withdrew himself in the deserts and prayed* (*autos de ēn hupochōrōn en tais erēmois kai proseuchomenos*). Peri-

phrastic imperfects. Literally, "But he himself was with-
drawing in the desert places and praying." The more the
crowds came as a result of the leper's story, the more Jesus
turned away from them to the desert regions and prayed
with the Father. It is a picture of Jesus drawn with vivid
power. The wild enthusiasm of the crowds was running
ahead of their comprehension of Christ and his mission and
message. *Hupochōreō* (perhaps with the notion of slipping
away secretly, *hupo-*) is a very common Greek verb, but in
the N.T. occurs in Luke alone. Elsewhere in the N.T.
anachōreō (to go back) appears.

17. *That* (*kai*). Use of *kai* = *hoti* (that) like the Hebrew
wav, though found in Greek also. *He* (*autos*). Luke sometimes has *autos* in the nominative as unemphatic "he" as
here, not "he himself." *Was teaching* (*ēn didaskōn*). Periphrastic imperfect again like our English idiom. *Were sitting
by* (*ēsan kathēmenoi*). Periphrastic imperfect again. There
is no "by" in the Greek. *Doctors of the law* (*nomodidaskaloi*).
A compound word formed after analogy of *hierodidaskalos*,
but not found outside of the N.T. and ecclesiastical writers,
one of the very few words apparently N.T. in usage. It
appears here and Acts 5:34 and I Tim. 1:7. It is not likely
that Luke and Paul made the word, but they simply used the
term already in current use to describe teachers and interpreters of the law. Our word "doctor" is Latin for
"teacher." These "teachers of the law" are called elsewhere
in the Gospels "scribes" (*grammateis*) as in Matthew and
Mark (see on Matt. 5:20; 23:34) and Luke 5:21; 19:47; 21:1;
22:2. Luke also employs *nomikos* (one skilled in the law,
nomos) as in 10:25. One thinks of our LL.D. (Doctors of
Civil and Canon Law), for both were combined in Jewish
law. They were usually Pharisees (mentioned here for the
first time in Luke) for which see on Matt. 3:7, 20. Luke will
often speak of the Pharisees hereafter. Not all the "Pharisees" were "teachers of the law" so that both terms often

occur together as in verse 21 where Luke has separate articles (*hoi grammateis kai hoi Pharisaioi*), distinguishing between them, though one article may occur as in Matt. 5:20 or no article as here in verse 17.   Luke alone mentions the presence here of these Pharisees and doctors of the law *"which were come"* (*hoi ēsan elēluthotes*, periphrastic past perfect active, *had come*).   *Out of every village of Galilee and Judea and Jerusalem* (*ek pasēs kōmēs tēs Galilaias kai Ioudaias kai Ierousalēm*).   Edersheim (*Jewish Social Life*) observes that the Jews distinguished Jerusalem as a separate district in Judea.   Plummer considers it hyperbole in Luke to use "every village."   But one must recall that Jesus had already made one tour of Galilee which stirred the Pharisees and rabbis to active opposition.   Judea had already been aroused and Jerusalem was the headquarters of the definite campaign now organized against Jesus.   One must bear in mind that John 4:1–4 shows that Jesus had already left Jerusalem and Judea because of the jealousy of the Pharisees. They are here on purpose to find fault and to make charges against Jesus.   One must not forget that there were many kinds of Pharisees and that not all of them were as bad as these legalistic and punctilious hypocrites who deserved the indictment and exposure of Christ in Matt. 23.   Paul himself is a specimen of the finer type of Pharisee which, however, developed into the persecuting fanatic till Jesus changed his whole life.   *The power of the Lord was with him to heal* (*dunamis Kuriou ēn eis to iāsthai auton*).   So the best texts.   It it neat Greek, but awkward English: "Then was the power of the Lord for the healing as to him (Jesus)."   Here *Kuriou* refers to Jehovah.   *Dunamis* (dynamite) is one of the common words for "miracles" (*dunameis*).   What Luke means is that Jesus had the power of the Lord God to heal with.   He does not mean that this power was intermittent.   He simply calls attention to its presence with Jesus on this occasion.

18. *That was palsied* (*hos ēn paralelumenos*).   Periphrastic

past perfect passive where Mark 2:3 and Matt. 9:2 have *paralutikon* (our paralytic). Luke's phrase is the technical medical term (Hippocrates, Galen, etc.) rather than Mark's vernacular word (Ramsay, *Luke the Physician*, pp. 57f.). *They sought* (*ezētoun*). Conative imperfect.

19. *By what way they might bring him in* (*poias eis enegkōsin auton*). Deliberative subjunctive of the direct question retained in the indirect. *The housetop* (*to dōma*). Very old word. The flat roof of Jewish houses was usually reached by outside stairway. Cf. Acts 10:9 where Peter went for meditation. *Through the tiles* (*dia tōn keramōn*). Common and old word for the tile roof. Mark 2:4 speaks of digging a hole in this tile roof. *Let him down* (*kathēkan auton*). First aorist (*k* aorist) effective active of *kathiēmi*, common verb. Mark 2:4 has historical present *chalōsi*, the verb used by Jesus to Peter and in Peter's reply (Luke 5:4f.). *With his couch* (*sun tōi klinidiōi*). Also in verse 24. Diminutive of *klinē* (verse 18) occurring in Plutarch and *Koinē* writers. Mark 2:4 has *krabatton* (pallet). It doubtless was a pallet on which the paralytic lay. *Into the midst before Jesus* (*eis to meson emprosthen tou Iēsou*). The four friends had succeeded, probably each holding a rope to a corner of the pallet. It was a moment of triumph over difficulties and surprise to all in the house (Peter's apparently, Mark 2:1).

20. *Their faith* (*tēn pistin autōn*). In all three Gospels. *Man* (*anthrōpe*). Mark and Matthew have "child" or "Son" (*teknon*). *Are forgiven* (*apheōntai*). This Doric form of the perfect passive indicative is for the Attic *apheintai*. It appears also in Luke 5:23; 7:47, 48; John 20:23; I John 2:12. Mark 2:6 and Matt. 9:2 have the present passive *aphientai*. Possibly this man's malady was due to his sin as is sometimes true (John 5:14). The man had faith along with that of the four, but he was still a paralytic when Jesus forgave his sins.

21. *But God alone* (*ei mē monos ho theos*). Mark has *heis* (one) instead of *monos* (alone).

22. *Perceiving* (*epignous*). Same form (second aorist active participle of *epiginōskō*, common verb for knowing fully) in Mark 2:8. *Reason ye* (*dialogizesthe*) as in Mark 2:8. Matt. 9:4 has *enthumeisthe*.

24. *He saith unto him that was palsied* (*eipen tōi paralelumenōi*). This same parenthesis right in the midst of the words of Jesus is in Mark 2:11 and Matt. 9:6, conclusive proof of interrelation between these documents. The words of Jesus are quoted practically alike in all three Gospels, the same purpose also *hina eidēte* (second perfect active subjunctive).

25. *Whereon he lay* (*eph' ho katekeito*). Imperfect, upon which he had been lying down. Luke uses this phrase instead of repeating *klinidion* (verse 24). *Glorifying God* (*doxazōn ton theon*). As one can well imagine.

26. *Amazement* (*ekstasis*). Something out of its place, as the mind. Here the people were almost beside themselves as we say with the same idiom. See on Mark 5:42. So they kept glorifying God (imperfect tense, *edoxazon*) and at the same time "were filled with fear" (*eplēsthēsan phobou*, aorist passive). *Strange things* (*paradoxa*). Our very word paradox, contrary to (*para*) received opinion (*doxa*). Plato, Xenophon, and Polybius use it. Here alone in the N.T.

27. *A publican named Levi* (*telōnen onomati Leuein*). Mark 2:13 has also "The son of Alphaeus" while Matt. 9:9 calls him "Matthew." He had, of course, both names. All three use the same words (*epi to telōnion*) for the place of toll. See discussion of *publican* (*telōnēs*) on Matt. 9:9. All three Gospels give the command of Jesus, *Follow me* (*akolouthei*).

28. *He forsook all* (*katalipōn panta*). This detail in Luke alone. He left his profitable business for the service of Christ. *Followed him* (*ēkolouthei autōi*). Imperfect active,

perhaps inchoative. He began at once to follow him and he kept it up. Both Mark 2:14 and Matt. 9:9 have the aorist (*ēkolouthēsen*), perhaps ingressive.

29. *A great feast* (*dochēn megalēn*). Here and in Luke 14:13 only in the N.T. The word *dochē*, from *dechomai*, means reception. Occurs in Plutarch and LXX. Levi made Jesus a big reception. *Publicans and others* (*telōnōn kai allōn*). Luke declines here to use "sinners" like Mark 2:15 and Matt. 9:10 though he does so in verse 30 and in 15:1. None but social outcasts would eat with publicans at such a feast or barbecue, for it was a very large affair. *Were sitting at meat with them* (*ēsan met' autōn katakeimenoi*). Literally, were reclining with them (Jesus and the disciples). It was a motley crew that Levi had brought together, but he showed courage as well as loyalty to Jesus.

30. *The Pharisees and their scribes* (*hoi Pharisaioi kai hoi grammateis autōn*). Note article with each substantive and the order, not "scribes and Pharisees," but "the Pharisees and the scribes of them" (the Pharisees). Some manuscripts omit "their," but Mark 2:16 (the scribes of the Pharisees) shows that it is correct here. Some of the scribes were Sadducees. It is only the Pharisees who find fault here. *Murmured* (*egogguzon*). Imperfect active. Picturesque onomatopoetic word that sounds like its meaning. A late word used of the cooing of doves. It is like the buzzing of bees, like *tonthorruzō* of literary Greek. They were not invited to this feast and would not have come if they had been. But, not being invited, they hang on the outside and criticize the disciples of Jesus for being there. The crowd was so large that the feast may have been served out in the open court at Levi's house, a sort of reclining garden party. *The publicans and sinners* (*tōn telōnōn kai hamartōlōn*). Here Luke is quoting the criticism of the critics. Note one article making one group of all of them.

31. *They that are whole* (*hoi hugiainontes*). Old Greek

word for good health from *hugiēs*, sound in body. So also
in Luke 7:10; 15:27; III John 2. This is the usual word for
good health used by Greek medical writers. Mark 2:17 and
Matt. 9:12 have *hoi ischuontes* (those who have strength).

32. *To repentance* (*eis metanoian*). Alone in Luke not
genuine in Mark 2:17 and Matt. 9:12. Only sinners would
need a call to repentance, a change of mind and life. For
the moment Jesus accepts the Pharisaic division between
"righteous" and "sinners" to score them and to answer
their criticism. At the other times he will show that they
only pretend to be "righteous" and are "hypocrites" in
reality. But Jesus has here blazed the path for all soul-
winners. The self-satisfied are the hard ones to win and
they often resent efforts to win them to Christ.

33. *Often* (*pukna*). Only in Luke. Common word for
thick, compact, often. *And make supplications* (*kai deēseis
poiountai*). Only in Luke. *But thine* (*hoi de soi*). Sharp
contrast between the conduct of the disciples of Jesus and
those of John and the Pharisees who here appear together
as critics of Christ and his disciples (Mark 2:18; Matt. 9:
14), though Luke does not bring that out sharply. It is
probable that Levi had his reception for Jesus on one of the
Jewish fast days and, if so, this would give special edge to
their criticism.

34. *Can ye* (*mē dunasthe*). So Luke, adding *make, poiēsai*,
where Mark and Matthew have *mē dunantai*. All three
have *mē* and expect the answer no.

35. *Then in those days* (*tote en ekeinais tais hēmerais*).
Here Mark 2:20 has "then in that day," and Matt. 9:15
only "then."

36. *Also a parable* (*kai parabolēn*). There are three parables here in the answer of Jesus (the bridegroom, the patch
on the garment, the wineskin). They are not called parables
save here, but they are parables and Luke's language means
that. *Rendeth* (*schisas*). This in Luke alone. Common

verb. Used of splitting rocks (Matt. 27:51). Our word schism comes from it. *Putteth it* (*epiballei*). So Matt. 9:16 when Mark 2:21 has *epiraptei* (sews on). The word for "piece" or "patch" (*epiblēma*) in all the three Gospels is from the verb *epiballō*, to clap on, and is in Plutarch, Arrian, LXX, though the verb is as old as Homer. See on Matthew and Mark for distinction between *kainos* (fresh), *neos* (new), and *palaios* (old). *He will rend the new* (*kai to kainon schisei*). Future active indicative. So the best MSS. *Will not agree* (*ou sumphōnēsei*). Future active indicative. So the best manuscripts again. *With the old* (*tōi palaiōi*). Associative instrumental case. Instead of this phrase in Luke, Mark 2:21 and Matt. 9:16 have "a worse rent" (*cheiron schisma*).

38. *Must be put* (*blēteon*). This verbal adjective in *-teos* rather than *-tos* appears here alone in the N.T. though it is common enough in Attic Greek. It is a survival of the literary style. This is the impersonal use and is transitive in sense here and governs the accusative "new wine" (*oinon neon*), though the agent is not expressed (Robertson, *Grammar*, p. 1097).

39. *The old is good* (*Ho palaios chrēstos estin*). So the best MSS. rather that *chrēstoteros*, comparative (better). Westcott and Hort wrongly bracket the whole verse, though occurring in Aleph, B C L and most of the old documents. It is absent in D and some of the old Latin MSS. It is the philosophy of the obscurantist, that is here pictured by Christ. "The prejudiced person will not even try the new, or admit that it has any merits. He knows that the old is pleasant, and suits him; and that is enough; he is not going to change" (Plummer). This is Christ's picture of the reactionary Pharisees.

CHAPTER VI

1. *On a sabbath* (*en sabbatōi*). This is the second sabbath on which Jesus is noted by Luke. The first was Luke 4:31–41. There was another in John 5:1–47. There is Western and Syrian (Byzantine) evidence for a very curious reading here which calls this sabbath "secondfirst" (*deuteroprōtōi*). It is undoubtedly spurious, though Westcott and Hort print it in the margin. A possible explanation is that a scribe wrote "first" (*prōtōi*) on the margin because of the sabbath miracle in Luke 6:6–11. Then another scribe recalled Luke 4:31 where a sabbath is mentioned and wrote "second" (*deuterōi*) also on the margin. Finally a third scribe combined the two in the word *deuteroprōtoi* that is not found elsewhere. If it were genuine, we should not know what it means. *Plucked* (*etillon*). Imperfect active. They were plucking as they went on through (*diaporeuesthai*). Whether wheat or barley, we do not know, not our "corn" (maize). *Did eat* (*ēsthion*). Imperfect again. See on Matt. 12:1f. and Mark 2:23f. for the separate acts in supposed violence of the sabbath laws. *Rubbing them in their hands* (*psōchontes tais chersin*). Only in Luke and only here in the N.T. This was one of the chief offences. "According to Rabbinical notions, it was reaping, threshing, winnowing, and preparing food all at once" (Plummer). These Pharisees were straining out gnats and swallowing camels! This verb *psōchō* is a late one for *psaō*, to rub.

3. *Not even this* (*oude touto*). This small point only in Luke. *What* (*ho*). Literally, *which*. Mark 2:25 and Matt. 12:3 have *ti* (what).

4. *Did take* (*labōn*). Second aorist active participle of *lambanō*. Not in Mark and Matthew. See Matt. 12:1–8

and Mark 2:23-28 for discussion of details about the shew-bread and the five arguments in defence of his conduct on the sabbath (example of David, work of the priests on the sabbath, prophecy of Hosea 6:6, purpose of the sabbath for man, the Son of Man lord of the sabbath). It was an over-whelming and crushing reply to these pettifogging ceremo-nialists to which they could not reply, but which increased their anger. Codex D transfers verse 5 to after verse 10 and puts here the following: "On the same day beholding one working on the sabbath he said to him: Man, if you know what you are doing, happy are you; but if you do not know, cursed are you and a transgressor of the law."

6. *On another sabbath* (*en heterōi sabbatōi*). This was a second (*heteron*, as it often means), but not necessarily the next, sabbath. This incident is given by all three synoptics (Mark 3:1-6; Matt. 12:9-14; Luke 6:6-11). See Matt. and Mark for details. Only Luke notes that it was on a sabbath. Was this because Luke as a physician had to meet this problem in his own practise? *Right hand* (*hē dexia*). This alone in Luke, the physician's eye for particulars.

7. *The scribes and the Pharisees* (*hoi grammateis kai hoi Pharisaioi*). Only Luke here though Pharisees named in Matt. 12:14 and Pharisees and Herodians in Mark 3:6. *Watched him* (*paretērounto auton*). Imperfect middle, were watching for themselves on the side (*para*). Mark 3:2 has the imperfect active *paretēroun*. Common verb, but the proposition *para* gave an extra touch, watching either assiduously like the physician at the bedside or insidiously with evil intent as here. *Would heal* (*therapeusei*). But the present active indicative (*therapeuei*) may be the correct text here. So Westcott and Hort. *That they might find out how to accuse him* (*hina heurōsin katēgorein autou*). Second aorist active subjunctive of *heuriskō* and the infinitive with it means to find out how to do a thing. They were determined

to make a case against Jesus. They felt sure that their presence would prevent any spurious work on the part of Jesus.

8. *But he knew their thoughts* (*autos de ēidei tous dialogismous autōn*). In Luke alone. Imperfect in sense, second past perfect in form *ēidei* from *oida*. Jesus, in contrast to these spies (Plummer), read their intellectual processes like an open book. *His hand withered* (*xēran tēn cheira*). Predicate position of the adjective. So in Mark 3:3. *Stand forth* (*stēthi*). Luke alone has this verb, second aorist active imperative. Mark 3:3 has *Arise into the midst* (*egeire eis to meson*). Luke has *Arise and step forth into the midst* (*egeire kai stēthi eis to meson*). Christ worked right out in the open where all could see. It was a moment of excitement when the man stepped forth (*estē*) there before them all.

9. *I ask you* (*eperōtō humās*). They had questions in their hearts about Jesus. He now asks in addition (*ep'*) an open question that brings the whole issue into the open. *A life* (*psuchēn*). So the Revised Version. The rabbis had a rule: *Periculum vitae pellit sabbatum.* But it had to be a Jew whose life was in peril on the sabbath. The words of Jesus cut to the quick. *Or to destroy it* (*ē apolesai*). On this very day these Pharisees were plotting to destroy Jesus (verse 7).

10. *He looked round about on them all* (*periblepsamenos*). First aorist middle participle as in Mark 3:5, the middle voice giving a personal touch to it all. Mark adds "with anger" which Luke here does not put in. All three Gospels have the identical command: *Stretch forth thy hand* (*exteinon tēn cheira sou*). First aorist active imperative. *Stretch out*, clean out, full length. All three Gospels also have the first aorist passive indicative *apekatestathē* with the double augment of the double compound verb *apokathistēmi*. As in Greek writers, so here the double compound means complete restoration to the former state.

11. *They were filled with madness (eplēsthēsan anoias)*
First aorist passive (effective) with genitive: In 5:26 we saw
the people filled with fear. Here is rage that is kin to insanity,
for *anoias* is lack of sense (*a* privative and *nous*, mind). An
old word, but only here and II Tim. 3:9 in the N.T. *Communed
(dielaloun)*, imperfect active, picturing their excited counsel-
lings with one another. Mark 3:6 notes that they bolted out
of the synagogue and outside plotted even with the Herodians
how to destroy Jesus, strange co-conspirators these against
the common enemy. *What they might do to Jesus (ti an
poiēsaien Iēsou)*. Luke puts it in a less damaging way than
Mark 3:6 and Matt. 12:14. This aorist optative with *an*
is the deliberative question like that in Acts 17:18 retained
in the indirect form here. Perhaps Luke means, not that
they were undecided about killing Jesus, but only as to the
best way of doing it. Already nearly two years before the
end we see the set determination to destroy Jesus. We see
it here in Galilee. We have already seen it at the feast in
Jerusalem (John 5:18) where "the Jews sought the more to
kill him." John and the Synoptics are in perfect agreement
as to the Pharisaic attitude toward Jesus.

12. *He went out into the mountains to pray (exelthein auton
eis to oros proseuxasthai)*. Note *ex-* where Mark 3:13 has
goeth up (anabainei). Luke alone has "to pray" as he
so often notes the habit of prayer in Jesus. *He continued all
night (en dianuktereuōn)*. Periphrastic imperfect active.
Here alone in the N.T., but common in the LXX and in late
Greek writers. Medical writers used it of whole night vigils.
In prayer to God (en tēi proseuchēi tou theou). Objective
genitive *tou theou*. This phrase occurs nowhere else. *Pros-
euchē* does not mean "place of prayer" or synagogue as in
Acts 16:13, but the actual prayer of Jesus to the Father all
night long. He needed the Father's guidance now in the
choice of the Apostles in the morning.

13. *When it was day (hote egeneto hēmera)*. When day

came, after the long night of prayer. *He chose from them twelve* (*eklexamenos ap' autōn dōdeka*). The same root (*leg*) was used for picking out, selecting and then for saying. There was a large group of "disciples" or "learners" whom he "called" to him (*prosephōnēsen*), and from among whom he chose (of himself, and for himself, indirect middle voice (*eklexamenos*). It was a crisis in the work of Christ. Jesus assumed full responsibility even for the choice of Judas who was not forced upon Jesus by the rest of the Twelve. "You did not choose me, but I chose you," (John 15:16) where Jesus uses *exelexasthe* and *exelexamēn* as here by Luke. *Whom also he named apostles* (*hous kai apostolous ōnomasen*). So then Jesus gave the twelve chosen disciples this appellation. Aleph and B have these same words in Mark 3:14 besides the support of a few of the best cursives, the Bohairic Coptic Version and the Greek margin of the Harclean Syriac. Westcott and Hort print them in their text in Mark 3:14, but it remains doubtful whether they were not brought into Mark from Luke 6:13 where they are undoubtedly genuine. See Matt. 10:2 where the connection with sending them out by twos in the third tour of Galilee. The word is derived from *apostellō*, to send (Latin, *mitto*) and apostle is missionary, one sent. Jesus applies the term to himself (*apesteilas*, John 17:3) as does Heb. 3:1. The word is applied to others, like Barnabas, besides these twelve including the Apostle Paul who is on a par with them in rank and authority, and even to mere messengers of the churches (II Cor. 8:23). But these twelve apostles stand apart from all others in that they were all chosen at once by Jesus himself "that they might be with him" (Mark 3:14), to be trained by Jesus himself and to interpret him and his message to the world. In the nature of the case they could have no successors as they had to be personal witnesses to the life and resurrection of Jesus (Acts 1:22). The selection of Matthias to succeed Judas cannot be called a mistake, but it automatically ceased. For dis-

cussion of the names and groups in the list see discussion on
Matt. 10:1–4 and Mark 3:14–19.

16. *Which was the traitor* (*hos egeneto prodotēs*). Who
became traitor, more exactly, *egeneto*, not *ēn*. He gave no
signs of treachery when chosen.

17. *He came down with them* (*katabas met' autōn*). Second
aorist active participle of *katabainō*, common verb. This
was the night of prayer up in the mountain (Mark 31:3; Luke
6:12) and the choice of the Twelve next morning. The going
up into the mountain of Matt. 5:1 may simply be a summary
statement with no mention of what Luke has explained or
may be a reference to the elevation, where he "sat down"
(Matt. 5:1), above the plain or "level place" (*epi topou
pedinou*) on the mountain side where Jesus "stood" or
"stopped" (*estē*). It may be a level place towards the foot
of the mountain. He stopped his descent at this level place
and then found a slight elevation on the mountain side and
began to speak. There is not the slightest reason for making
Matthew locate this sermon on the mountain and Luke in the
valley as if the places, audiences, and topics were different.
For the unity of the sermon see discussion on Matt. 5:1f.
The reports in Matthew and Luke begin alike, cover the same
general ground and end alike. The report in Matthew is
longer chiefly because in Chapter 5, he gives the argument
showing the contrast between Christ's conception of righteousness and that of the Jewish rabbis. Undoubtedly, Jesus
repeated many of the crisp sayings here at other times as in
Luke 12, but it is quite gratuitous to argue that Matthew
and Luke have made up this sermon out of isolated sayings
of Christ at various times. Both Matthew and Luke give
too much that is local of place and audience for that idea.
Matt. 5:1 speaks of "the multitudes" and "his disciples."
Luke 6:17 notes "a great multitude of his disciples, and a
great number of the people from all Judea and Jerusalem,
and the sea coast of Tyre and Sidon." They agree in the

presence of disciples and crowds besides the disciples from
whom the twelve apostles were chosen. It is important to
note how already people were coming from " the sea coast
of Tyre and Sidon " "to hear him and to be healed (*iathēnai*,
first aorist passive of *iaomai*) of their diseases."

18. *With unclean spirits (apo pneumatōn akathartōn)*. In an
amphibolous position for it can be construed with "troubled,"
(present passive participle *enochloumenoi*) or with "were
healed" (imperfect passive, *etherapeuonto*). The healings
were repeated as often as they came. Note here both verbs,
iaomai and *therapeuō*, used of the miraculous cures of Jesus.
Therapeuō is the verb more commonly employed of regular
professional cures, but no such distinction is made here.

19. *Sought to touch him (ezētoun haptesthai autou)*. Imperfect active. One can see the surging, eager crowd pressing
up to Jesus. Probably some of them felt that there was a
sort of virtue or magic in touching his garments like the
poor woman in Luke 8:43f. (Mark 5:23 = Matt. 9:21). *For
power came forth from him (hoti dunamis par' autou exērcheto)*.
Imperfect middle, *power was coming out from him*. This
is the reason for the continual approach to Jesus. *And
healed them all (kai iāto pantas)*. Imperfect middle again.
Was healing all, kept on healing all. The preacher today
who is not a vehicle of power from Christ to men may
well question why that is true. Undoubtedly the failure to
get a blessing is one reason why many people stop going to
church. One may turn to Paul's tremendous words in Phil.
4:13: "I have strength for all things in him who keeps on
pouring power into me" (*panta ischuō en tōi endunamounti
me*). It was at a time of surpassing dynamic spiritual energy
when Jesus delivered this greatest of all sermons so far as
they are reported to us. The very air was electric with
spiritual power. There are such times as all preachers
know.

20. *And he lifted up his eyes (kai autos eparas tous opthal-*

mous autou). First aorist active participle from *epairō*. Note also Luke's favourite use of *kai autos* in beginning a paragraph. Vivid detail alone in Luke. Jesus looked the vast audience full in the face. Matt. 5:2 mentions that "he opened his mouth and taught them" (began to teach them, inchoative imperfect, *edidasken*). He spoke out so that the great crowd could hear. Some preachers do not open their mouths and do not look up at the people, but down at the manuscript and drawl along while the people lose interest and even go to sleep or slip out. *Ye poor* (*hoi ptōchoi*). *The poor*, but "yours" (*humetera*) justifies the translation "ye." Luke's report is direct address in all the four beatitudes and four woes given by him. It is useless to speculate why Luke gives only four of the eight beatitudes in Matthew or why Matthew does not give the four woes in Luke. One can only say that neither professes to give a complete report of the sermon. There is no evidence to show that either saw the report of the other. They may have used a common source like Q (the Logia of Jesus) or they may have had separate sources. Luke's first beatitude corresponds with Matthew's first, but he does not have "in spirit" after "poor." Does Luke represent Jesus as saying that poverty itself is a blessing? It can be made so. Or does Luke represent Jesus as meaning what is in Matthew, poverty of spirit? *The kingdom of God* (*hē basileia tou theou*). Matt. 5:3 has "the kingdom of heaven" which occurs alone in Matthew though he also has the one here in Luke with no practical difference. The rabbis usually said "the kingdom of heaven." They used it of the political Messianic kingdom when Judaism of the Pharisaic sort would triumph over the world. The idea of Jesus is in the sharpest contrast to that conception here and always. See on Matt. 3:2 for discussion of the meaning of the word "kingdom." It is the favourite word of Jesus for the rule of God in the heart here and now. It is both present and future and will reach a glorious consummation.

Some of the sayings of Christ have apocalyptic and eschatological figures, but the heart of the matter is here in the
spiritual reality of the reign of God in the hearts of those
who serve him. The kingdom parables expand and enlarge
upon various phases of this inward life and growth.

21. *Now* (*nun*). Luke adds this adverb here and in the
next sentence after "weep." This sharpens the contrast
between present sufferings and the future blessings. *Filled*
(*chortasthēsesthe*). Future passive indicative. The same
verb in Matt. 5:6. Originally it was used for giving fodder
(*chortos*) to animals, but here it is spiritual fodder or food
except in Luke 15:16 and 16:21. Luke here omits "and
thirst after righteousness." *Weep* (*klaiontes*). Audible
weeping. Where Matt. 5:4 has "mourn" (*penthountes*).
Shall laugh (*gelasete*). Here Matt. 5:4 has "shall be com-
forted." Luke's words are terse.

22. *When they shall separate you* (*hotan aphorisōsin humās*).
First aorist active subjunctive, from *aphorizō*, common verb
for marking off a boundary. So either in good sense or bad
sense as here. The reference is to excommunication from
the congregation as well as from social intercourse. *Cast
out your name as evil* (*exbalōsin to onoma humōn hōs ponēron*).
Second aorist active subjunctive of *ekballō*, common verb.
The verb is used in Aristophanes, Sophocles, and Plato of
hissing an actor off the stage. The name of Christian or
disciple or Nazarene came to be a byword of contempt
as shown in the Acts. It was even unlawful in the Neronian
persecution when Christianity was not a *religio licita*. *For
the Son of man's sake* (*heneka tou huiou tou anthrōpou*).
Jesus foretold what will befall those who are loyal to him.
The Acts of the Apostles is a commentary on this prophecy.
This is Christ's common designation of himself, never of
others save by Stephen (Acts 7:56) and in the Apocalypse
(Rev. 1:13; 14:14). But both Son of God and Son of man
apply to him (John 1:50, 52; Matt. 26:63f.). Christ was a

real man though the Son of God. He is also the representative man and has authority over all men.

23. *Leap for joy* (*skirtēsate*). Old verb and in LXX, but
only in Luke in the N.T. (here and 1:41, 44). It answers to
Matthew's (5:12) "be exceeding glad." *Did* (*epoioun*).
Imperfect active, the habit of "their fathers" (peculiar to
both here). Matt. 5:12 has "persecuted." Thus they will
receive a prophet's reward (Matt. 1:41).

24. *But woe unto you that are rich* (*Plēn ouai humin tois
plousiois*). Sharp contrast (*plēn*). As a matter of fact the
rich Pharisees and Sadducees were the chief opposers of
Christ as of the early disciples later (James 5:1–6). *Ye have
received* (*apechete*). Receipt in full *apechō* means as the
papyri show. *Consolation* (*paraklēsin*). From *parakaleō*,
to call to one's side, to encourage, to help, to cheer.

25. *Now* (*nun*). Here twice as in verse 21 in contrast with
future punishment. The joys and sorrows in these two
verses are turned round, measure for measure reversed.
The Rich Man and Lazarus (Luke 16:19–31) illustrate these
contrasts in the present and the future.

26. *In the same manner did their fathers* (*ta auta epoioun
hoi pateres autōn*). Literally, their fathers did the same
things to the false prophets. That is they spoke well (*kalōs*),
finely of false prophets. Praise is sweet to the preacher but
all sorts of preachers get it. *Of you* (*humas*). Accusative
case after words of speaking according to regular Greek
idiom, to speak one fair, to speak well of one.

27. *But I say unto you that hear* (*Alla humin legō tois
akouousin*). There is a contrast in this use of *alla* like that
in Matt. 5:44. This is the only one of the many examples
given by Matthew in Chapter 5 of the sharp antithesis between what the rabbis taught and what Jesus said. Perhaps
that contrast is referred to by Luke. If necessary, *alla*
could be co-ordinating or paratactic conjunction as in II Cor.
7:11 rather than adversative as apparently here. See Matt.

5:43f. Love of enemies is in the O.T., but Jesus ennobles the word, *agapaō*, and uses it of love for one's enemies.

28. *That despitefully use you* (*tōn epēreazontōn humās*). This old verb occurs here only in the N.T. and in I Pet. 3:16, not being genuine in Matt. 5:44.

29. *On the cheek* (*epi tēn siagona*). Matt. 5:39 has "right." Old word meaning jaw or jawbone, but in the N.T. only here and Matt. 5:39, which see for discussion. It seems an act of violence rather than contempt. Sticklers for extreme literalism find trouble with the conduct of Jesus in John 18:22f. where Jesus, on receiving a slap in the face, protested against it. *Thy cloke* (*to himation*), *thy coat* (*ton chitōna*). Here the upper and more valuable garment (*himation*) is first taken, the under and less valuable *chitōn* last. In Matt. 5:40 the process (apparently a legal one) is reversed. *Withhold not* (*mē kōluseis*). Aorist subjunctive in prohibition against committing an act. Do not hinder him in his robbing. It is usually useless anyhow with modern armed bandits.

30. *Ask them not again* (*mē apaitei*). Here the present active imperative in a prohibition, do not have the habit of asking back. This common verb only here in the N.T., for *aitousin* is the correct text in Luke 12:20. The literary flavour of Luke's *Koiné* style is seen in his frequent use of words common in the literary Greek, but appearing nowhere else in the N.T.

31. *As ye would* (*kathōs thelete*). In Matt. 7:12 the Golden Rule begins: *Panta hosa ean thelēte*. Luke has "likewise" (*homoiōs*) where Matthew has *houtōs*. See on Matthew for discussion of the saying.

32. *What thank have ye?* (*poia hūmin charis estin;*). What grace or gratitude is there to you? Matt. 5:46 has *misthon* (reward).

33. *Do good* (*agathopoiēte*). Third-class condition, *ean* and present subjunctive. This verb not in old Greek, but

in LXX. *Even sinners* (*kai hoi hamartōloi*). Even the sinners, the article distinguishing the class. Matt. 5:46 has "even the publicans" and 5:47 "even the Gentiles." That completes the list of the outcasts for "sinners" includes "harlots" and all the rest.

34. *If ye lend* (*ean danisēte*). Third-class condition, first aorist active subjunctive from *danizō* (old form *daneizō*) to lend for interest in a business transaction (here in active to lend and Matt. 5:42 middle to borrow and nowhere else in N.T.), whereas *kichrēmi* (only Luke 11:5 in N.T.) means to loan as a friendly act. *To receive again as much* (*hina apolabōsin ta isa*). Second aorist active subjunctive of *apolambanō*, old verb, to get back in full like *apechō* in 6:24. Literally here, "that they may get back the equal" (principal and interest, apparently). It could mean "equivalent services." No parallel in Matthew.

35. *But* (*plēn*). Plain adversative like *plēn* in verse 24. Never despairing (*mēden apelpizontes*). *Mēden* is read by A B L Bohairic and is the reading of Westcott and Hort. The reading *mēdena* is translated "despairing of no man." The Authorized Version has it "hoping for nothing again," a meaning for *apelpizō* with no parallel elsewhere. Field (*Otium Nor.* iii. 40) insists that all the same the context demands this meaning because of *apelpizein* in verse 34, but the correct reading there is *elpizein*, not *apelpizein*. Here Field's argument falls to the ground. The word occurs in Polybius, Diodorus, LXX with the sense of despairing and that is the meaning here. D and Old Latin documents have *nihil desperantes*, but the Vulgate has *nihil inde sperantes* (hoping for nothing thence) and this false rendering has wrought great havoc in Europe. "On the strength of it Popes and councils have repeatedly condemned the taking of any interest whatever for loans. As loans could not be had without interest, and Christians were forbidden to take it, money lending passed into the hands of the Jews, and

added greatly to the unnatural detestation in which Jews
were held" (Plummer). By "never despairing" or "giving
up nothing in despair" Jesus means that we are not to despair
about getting the money back. We are to help the apparently hopeless cases. Medical writers use the word for des-
perate or hopeless cases. *Sons of the Most High* (*huoi Hupsistou*). In 1:32 Jesus is called "Son of the Highest" and
here all real children or sons of God (Luke 20:36) are so
termed. See also 1:35, 76 for the use of "the Highest" of
God. He means the same thing that we see in Matt. 5:45, 48
by "your Father." *Toward the unthankful and evil* (*epi
tous acharistous kai ponērous*). God the Father is kind towards the unkind and wicked. Note the one article with
both adjectives.

36. *Even as your Father* (*kathōs ho patēr humōn*). In Matt.
5:48 we have *hōs ho patēr humōn*. In both the perfection of
the Father is placed as the goal before his children. In
neither case is it said that they have reached it.

37. *And judge not* (*kai mē krinete*). *Mē* and the present
active imperative, forbidding the habit of criticism. The
common verb *krinō*, to separate, we have in our English words
critic, criticism, criticize, dis-criminate. Jesus does not
mean that we are not to form opinions, but not to form them
rashly, unfairly, like our prejudice. *Ye shall not be judged*
(*ou mē krithēte*). First aorist passive subjunctive with
double negative *ou mē*, strong negative. *Condemn not*
(*mē katadikazete*). To give judgment (*dikē, dixazō*) against
(*kata*) one. *Mē* and present imperative. Either cease doing
or do not have the habit of doing it. Old verb. *Ye shall not
be condemned* (*ou mē katadikasthēte*). First aorist passive indicative again with the double negative. Censoriousness is
a bad habit. *Release* (*apoluete*). Positive command the
opposite of the censoriousness condemned.

38. *Pressed down* (*pepiesmenon*). Perfect passive participle from *piezō*, old verb, but here alone in the N.T.,

though the Doric form *piazo*, to seize, occurs several times
(John 7:30, 32, 44). *Shaken together (sesaleumenon)*. Perfect
passive participle again from common verb *saleuo*. *Running
over (huperekchunnomenon)*. Present middle participle of
this double compound verb not found elsewhere save in A Q
in Joel 2:24. *Chuno* is a late form of *cheo*. There is asyndeton here, no conjunction connecting these participles. The
present here is in contrast to the two preceding perfects.
The participles form an epexegesis or explanation of the
"good measure" (*metron kalon*). *Into your bosom (eis ton
kolpon humon)*. The fold of the wide upper garment bound
by the girdle made a pocket in common use (Ex. 4:6; Prov.
6:27; Psa. 79:12; Isa. 65:6f.; Jer. 32:18). So Isa. 65:7: *I will
measure their former work unto their bosom*. *Shall be measured to you again (antimetrethesetai)*. Future passive indicative of the verb here only in the N.T. save late MSS. in
Matt. 7:2. Even here some MSS. have *metrethesetai*. The
anti has the common meaning of in turn or back, measured
back to you in requital.

39. *Also a parable (kai parabolen)*. Plummer thinks
that the second half of the sermon begins here as indicated
by Luke's insertion of "And he spake (*eipen de*) at this
point. Luke has the word parable some fifteen times both
for crisp proverbs and for the longer narrative comparisons.
This is the only use of the term parable concerning the metaphors in the Sermon on the Mount. But in both Matthew
and Luke's report of the discourse there are some sixteen
possible applications of the word. Two come right together:
The blind leading the blind, the mote and the beam. Matthew gives the parabolic proverb of the blind leading the
blind later (15:14). Jesus repeated these sayings on various
occasions as every teacher does his characteristic ideas.
So Luke 6:40 = Matt. 10:24, Luke 6:45 = Matt. 12:34f.
Can (Meti dunatai). The use of *meti* in the question shows
that a negative answer is expected. *Guide (hodegein)*.

Common verb from *hodēgos* (guide) and this from *hodos*
(way) and *hēgeomai*, to lead or guide. *Shall they not both
fall?* (*ouchi amphoteroi empesountai;*). *Ouchi*, a sharpened
negative from *ouk*, in a question expecting the answer Yes.
Future middle indicative of the common verb *empiptō*. *Into
a pit* (*eis bothunon*). Late word for older *bothros*.

40. *The disciple is not above his master* (*ouk estin mathētēs
huper ton didaskalon*). Literally, a learner (or pupil) is
not above the teacher. Precisely so in Matt. 10:24 where
"slave" is added with "lord." But here Luke adds: "But
everyone when he is perfected shall be as his master"
(*katērtismenos de pās estai hōs ho didaskalos autou*). The state
of completion, perfect passive participle, is noted in *katērtismenos*. The word is common for mending broken things or
nets (Matt. 4:21) or men (Gal. 6:1). So it is a long process
to get the pupil patched up to the plane of his teacher.

41. *Mote* (*karphos*) and *beam* (*dokon*). See on Matt. 7:3–5
for discussion of these words in this parabolic proverb kin to
several of ours today.

42. *Canst thou say* (*dunasai legein*). Here Matt. 7:4 has
wilt thou say (*ereis*). *Beholdest not* (*ou blepōn*). Matt. 7:4
has "lo" (*idou*). *Thou hypocrite* (*hupokrita*). Contrast to
the studied politeness of "brother" (*adelphe*) above. Powerful picture of blind self-complacence and incompetence, the
keyword to argument here.

44. *Is known* (*ginōsketai*). The fruit of each tree reveals
its actual character. It is the final test. This sentence is
not in Matt. 7:17–20, but the same idea is in the repeated
saying (Matt. 7:16, 20): "By their fruits ye shall know
them," where the verb *epignōsesthe* means full knowledge.
The question in Matt. 7:16 is put here in positive declarative form. The verb is in the plural for "men" or "people,"
sullegousin. See on Matt. 7:16. *Bramble bush* (*batou*).
Old word, quoted from the LXX in Mark 12:26, Luke 20:
37 (from Ex. 3:6) about the burning bush that Moses saw,

and by Stephen (Acts 7:30, 35) referring to the same incident. Nowhere else in the N.T. "Galen has a chapter on
its medicinal uses, and the medical writings abound in
prescriptions of which it is an ingredient" (Vincent). *Gather*
(*trugōsin*). A verb common in Greek writers for gathering
ripe fruit. In the N.T. only here and Rev. 14:18f. *Grapes*
(*staphulēn*). Cluster of grapes.

45. *Bringeth forth* (*propherei*). In a similar saying repeated later. Matt. 12:34f. has the verb *ekballei* (throws out,
casts out), a bolder figure. "When men are natural, heart
and mouth act in concert. But otherwise the mouth sometimes professes what the heart does not feel" (Plummer).

46. *And do not* (*kai ou poieite*). This is the point about
every sermon that counts. The two parables that follow
illustrate this point.

47. *Hears and does* (*akouōn kai poiōn*). Present active
participles. So in Matt. 7:24. (Present indicative.) *I will
show you* (*hupodeixō humin*). Only in Luke, not Matthew.

48. *Digged and went deep* (*eskapsen kai ebathunen*). Two
first aorist indicatives. Not a *hendiadys* for dug deep.
Skaptō, to dig, is as old as Homer, as is *bathunō*, to make deep.
And laid a foundation (*kai ethēken themelion*). That is the
whole point. This wise builder struck the rock before he
laid the foundation. *When a flood arose* (*plēmmurēs genomenēs*). Genitive absolute. Late word for flood, *plēmmura*,
only here in the N.T., though in Job 40:18. *Brake against*
(*proserēxen*). First aorist active indicative from *prosrēgnumi*
and in late writers *prosrēssō*, to break against. Only here
in the N.T. Matt. 7:25 has *prosepesan*, from *prospiptō*,
to fall against. *Could not shake it* (*ouk ischusen saleusai
autēn*). Did not have strength enough to shake it. *Because
it had been well builded* (*dia to kalōs oikodomēsthai autēn*).
Perfect passive articular infinitive after *dia* and with accusative of general reference.

49. *He that heareth and doeth not* (*ho de akousas kai mē*

poiēsas). Aorist active participle with article. Particular case singled out (punctiliar, aorist). *Like a man* (*homoios estin anthrōpōi*). Associative instrumental case after *homoios* as in verse 47. *Upon the earth* (*epi tēn gēn*). Matt. 7:26 has "upon the sand" (*epi tēn ammon*), more precise and worse than mere earth. But not on the rock. *Without a foundation* (*chōris themeliou*). The foundation on the rock after deep digging as in verse 48. *It fell in* (*sunepesen*). Second aorist active of *sunpiptō*, to fall together, to collapse. An old verb from Homer on, but only here in the N.T. *The ruin* (*to rēgma*). The crash like a giant oak in the forest resounded far and wide. An old word for a rent or fracture as in medicine for laceration of a wound. Only here in the N.T.

CHAPTER VII

1. *After* (*epeidē, epei* and *dē*). This conjunction was written *epei dē* in Homer and is simple *epei* with the intensive *dē* added and even *epei dē per* once in N.T. (Luke 1:1). This is the only instance of the temporal use of *epeidē* in the N.T. The causal sense occurs only in Luke and Paul, for *epei* is the correct text in Matt. 21:46. *Had ended* (*eplērōsen*). First aorist active indicative. There is here a reference to the conclusion of the Sermon on the Mount, but with nothing concerning the impression produced by the discourse such as is seen in Matt. 7:28. This verse really belongs as the conclusion of Chapter 6, not as the beginning of Chapter 7. *In the ears of the people* (*eis tas akoas tou laou*). *Akoē* from *akouō*, to hear, is used of the sense of hearing (I Cor. 12:17), the ear with which one hears (Mark 7:35; Heb. 5:11), the thing heard or the report (Rom. 10:16) or oral instruction (Gal. 3:2, 5). Both Matt. 8:5–13 and Luke 7:1–10 locate the healing of the centurion's servant in Capernaum where Jesus was after the Sermon on the Mount.

2. *Centurion's servant* (*Hekatontarchou tinos doulos*). Slave of a certain centurion (Latin word *centurio*, commander of a century or hundred). Mark 15:39, 44 has the Latin word in Greek letters, *kenturiōn*. The centurion commanded a company which varied from fifty to a hundred. Each cohort had six centuries. Each legion had ten cohorts or bands (Acts 10:1). The centurions mentioned in the N.T. all seem to be fine men as Polybius states that the best men in the army had this position. See also Luke 23:47. The Greek has two forms of the word, both from *hekaton*, hundred, and *archō*, to rule, and they appear to be used interchangeably. So we have *hekatontarchos;* here, the form is

97

-*archos*, and *hekatontarchēs*, the form is -*archēs* in verse 6.
The manuscripts differ about it in almost every instance.
The -*archos* form is accepted by Westcott and Hort only in
the nominative save the genitive singular here in Luke 7:2
and the accusative singular in Acts 22:25. See like variation between them in Matt. 8:5 and 8 (-*archos*) and 13
(*archēi*). So also -*archon* (Acts 22:25) and -*archēs* (Acts
22:26). *Dear to him* (*autōi entimos*). Held in honour, prized,
precious, dear (Luke 14:8; I Pet. 2:4; Phil. 2:29), common
Greek word. Even though a slave he was dear to him. *Was
sick* (*kakōs echōn*). Having it bad. Common idiom. See
already Matt. 4:24, 8:16; Mark 2:17; Luke 5:31, etc. Matt.
8:6 notes that the slave was a paralytic. *And at the point
of death* (*ēmellen teleutāin*). Imperfect active of *mellō* (note
double augment *ē*) which is used either with the present infinitive as here, the aorist (Rev. 3:16), or even the future because of the future idea in *mellō* (Acts 11:28; 24:15). He
was about to die.

3. *Sent unto him elders of the Jews* (*apesteilen pros auton
presbuterous tōn Ioudaiōn*). Matt. 8:5 says "the centurion
came unto him." For discussion of this famous case of
apparent discrepancy see discussion on Matthew. One possible solution is that Luke tells the story as it happened with
the details, whereas Matthew simply presents a summary
statement without the details. What one does through
another he does himself. *Asking him* (*erōtōn auton*). Present active participle, masculine singular nominative, of
the verb *erōtaō* common for asking a question as in the old
Greek (Luke 22:68). But more frequently in the N.T. the
verb has the idea of making a request as here. This is not a
Hebraism or an Aramaism, but is a common meaning of
the verb in the papyri (Deissmann, *Light from the Ancient
East*, p. 168). It is to be noted here that Luke represents
the centurion himself as "asking" through the elders of
the Jews (leading citizens). In Matt. 8:6 the verb is

parakalōn (beseeching). *That he would come and save (hopōs elthōn diasōsei).* *Hina* is the more common final or sub-final (as here) conjunction, but *hopōs* still occurs. *Diasōsei* is effective aorist active subjunctive, to bring safe through as in a storm (Acts 28: 1, 4). Common word.

4. *Besought (parekaloun).* Imperfect active, began and kept on beseeching. This is the same verb used by Matthew in 8:5 of the centurion himself. *Earnestly (spoudaiōs).* From *spoudē* haste. So eagerly, earnestly, zealously, for time was short. *That thou shouldst do this for him (hōi parexei touto).* Second future middle singular of *parechō*. Old and common verb, furnish on thy part. *Hōi* is relative in dative case almost with notion of contemplated result (Robertson, *Grammar*, p. 961).

5. *For (gar).* This clause gives the reason why the elders of the Jews consider him "worthy" (*axios*, drawing down the scale, *axis, agō*). He was hardly a proselyte, but was a Roman who had shown his love for the Jews. *Himself (autos).* All by himself and at his own expense. *Us (hēmin).* Dative case, for us. It is held by some archaeologists that the black basalt ruins in Tell Hum are the remains of the very synagogue (*tēn sunagōgēn*). Literally, *the synagogue,* the one which we have, the one for us.

6. *Went with them (eporeueto sun autois).* Imperfect indicative middle. He started to go along with them. *Now (ēdē).* Already like Latin *jam.* In I Cor. 4:8 *nun ēdē* like *jam nunc.* *Sent friends (epempsen philous).* This second embassy also, wanting in Matthew's narrative. He "puts the message of both into the mouth of the centurion himself" (Plummer). Note saying (*legōn*), present active singular participle, followed by direct quotation from the centurion himself. *Trouble not thyself (Mē skullou).* Present middle (direct use) imperative of *skullō*, old verb originally meaning to skin, to mangle, and then in later Greek to vex, trouble, annoy. Frequent in the papyri in this latter sense.

For I am not worthy that (ou gar hikanos eimi hina). The same word *hikanos*, not *axios*, as in Matt. 8:8, which see for discussion, from *hikō, hikanō*, to fit, to reach, be adequate for. *Hina* in both places as common in late Greek. See Matt. 8:8 also for "roof" (*stegēn*, covering).

7. *Wherefore neither thought I myself worthy to come unto thee (dio oude emauton ēxiōsa pros se elthein)*. Not in Matthew because he represents the centurion as coming to Jesus. *Speak the word (eipe logōi)*. As in Matt. 8:8. Second aorist active imperative with instrumental case, speak with a word. *My servant shall be healed (iathētō ho pais mou)*. Imperative first aorist passive, let be healed. *Pais* literally means "boy," an affectionate term for the "slave," *doulos* (verse 2), who was "dear" to him.

8. *"Set" (tassomenos)*. Genuine here, though doubtful in Matt. 8:9 where see discussion of this vivid and characteristic speech of the centurion.

9. *Turned (strapheis)*. Second aorist passive participle of *strephō*, to turn. Common verb. A vivid touch not in Matthew's account. In both Matthew and Luke Jesus marvels at the great faith of this Roman centurion beyond that among the Jews. As a military man he had learned how to receive orders and to execute them and hence to expect obedience to his commands. He recognized Jesus as Master over disease with power to compel obedience.

10. *Whole (hugiainonta)*. Sound, well. See Luke 5:31.

11. *Soon afterwards (en tōi hexēs)*. According to this reading supply *chronōi*, time. Other MSS. read *tēi hexēs* (supply *hēmerāi*, day). *Hexēs* occurs in Luke and Acts in the N.T. though old adverb of time. *That (Hoti)*. Not in the Greek, the two verbs *egeneto* and *eporeuthē* having no connective (asyndeton). *Went with him (suneporeuonto autōi)*. Imperfect middle picturing the procession of disciples and the crowd with Jesus. Nain is not mentioned elsewhere in the N.T. There is today a hamlet about two miles west of

Endor on the north slope of Little Hermon. There is a burying-place still in use. Robinson and Stanley think that the very road on which the crowd with Jesus met the funeral procession can be identified.

12. *Behold* (*kai idou*). The *kai* introduces the apodosis of the temporal sentence and has to be left out in translations. It is a common idiom in Luke, *kai idou*. *There was carried out* (*exekomizeto*). Imperfect passive indicative. Common verb in late Greek for carrying out a body for burial, though here only in the N.T. (*ekkomizō*). Rock tombs outside of the village exist there today. *One that was dead* (*tethnē-kōs*). Perfect active participle of *thnēskō*, to die. *The only son of his mother* (*monogenēs huios tēi mētri autou*). Only begotten son to his mother (dative case). The compound adjective *monogenēs* (*monos* and *genos*) is common in the old Greek and occurs in the N.T. about Jesus (John 3:16, 18). The "death of a widow's only son was the greatest misfortune conceivable" (Easton). *And she was a widow* (*kai autē ēn chēra*). This word *chēra* gives the finishing touch to the pathos of the situation. The word is from *chēros*, bereft. The mourning of a widow for an only son is the extremity of grief (Plummer). *Much people* (*ochlos hikanos*). Considerable crowd as often with this adjective *hikanos*. Some were hired mourners, but the size of the crowd showed the real sympathy of the town for her.

13. *The Lord saw her* (*idōn autēn ho kurios*). The Lord of Life confronts death (Plummer) and Luke may use *Kurios* here purposely. *Had compassion* (*esplagchthē*). First aorist (ingressive) passive indicative of *splagchnizomai*. Often love and pity are mentioned as the motives for Christ's miracles (Matt. 14:14; 15:32, etc.). It is confined to the Synoptics in the N.T. and about Christ save in the parables by Christ. *Weep not* (*mē klaie*). Present imperative in a prohibition. Cease weeping.

14. *Touched the bier* (*hēpsato tou sorou*). An urn for the

bones or ashes of the dead in Homer, then the coffin (Gen.
5:26), then the funeral couch or bier as here. Only here in
the N.T. Jesus touched the bier to make the bearers stop,
which they did (*stood still, estēsan*), second aorist active
indicative of *histēmi*.

15. *Sat up* (*anekathisen*). First aorist active indicative.
The verb in the N.T. only here and Acts 9:40. Medical
writers often used it of the sick sitting up in bed (Hobart,
Med. Lang. of St. Luke, p. 11). It is objected that the sym-
metry of these cases (daughter of Jairus raised from the death-
bed, this widow's son raised from the bier, Lazarus raised
from the tomb) is suspicious, but no one Gospel gives all
three (Plummer). *Gave him to his mother* (*edōken auton tēi
mētri autou*). Tender way of putting it. "For he had
already ceased to belong to his mother" (Bengel). So in
Luke 9:42.

16. *Fear seized all* (*elaben de phobos pantas*). Aorist active
indicative. At once. *They glorified God* (*edoxazon ton theon*).
Imperfect active, inchoative, began and increased.

17. *This report* (*ho logos houtos*). That God had raised
up a great prophet who had shown his call by raising the
dead.

18. *And the disciples of John told him* (*kai apēggeilan
Iōanēi hoi mathētai autou*). Literally, and his disciples
announced to John. Such news (verse 17) was bound to come
to the ears of the Baptist languishing in the dungeon of
Machaerus (Luke 3:20). Luke 7:18–35 runs parallel with
Matt. 11:2–19, a specimen of Q, the non-Marcan portion of
Matthew and Luke.

19. *Calling unto him* (*proskalesamenos*). First aorist middle
(indirect) participle. *Two* (*duo tinas*). Certain two. Not
in Matt. 11:2. *Saying* (*legōn*). John saying by the two
messengers. The message is given precisely alike in Matt.
11:3, which see. In both we have *heteron* for "another,"
either a second or a different kind. In verse 20 Westcott and

Hort read *allon* in the text, *heteron* in the margin. *Prosdokō-men*, may be present indicative or present subjunctive (deliberative), the same contract form (*ao* = *ō*, *aō ō*).

21. *In that hour he cured* (*en ekeinēi tēi horāi etherapeusen*). This item is not in Matthew. Jesus gave the two disciples of John an example of the direct method. They had heard. Then they saw for themselves. *Diseases* (*nosōn*), *plagues* (*mastigōn*), *evil spirits* (*pneumatōn ponērōn*), all kinds of bodily ills, and he singles out the *blind* (*tuphlois*) to whom in particular he bestowed sight (*echarizato blepein*), gave as a free gift (from *charis*, grace) seeing (*blepein*).

22. *What things ye have seen and heard* (*ha eidete kai ēkousate*). In Matt. 11:4, present tense "which ye do hear and see." Rest of verse 22 and 23 as in Matt. 11:4-6, which see for details. Luke mentions no raisings from the dead in verse 21, but the language is mainly general, while here it is specific. *Skandalizomai* used here has the double notion of to trip up and to entrap and in the N.T. always means causing to sin.

24. *When the messengers of John were departed* (*apelthontōn tōn aggelōn Iōanou*). Genitive absolute of aorist active participle. Matt. 11:7 has the present middle participle *poreuomenōn*, suggesting that Jesus began his eulogy of John as soon as the messengers (angels, Luke calls them) were on their way. The vivid questions about the people's interest in John are precisely alike in both Matthew and Luke.

25. *Gorgeously apparelled* (*en himatismōi endoxōi*). In splendid clothing. Here alone in this sense in the N.T. *And live delicately* (*truphēi*). From *thruptō* to break down, to enervate, an old word for luxurious living. See the verb *truphaō* in James 5:5. *In kings' courts* (*en tois basileiois*). Only here in the N.T. Matt. 11:8 has it "in kings' houses." Verses 26 and 27 are precisely alike in Matt. 11 9 and 10, which see for discussion.

26. *A prophet?* (*prophētēn;*). A real prophet will always get

a hearing if he has a message from God. He is a for-speaker, forth-teller (*pro-phētēs*). He may or may not be a fore-teller. The main thing is for the prophet to have a message from God which he is willing to tell at whatever cost to himself. The word of God came to John in the wilderness of Judea (Luke 3:2). That made him a prophet. There is a prophetic element in every real preacher of the Gospel. Real prophets become leaders and moulders of men.

28. *There is none* (*oudeis estin*). No one exists, this means. Matt. 11:11 has *ouk egēgertai* (hath not arisen). See Matthew for discussion of "but little" and "greater."

29. *Justified God* (*edikaiōsan ton theon*). They considered God just or righteous in making these demands of them. Even the publicans did. They submitted to the baptism of John (*baptisthentes to baptisma tou Iōanou*. First aorist passive participle with the cognate accusative retained in the passive. Some writers consider verses 29 and 30 a comment of Luke in the midst of the eulogy of John by Jesus. This would be a remarkable thing for so long a comment to be interjected. It is perfectly proper as the saying of Jesus.

30. *Rejected for themselves* (*ethetēsan eis heautous*). The first aorist active of *atheteō* first seen in LXX and Polybius. Occurs in the papyri. These legalistic interpreters of the law refused to admit the need of confession of sin on their part and so set aside the baptism of John. They annulled God's purposes of grace so far as they applied to them. *Being not baptized by him* (*mē baptisthentes hup' autou*. First aorist passive participle. *Mē* is the usual negative of the participle in the *Koiné*.

31. *And to what are they like?* (*kai tini eisin homoioi;*). This second question is not in Matt. 11:16. It sharpens the point. The case of *tini* is associative instrumental after *homoioi*. See discussion of details in Matthew.

32. *And ye did not weep* (*kai ouk eklausate*). Here Matt. 11:17 has "and ye did not mourn (or beat your breast, *ouk*

ekopsasthe). They all did it at funerals. These children
would not play wedding or funeral.

33. *John the Baptist is come* (*elēluthen*). Second perfect
active indicative where Matt. 11:18 has *ēlthen* second aorist
active indicative. So as to verse 34. Luke alone has
"bread" and "wine." Otherwise these verses like Matt.
11:18 and 19, which see for discussion of details. There are
actually critics today who say that Jesus was called the
friend of sinners and even of harlots because he loved them
and their ways and so deserved the slur cast upon him by his
enemies. If men can say that today we need not wonder
that the Pharisees and lawyers said it then to justify their
own rejection of Jesus.

35. *Of all her children* (*apo pantōn tōn teknōn autēs*). Here
Matt. 11:19 has "by her works" (*apo tōn ergōn autēs*). Aleph
has *ergōn* here. The use of "children" personifies wisdom as
in Prov. 8 and 9.

36. *That he would eat with him* (*hina phagēi met' autou*).
Second aorist active subjunctive. The use of *hina* after
erōtaō (see also Luke 16:27) is on the border between the
pure object clause and the indirect question (Robertson,
Grammar, p. 1046) and the pure final clause. Luke has two
other instances of Pharisees who invited Jesus to meals
(11:37; 14:1) and he alone gives them. This is the Gospel of
Hospitality (Ragg). Jesus would dine with a Pharisee or
with a publican (Luke 5:29 = Mark 2:15 = Matt. 9:10) and
even invited himself to be the guest of Zaccheus (Luke 9:5).
This Pharisee was not as hostile as the leaders in Jerusalem.
It is not necessary to think this Pharisee had any sinister
motive in his invitation though he was not overly friendly
(Plummer).

37. *A woman which was in the city, a sinner* (*gunē hētis en
tēi polei hamartōlos*). Probably in Capernaum. The use of
hētis means "Who was of such a character as to be" (cf. 8:3)
and so more than merely the relative *hē*, who, that is,

"who was a sinner in the city," a woman of the town, in other words, and known to be such. *Hamartōlos*, from *hamartanō*, to sin, means devoted to sin and uses the same form for feminine and masculine. It is false and unjust to Mary Magdalene, introduced as a new character in Luke 8:2, to identify this woman with her. Luke would have no motive in concealing her name here and the life of a courtesan would be incompatible with the sevenfold possession of demons. Still worse is it to identify this courtesan not only with Mary Magdalene, but also with Mary of Bethany simply because it is a Simon who gives there a feast to Jesus when Mary of Bethany does a beautiful deed somewhat like this one here (Mark 14:3–9 = Matt. 26:6–13 = John 12; 2–8). Certainly Luke knew full well the real character of Mary of Bethany (10:38–42) so beautifully pictured by him. But a falsehood, once started, seems to have more lives than the cat's proverbial nine. The very name Magdalene has come to mean a repentant courtesan. But we can at least refuse to countenance such a slander on Mary Magdalene and on Mary of Bethany. This sinful woman had undoubtedly repented and changed her life and wished to show her gratitude to Jesus who had rescued her. Her bad reputation as a harlot clung to her and made her an unwelcome visitor in the Pharisee's house. *When she knew* (*epignousa*). Second aorist active participle from *epiginōskō*, to know fully, to recognize. She came in by a curious custom of the time that allowed strangers to enter a house uninvited at a feast, especially beggars seeking a gift. This woman was an intruder whereas Mary of Bethany was an invited guest. "Many came in and took their places on the side seats, uninvited and yet unchallenged. They spoke to those at table on business or the news of the day, and our host spoke freely to them" (Trench in his *Parables*, describing a dinner at a Consul's house at Damietta). *He was sitting at meat* (*katakeitai*). Literally, he is reclining (present tense retained in indirect discourse in Greek). *An alabaster cruse of ointment* (*alabastron murou*). See on Matt. 26:7 for discussion of *alabastron* and *murou*.

38. *Standing behind at his feet* (*stāsa opisō para tous podas autou*). Second aorist active participle from *histēmi* and intransitive, first aorist *estēsa* being transitive. The guest removed his sandals before the meal and he reclined on the left side with the feet outward. She was standing beside (*para*) his feet *weeping* (*klaiousa*). She was drawn irresistibly by gratitude to Jesus and is overcome with emotion before she can use the ointment; her tears (*tois dakrusin*, instrumental case of *dakru*) take the place of the ointment. *Wiped them with the hair of her head* (*tais thrixin tēs kephalēs autēs exemassen*). Inchoative imperfect of an old verb *ekmassō*, to rub out or off, began to wipe off, an act of impulse evidently and of embarrassment. "Among the Jews it was a shameful thing for a woman to let down her hair in public; but she makes this sacrifice" (Plummer). So Mary of Bethany wiped the feet of Jesus with her hair (John 12:3) with a similar sacrifice out of her great love for Jesus. This fact is relied on by some to prove that Mary of Bethany had been a woman of bad character, surely an utter failure to recognize Mary's motive and act. *Kissed* (*katephilei*). Imperfect active of *kataphileō*, to kiss repeatedly (force of *kata*), and accented by the tense of continued action here. The word in the N.T. occurs here, of the prodigal's father (15:20), of the kiss of Judas (Mark 14:45 = Matt. 26:49), of the Ephesian elders (Acts 20:37). "Kissing the feet was a common mark of deep reverence, especially to leading rabbis" (Plummer). *Anointed them with the ointment* (*ēleiphen tōi murōi*). Imperfect active again of *aleiphō*, a very common verb. *Chriō* has a more religious sense. The anointing came after the burst of emotional excitement.

39. *This man* (*houtos*). Contemptuous, this fellow. *If he were a* (*the*) *prophet* (*ei ēn* [*ho*] *prophētēs*). Condition of the

second class, determined as unfulfilled. The Pharisee assumes that Jesus is not a prophet (or the prophet, reading of
B, that he claims to be). A Greek condition puts the thing
from the standpoint of the speaker or writer. It does not
deal with the actual facts, but only with the statement about
the facts. *Would have perceived* (*eginōsken an*). Wrong
translation, would now perceive or know (which he assumes
that Jesus does not do). The protasis is false and the conclusion also. He is wrong in both. The conclusion (apodosis),
like the condition, deals here with the present situation and
so both use the imperfect indicative (*an* in the conclusion,
a mere device for making it plain that it is not a condition
of the first class). *Who and what manner of woman* (*tis kai
potapē hē gunē*). She was notorious in person and character.

40. *Answering* (*apokritheis*). First aorist passive participle, redundant use with *eipen*. Jesus answers the thoughts
and doubts of Simon and so shows that he knows all about
the woman also. Godet notes a tone of Socratic irony here.

41. *A certain lender* (*danistēi tini*). A lender of money
with interest. Here alone in the N.T. though a common
word. *Debtors* (*chreophiletai*). From *chreō* (debt, obligation)
and *opheilō*, to owe. Only here and 16:5 in the N.T., though
common in late Greek writers. *Owed* (*ōpheilen*). Imperfect
active and so unpaid. Five hundred *dēnaria* and fifty like
two hundred and fifty dollars and twenty-five dollars.

42. *Will love him most* (*pleion agapēsei auton*). Strictly,
comparative *more, pleion*, not superlative *pleista*, but most
suits the English idiom best, even between two. Superlative
forms are vanishing before the comparative in the *Koinē*.
This is the point of the parable, the attitude of the two debtors toward the lender who forgave both of them (Plummer).

43. *I suppose* (*hupolambanō*). Old verb, originally to
take up from under, to bear away as on high, to take up in
speech (Luke 10:30), to take up in mind or to assume as here
and Acts 2:15. Here with an air of supercilious indifference

(Plummer). *The most (to pleion).* The more. *Rightly (orthōs).* Correctly. Socrates was fond of *panu orthōs.* The end of the argument.

44. *Turning (strapheis).* Second aorist passive participle. *Seest thou (blepeis).* For the first time Jesus looks at the woman and he asks the Pharisee to look at her. She was behind Jesus. Jesus was an invited guest. The Pharisee had neglected some points of customary hospitality. The contrasts here made have the rhythm of Hebrew poetry. In each contrast the first word is the point of defect in Simon: *water* (44), *kiss* (45), *oil* (46).

45. *Hath not ceased to kiss (ou dielipen kataphilousa).* Supplementary participle.

46. *With ointment (murōi).* Instrumental case. She used the costly ointment even for the feet of Jesus.

47. *Are forgiven (apheōntai).* Doric perfect passive form. See Luke 5:21, 23. *For she loved much (hoti ēgapēsen polu).* Illustration or proof, not reason for the forgiveness. Her sins had been already forgiven and remained forgiven. *But to whom little is forgiven, the same loveth little (Hōi de oligon aphietai oligon agapāi).* This explanation proves that the meaning of *hoti* preceding is proof, not cause.

48. *Are forgiven (apheōntai).* As in verse 47. Remain forgiven, Jesus means, in spite of the slur of the Pharisee.

49. *Who even forgiveth sins (hos kai hamartias aphiēsin).* Present indicative active of same verb, *aphiēmi.* Once before the Pharisees considered Jesus guilty of blasphemy in claiming the power to forgive sins (Luke 5:21). Jesus read their inmost thoughts as he always does.

CHAPTER VIII

1. *Soon afterwards (en tōi kathexēs).* In 7:11 we have *en tōi hexēs.* This word means one after the other, successively, but that gives no definite data as to the time, only that this incident in 8:1–3 follows that in 7:36–50. Both in Luke alone. *That (kai).* One of Luke's idioms with *kai egeneto* like Hebrew *wav. Went about (diōdeuen).* Imperfect active of *diodeuō,* to make one's way through (*dia, hodos*), common in late Greek writers. In the N.T. here only and Acts 17:1. *Through cities and villages (kata polin kai kōmēn).* Distributive use of *kata* (up and down). The clause is amphibolous and goes equally well with *diōdeuen* or with *kērussōn* (heralding) *kai euaggelizomenos* (evangelizing, gospelizing). This is the second tour of Galilee, this time the Twelve with him.

2. *Which had been healed (hai ēsan tetherapeumenai).* Periphrastic past perfect passive, suggesting that the healing had taken place some time before this tour. These women all had personal grounds of gratitude to Jesus. *From whom seven devils (demons) had gone out (aph' hēs daimonia hepta exelēluthei).* Past perfect active third singular for the *daimonia* are neuter plural. This first mention of Mary Magdalene describes her special cause of gratitude. This fact is stated also in Mark 16:9 in the disputed close of the Gospel. The presence of seven demons in one person indicates special malignity (Mark 5:9). See Matt. 12:45 for the parable of the demon who came back with seven other demons worse than the first. It is not known where Magdala was, whence Mary came.

3. *Joanna (Iōana).* Her husband *Chuzā,* steward (*epitropou*) of Herod, is held by some to be the nobleman (*basilikos*) of John 4:46–53 who believed and all his house. At

any rate Christ had a follower from the household of Herod
Antipas who had such curiosity to see and hear him. One
may recall also Manaen (Acts 13:1), Herod's foster brother.
Joanna is mentioned again with Mary Magdalene in Luke
24:10. *Who ministered unto them (haitines diēkonoun autois).*
Imperfect active of *diakoneō*, common verb, but note augment as if from *dia* and *akoneō*, but from *diakonos* and that
from *dia* and *konis* (dust). The very fact that Jesus now
had twelve men going with him called for help from others
and the women of means responded to the demand. *Of their
substance (ek tōn huparchontōn autais).* From the things
belonging to them. This is the first woman's missionary
society for the support of missionaries of the Gospel. They
had difficulties in their way, but they overcame these, so
great was their gratitude and zeal.

4. *By a parable (dia parabolēs).* Mark 4:2 says "in parables" as does Matt. 13:3. This is the beginning of the first
great group of parables as given in Mark 4:1–34 and Matt.
13:1-53. There are ten of these parables in Mark and Matthew and only two in Luke 8:4–18 (The Sower and the Lamp,
8:16) though Luke also has the expression "in parables"
(8:10). See Matt. 13 and Mark 4 for discussion of the word
parable and the details of the Parable of the Sower. Luke
does not locate the place, but he mentions the great crowds
on hand, while both Mark and Matthew name the seaside
as the place where Jesus was at the start of the series of
parables.

5. *His seed (ton sporon autou).* Peculiar to Luke. *Was
trodden under foot (katepatēthē).* First aorist passive indicative of *katapateō*. Peculiar to Luke here. *Of the heavens
(tou ouranou).* Added in Luke.

6. *Upon the rock (epi tēn petran).* Mark 4:5 "the rocky
ground" (*epi to petrōdes*), Matt. 13:5 "the rocky places.
As soon as it grew (phuen).* Second aorist passive participle
of *phuō*, an old verb to spring up like a sprout. *Witherea*

away (*exēranthē*). First aorist passive indicative of *zērainō*, old verb, to dry up. *Moisture* (*ikmada*). Here only in the N.T., though common word.

7. *Amidst the thorns* (*en mesōi tōn akanthōn*). Mark 4:7 has *eis* (among) and Matt. 13:7 has *epi* "upon." *Grew with it* (*sunphueisai*). Same participle as *phuen* above with *sun-* (together). *Choked* (*apepnixan*). From *apopnigō*, to choke off as in Matt. 13:7. In Mark 4:7 the verb is *sunepnixan* (choked together).

8. *A hundredfold* (*hekatonplasiona*). Luke omits the thirty and sixty of Mark 4:8 and Matt. 13:8. *He cried* (*ephōnei*). Imperfect active, and in a loud voice, the verb means. The warning about hearing with the ears occurs also in Mark 4:9 and Matt. 13:9.

9. *Asked* (*epērōtōn*). Imperfect of *eperōtaō* (*epi* and *erōtaō*) where Mark 4:10 has *ērōtōn* (uncompounded imperfect), both the tense and the use of *epi* indicate eager and repeated questions on the part of the disciples, perhaps dimly perceiving a possible reflection on their own growth. *What this parable might be* (*tis hautē eiē hē parabolē*). A mistranslation, What this parable was (or meant). The optative *eiē* is merely due to indirect discourse, changing the indicative *estin* (is) of the direct question to the optative *eiē* of the indirect, a change entirely with the writer or speaker and without any change of meaning (Robertson, *Grammar*, pp. 1043f.).

10. *The mysteries* (*ta mustēria*). See for this word on Matt. 13:11 = Mark 4:11. Part of the mystery here explained is how so many people who have the opportunity to enter the kingdom fail to do so because of manifest unfitness. *That* (*hina*). Here Mark 4:11 also has *hina* while Matt. 13:13 has *hoti* (because). On the so-called causal use of *hina* as here equal to *hoti* see discussion on Matt. 13:13 and Mark 4:11. Plummer sensibly argues that there is truth both in the causal *hoti* of Matthew and the final *hina* of Mark

and Matthew. "But the principle that he who hath shall receive more, while he who hath not shall be deprived of what he seemeth to have, explains both the *hina* and the *hoti*. Jesus speaks in parables because the multitudes see without seeing and hear without hearing. But He also speaks in parable *in order that* they may see without seeing and hear without hearing." Only for "hearing" Luke has "understand" *suniōsin*, present subjunctive from a late omega form *suniō* instead of the *-mi* verb *suniēmi*.

11. *Is this* (*estin de hautē*). Means this. Jesus now proceeds to interpret his own parable. *The seed is the word of God* (*ho sporos estin ho logos tou theou*). The article with both subject and predicate as here means that they are interchangeable and can be turned round: The word of God is the seed. The phrase "the word of God" does not appear in Matthew and only once in Mark (7:13) and John (10:35), but four times in Luke (5:1; 8:11, 21; 11:28) and twelve times in Acts. In Mark 4:14 we have only "the word." In Mark 3:31 we have "the will of God," and in Matt. 12:46 "the will of my Father" where Luke 8:21 has "the word of God." This seems to show that Luke has the subjective genitive here and means the word that comes from God.

12. *Those by the wayside* (*hoi para tēn hodon*). As in Mark 4:15 = Matt. 19 so here the people who hear the word = the seed are discussed by metonymy. *The devil* (*ho diabolos*). The slanderer. Here Mark 4:15 has Satan. *From their heart* (*apo tēs kardias autōn*). Here Mark has "in them." It is the devil's business to snatch up the seed from the heart before it sprouts and takes root. Every preacher knows how successful the devil is with his auditors. Matt. 13:19 has it "sown in the heart." *That they may not believe and be saved* (*hina mē pisteusantes sōthōsin*). Peculiar to Luke. Negative purpose with aorist active participle and first aorist (ingressive) passive subjunctive. Many reasons are offered today for the failure of preachers to win souls. Here is the

main one, the activity of the devil during and after the
preaching of the sermon. No wonder then that the sower
must have good seed and sow wisely, for even then he can
only win partial success.

13. *Which for a while believe* (*hoi pros kairon pisteuousin*).
Ostensibly they are sincere and have made a real start in
the life of faith. *They fall away* (*aphistantai*). Present
middle indicative. They stand off, lose interest, stop coming
to church, drop out of sight. It is positively amazing the
number of new church members who "stumble" as Mark
4:17 has it (*skandalizontai*), do not like the pastor, take
offence at something said or done by somebody, object to
the appeals for money, feel slighted. The "season of trial"
becomes a "season of temptation" (*en kairōi peirasmou*) for
these superficial, emotional people who have to be periodi-
cally rounded up if kept within the fold.

14. *They are choked* (*sunpnigontai*). Present passive indicative of this powerfully vivid compound verb *sunpnigō*
used in Mark 4:19 = Matt. 13:22, only there these worldly
weeds choke the word while here the victims themselves are
choked. Both are true. Diphtheria will choke and strangle
the victim. Who has not seen the promise of fair flower and
fruit choked into yellow withered stalk without fruit "as
they go on their way" (*poreuomenoi*). *Bring no fruit to
perfection* (*ou telesphorousin*). Compound verb common in
the late writers (*telos, phoreō*). To bring to completion.
Used of fruits, animals, pregnant women. Only here in the
N.T.

15. *In an honest and good heart* (*en kardiāi kalēi kai aga-
thēi*). Peculiar to Luke. In verse 8 the land (*gēn*) is called
agathēn (really good, generous) and in verse 15 we have *en
tēi kalēi gēi* (*in the beautiful or noble land*). So Luke uses both
adjectives of the heart. The Greeks used *kalos k' agathos* of
the high-minded gentleman. It is probable that Luke knew
this idiom. It occurs here alone in the N.T. It is not easy

to translate. We have such phrases as "good and true," "sound and good," "right and good," no one of which quite suits the Greek. Certainly Luke adds new moral qualities not in the Hellenic phrase. The English word "honest" here is like the Latin *honestus* (fair, noble). The words are to be connected with "hold fast" (*katechousin*), "hold it down" so that the devil does not snatch it away, having depth of soil so that it does not shrivel up under the sun, and is not choked by weeds and thorns. It bears fruit (*karpophorousin*, an old expressive verb, *karpos* and *phoreō*). That is the proof of spiritual life. *In patience* (*en hupomonēi*). There is no other way for real fruit to come. Mushrooms spring up overnight, but they are usually poisonous. The best fruits require time, cultivation, patience.

16. *When he hath lighted a lamp* (*luchnon hapsas*). It is a portable lamp (*luchnon*) that one lights (*hapsas* aorist active participle of *haptō*, to kindle, fasten to, light). *With a vessel* (*skeuei*, instrumental case of *skeuos*). Here Mark 4:21 has the more definite figure "under the bushel" as has Matt. 5:15. *Under the bed* (*hupokatō klinēs*). Here Mark 4:21 has the regular *hupo tēn klinēn* instead of the late compound *hupokatō*. Ragg notes that Matthew distributes the sayings of Jesus given here by Luke 8:16–18 = Mark 4:21–25 concerning the parable of the lamp and gives them in three separate places (Matt. 5:15; 10:26; 13:12). That is true, but it does not follow that Mark and Luke have bunched together separate sayings or that Matthew has scattered sayings delivered only on one occasion. One of the slowest lessons for some critics to learn is that Jesus repeated favourite sayings on different occasions and in different groupings just as every popular preacher and teacher does today. See on Mark 4:21 for further discussion of the lamp and stand. *May see the light* (*Blepōsin to phōs*). In Matt. 5:16 Jesus has it "may see your good works." The purpose of light is to let one see something else, not the light. Note present subjunctive

(*blepōsin*), linear action "Jesus had kindled a light within them. They must not hide it, but must see that it spreads to others" (Plummer). The parable of the lamp throws light on the parable of the sower.

17. *That shall not be known* (*ho ou mē gnōsthēi*). Peculiar to Luke. First aorist passive subjunctive of *ginōskō* with the strong double negative *ou mē*. See on Mark 4:22 for discussion of *krupton* and *apokruphon*.

18. *How ye hear* (*pōs akouete*). The manner of hearing. Mark 4:24 has "what ye hear" (*ti akouete*), the matter that is heard. Both are supremely important. Some things should not be heard at all. Some that are heard should be forgotten. Others should be treasured and practised. *For whosoever hath* (*Hos an gar echēi*). Present active subjunctive of the common verb *echō* which may mean "keep on having" or "acquiring." See on Mark 4:25 for discussion. *Thinketh he hath* (*dokei echein*), or *seems to acquire or to hold*. Losses in business illustrate this saying as when we see their riches take wings and fly away. So it is with hearing and heeding. Self-deception is a common complaint.

19. *His mother and brethren* (*hē mētēr kai hoi adelphoi autou*). Mark 3:31–35 and Matt. 12:46–50 place the visit of the mother and brothers of Jesus before the parable of the sower. Usually Luke follows Mark's order, but he does not do so here. At first the brothers of Jesus (younger sons of Joseph and Mary, I take the words to mean, there being sisters also) were not unfriendly to the work of Jesus as seen in John 2:12 when they with the mother of Jesus are with him and the small group (half dozen) disciples in Capernaum after the wedding in Cana. But as Jesus went on with his work and was rejected at Nazareth (Luke 4:16–31), there developed an evident disbelief in his claims on the part of the brothers who ridiculed him six months before the end (John 7:5). At this stage they have apparently come with Mary to take Jesus home out of the excitement of the crowds,

perhaps thinking that he is beside himself (Mark 3:21).
They hardly believed the charge of the rabbis that Jesus
was in league with Beelzebub. Certainly the mother of
Jesus could give no credence to that slander. But she herself was deeply concerned and wanted to help him if possible.
See discussion of the problem in my little book *The Mother
of Jesus* and also on Mark 3:31 and Matt. 12:46. *Come to
him (suntuchein).* Second aorist active infinitive of *sun-
tugchanō*, an old verb, though here alone in the N.T., meaning to meet with, to fall in with as if accidentally, here with
associative instrumental case *autōi*.

20. *Was told (apēggelē).* Second aorist passive indicative
of *apaggellō*, to bring word or tidings. Common verb. See
on Mark 3:32 and Matt. 12:47 for details.

21. *These which hear the word of God and do it (hoi ton
logon tou theou akouontes kai poiountes).* The absence of the
article with "mother" and "brothers" probably means, as
Plummer argues, "Mother to me and brothers to me are
those who &c." No one is a child of God because of human
parentage (John 1:13). "Family ties are at best temporal;
spiritual ties are eternal" (Plummer). Note the use of
"hear and do" together here as in Matt. 7:24 = Luke 6:47
at the close of the Sermon on the Mount. The parable of
the sower is almost like a footnote to that sermon. Later
Jesus will make "doing" a test of friendship for him (John
15:14).

22. *And they launched forth (kai anēchthēsan).* First aorist
passive indicative of *anagō*, an old verb, to lead up, to put
out to sea (looked at as going up from the land). This nautical sense of the verb occurs only in Luke in the N.T. and
especially in the Acts (13:13; 16:11; 18:21; 20:3, 13; 21:1, 2;
27:2, 4, 12, 21; 28:10f.).

23. *He fell asleep (aphupnōsen).* First aorist (ingressive)
active indicative of *aphupnoō*, to put to sleep, to fall off to
sleep, a late verb for which the older Greek used *kathupnoō*.

Originally *aphupnoō* meant to waken from sleep, then to fall off to sleep (possibly a medical use). This is the only passage which speaks of the sleep of Jesus. Here only in the N.T. *Came down (katebē)*. Second aorist active indicative of *katabainō*, common verb. It was literally true. These wind storms (*lailaps*. So also Mark 4:37) rushed from Hermon down through the Jordan gorge upon the Sea of Galilee and shook it like a tempest (Matt. 8:24). Mark's (4:37) vivid use of the dramatic present *ginetai* (ariseth) is not so precise as Luke's "came down." See on Matt. 8:24. These sudden squalls were dangerous on this small lake. *They were filling (suneplērounto)*. Imperfect passive. It was the boat that was being filled (Mark 4:37) and it is here applied to the navigators as sailors sometimes spoke. An old verb, but in the N.T. used only by Luke (8:23; 9:51; Acts 2:1). *Were in jeopardy (ekinduneuon)*. Imperfect active, vivid description. Old verb, but in the N.T. only here, Acts 19:27; I Cor. 15:30.

24. *Master, Master (Epistata, epistata)*. See on Luke 5:5 for discussion. Mark 4:38 has *Teacher (Didaskale)*, Matt. 8:25 has *Lord (Kurie)*. The repetition here shows the uneasiness of the disciples. *We perish (apollumetha)*. So in Mark 4:38 and Matt. 8:25. Linear present middle indicative, we are perishing. *The raging of the water (tōi kludoni tou hudatos)*. *Kludōn*, common Greek word, is a boisterous surge, a violent agitation. Here only in the N.T. save James 1:6. *Kuma* (Mark 4:37) is the regular swell or wave. *A calm (galēnē)*. Only in the parallels in the N.T., though common word. Here Mark 4:39 and Matt. 8:26 add *great (megalē)*. *That (hoti)*. This use of *hoti* as explanatory of the demonstrative pronoun *houtos* occurs in the parallels Mark 4:36 = Matt. 8:27 and also in Luke 4:36. It is almost result. *He commandeth (epitassei)*. Peculiar to Luke.

26. *They arrived (katepleusan)*. First aorist active indicative of *katapleō*, common verb, but here only in the N.T.

Literally, *they sailed down* from the sea to the land, the opposite of *launched forth* (*anēchthēsan*) of verse 22. So we today use like nautical terms, to bear up, to bear down. *The Gerasenes* (*tōn Gerasēnōn*). This is the correct text here as in Mark 5:1 while Gadarenes is correct in Matt. 8:28. See there for explanation of this famous discrepancy, now cleared up by Thomson's discovery of Khersa (*Gersa*) on the steep eastern bank and in the vicinity of Gadara. *Over against Galilee* (*antipera tēs Galilaias*). Only here in the N.T. The later Greek form is *antiperan* (Polybius, etc.). Some MSS. here have *peran* like Mark 5:1 = Matt. 8:28.

27. *And for a long time* (*kai chronōi hikanōi*). The use of the associative instrumental case in expressions of time is a very old Greek idiom that still appears in the papyri (Robertson, *Grammar*, p. 527). *He had worn no clothes* (*ouk enedusato himation*). First aorist middle indicative, constative aorist, viewing the "long time" as a point. Not pluperfect as English has it and not for the pluperfect, simply "and for a long time he did not put on himself (indirect middle) any clothing." The physician would naturally note this item. Common verb *enduō* or *endunō*. This item in Luke alone, though implied by Mark 5:15 "clothed" (*himatismenon*). *And abode not in any house* (*kai en oikiāi ouk emenen*). Imperfect active. Peculiar to Luke, though implied by the mention of tombs in all three (Mark 5:3 = Matt. 8:28 = Luke 8:27).

28. *Fell down* (*prosepesen*). Second aorist active of *prospiptō*, to fall forward, towards, prostrate before one as here. Common verb. Mark 5:6 has *prosekunēsen* (worshipped). *The Most High God* (*tou theou tou hupsistou*). Uncertain whether *tou theou* genuine or not. But "the Most High" clearly means God as already seen (Luke 1:32, 35, 36; 6:35). The phrase is common among heathen (Num. 24:16; Micah. 6:6; Isa. 14:14). The demoniac may have been a Gentile, but it is the demon here speaking. See on Mark

2:7 = Matt. 8:29 for the Greek idiom (*ti emoi kai soi*). "What have I to do with thee?" See there also for "Torment me not."

29. *For he commanded* (*parēggellen gar*). Imperfect active, correct text, for he was commanding. *Oftentimes* (*pollois chronois*). Or "for a long time" like *chronōi pollōi* of verse 27 (see Robertson, *Grammar*, p. 537, for the plural here). *It had seized* (*sunērpakei*). Past perfect active of *sunarpazō*, to lay hold by force. An old verb, but only in Luke in the N.T. (Luke 8:29; Acts 6:12; 19:29; 27:15). *Was kept under guard* (*edesmeueto*). Imperfect passive of *desmeuō* to put in chains, from *desmos*, bond, and that from *deō* to bind. Old, but rather rare verb. Only here and Acts 22:4 in this sense. In Matt. 23:4 it means to bind together. Some MSS. read *desmeō* in Luke 8:29. *Breaking the bands asunder* (*diarēssōn ta desma*). Old verb, the preposition *dia* (in two) intensifying the meaning of the simple verb *rēssō* or *rēgnumi*, to rend. *Was driven* (*ēlauneto*). Imperfect passive of *elaunō*, to drive, to row, to march (Xenophon). Only five times in the N.T. Here alone in Luke and peculiar to Luke in this incident.

30. *Legion* (*Legiōn*). See on Mark 5:9.

31. *Into the abyss* (*eis tēn abusson*). Rare old word common in LXX from *a* privative and *bathus* (deep). So bottomless place (supply *chōra*). The deep sea in Gen. 1:2; 7:11. The common receptacle of the dead in Rom. 10:7 and especially the abode of demons as here and Rev. 9:1–11; 11:7; 17:8; 20:1, 3.

32. *A herd of many swine* (*agelē choirōn hikanōn*). Word *herd* (*agelē*) old as Homer, but in N.T. only here and parallels (Mark 5:11 = Matt. 8:30). Luke shows his fondness for adjective *hikanos* here again (see verse 27) where Mark has *megalē* and Matthew *pollōn*.

33. *Rushed down the steep* (*hōrmēsen kata tou krēmnou*). Ablative with *kata* as in Mark 5:13 and Matt. 8:32 and the

same vivid verb in each account, to hurl impetuously, to rush. *Were choked (apepnigē).* Second aorist (constative) passive indicative third singular (collective singular) where Mark 5:13 has the picturesque imperfect *epnigonto.*

34. *Saw what had come to pass (idontes to gegonos).* This item only in Luke. Note the neat Greek idiom *to gegonos,* articular second perfect active participle of *ginomai.* Repeated in verse 35 and in Mark 5:14. Note numerous participles here in verse 35 as in Mark 5:15.

36. *He that was possessed with devils (demons)* (only two words in Greek, *ho daimonistheis,* the demonized). *Was made whole (esōthē).* First aorist passive indicative of *sōzō* to save from *sōs* (safe and sound). This is additional information to the news carried to them in verse 34.

37. *Were holden with great fear (phoboi megaloi suneichonto).* Imperfect passive of *sunechō* with the instrumental case of *phobos.* See a similar use of this vigorous verb in Luke 12:50 of Jesus and in Phil. 1:23 of Paul.

38. *From whom the devils (demons) were gone out (aph' hou exelēluthei ta daimonia).* Past perfect active of *exerchomai,* state of completion in the past. *Prayed him (edeeito autou).* Imperfect middle, kept on begging.

39. *Throughout the whole city (kath' holēn tēn polin).* Mark 5:20 has it "in Decapolis." He had a great story to tell and he told it with power. The rescue missions in our cities can match this incident with cases of great sinners who have made witnesses for Christ.

40. *Welcomed (apedexato).* Peculiar to Luke. To receive with pleasure, from *apodechomai,* a common verb. *For they were all waiting for him (ēsan gar pantes prosdokōntes auton).* Periphrastic imperfect active of *prosdokaō,* an old verb for eager expectancy, a vivid picture of the attitude of the people towards Jesus. Driven from Decapolis, he is welcomed in Capernaum.

41. *Was (hupērchen).* Imperfect of *huparchō* in sense of

ēn as in modern Greek. Common in Luke, and Acts, but not in other Gospels.

42. An only daughter (*thugatēr monogenēs*). The same adjective used of the widow's son (7:12) and the epileptic boy (9:38) and of Jesus (John 1:18; 3:16). *She lay a dying* (*apethnēsken*). Imperfect active, she was dying. Matt. 9:18 has it that she has just died. *Thronged* (*sunepnigon*). Imperfect active of *sumpnigō*, to press together, the verb used of the thorns choking the growing grain (Luke 8:14). It was a jam.

43. *Had spent all her living upon physicians* (*eis iatrous prosanalōsasa holon ton bion*). First aorist active participle of an old verb *prosanaliskō*, only here in the N.T. But Westcott and Hort reject this clause because it is not in B D Syriac Sinaitic. Whether genuine or not, the other clause in Mark 5:26 certainly is not in Luke: "had suffered many things of many physicians." Probably both are not genuine in Luke who takes care of the physicians by the simple statement that it was a chronic case: *could not be healed of any* (*ouk ischusen ap' oudenos therapeuthēnai*). He omitted also what Mark has: "and was nothing bettered but rather grew worse."

44. *The border of his garment* (*tou kraspedou tou himatiou*). Probably the tassel of the overgarment. Of the four corners two were in front and two behind. See on Matt. 9:20. *Stanched* (*estē*). Second aorist active indicative, *stopped* at once (effective aorist).

45. *Press thee and crush thee* (*sunechousin se kai apothlibousin*). Hold thee together, hold thee in (*sunechō*, see verse 37). Crush thee (*apothlibō*) here only in the N.T., a verb used of pressing out grapes in Diodorus and Josephus. Mark 5:31 has *sunthlibō*, to press together.

46. *For I perceived that power had gone forth from me* (*egō gar egnōn dunamin exelēluthuian ap' emou*). *Egnōn* is second aorist active indicative of *ginōskō*, knowledge by personal

experience as here. It is followed by the second perfect active participle *exeleluthuian* in indirect discourse (Robertson, *Grammar*, pp. 1040–42). Jesus felt the sensation of power already gone. Who does not know what this sense of "goneness" or exhaustion of nervous energy means?

47. *Trembling* (*tremousa*). Vivid touch of the feeling of this sensitive woman who now had to tell everybody of her cure, "in the presence of all the people" (*enōpion pantos tou laou*). She faced the widest publicity for her secret cure.

49. *From the ruler of the synagogue's house* (*para tou archisunagōgou*). The word "house" is not in the Greek here as in Mark 5:35 where *apo* is used rather than *para*, as here. But the ruler himself had come to Jesus (Luke 8:41) and this is the real idea. Trouble not (*mēketi skulle*). See on Luke 7:6 for this verb and also Mark 5:35 and Matt 9:36.

50. *And she shall be made whole* (*kai sōthēsetai*). This promise in addition to the words in Mark 5:36. See there for discussion of details.

53. *Knowing that she was dead* (*eidotes hoti apethanen*). That she died (*apethanen*), second aorist active indicative of *apothnēskō*.

54. *Called* (*ephōnēsen*). Certainly not to wake up the dead, but to make it plain to all that she rose in response to his elevated tone of voice. Some think that the remark of Jesus in verse 52 (= Mark 5:39 = Matt. 9:24) proves that she was not really dead, but only in a trance. It matters little. The touch of Christ's hand and the power of his voice restored her to life. *Maiden* (*hē pais*) rather than Mark's (5:41) *to korasion* (vernacular *Koinē*).

55. *Her spirit returned* (*epestrepsen to pneuma autēs*). The life came back to her at once. *Be given her to eat* (*autēi dothēnai phagein*). The first infinitive *dothēnai* is an indirect command. The second *phagein* (second aorist active of *esthiō*) is epexegetic purpose.

CHAPTER IX

1. *He called the twelve together* (*sunkalesamenos tous dō-deka*). Mark 6:7 and Matt. 10:1 have *proskaleōmai*, to call to him. Both the indirect middle voice.

2. *He sent them forth* (*apesteilen autous*). First aorist active indicative of *apostellō*. *To preach the kingdom of God and to heal the sick* (*kērussein tēn basileian tou theou kai iās-thai*). Present indicative for the continuous functions during this campaign. This double office of herald (*kērussein*) and healer (*iāsthai*) is stated directly in Matt. 10:7-8. Note the verb *iaomai* for healing here, though *therapeuein* in verse 1, apparently used interchangeably.

3. *Neither staff* (*mēte rabdon*). For the apparent contradiction between these words (= Matt. 10:10) and Mark 6:8 see discussion there. For *pēran* (wallet) see also on Mark 6:8 (= Matt. 10:10) for this and other details here.

5. *As many as receive you not* (*hosoi an mē dechōntai humas*). Indefinite relative plural with *an* and present middle subjunctive and the negative *mē*. Here Matt. 10:14 has the singular (whosoever) and Mark 6:11 has "whatsoever place." *For a testimony against them* (*eis marturion ep' autous*). Note use of *ep' autous* where Mark 6:11 has simply the dative *autois* (disadvantage), really the same idea.

6. *Went* (*diērchonto*). Imperfect middle, continuous and repeated action made plainer also by three present participles (*exerchomenoi, euaggelizomenoi, therapeuontes*), describing the wide extent of the work through all the villages (*kata tas kōmas*, distributive use of *kata*) everywhere (*pantachou*) in Galilee.

7. *All that was done* (*ta ginomena panta*). Present middle participle, "all that was coming to pass." *He was much*

perplexed (*diēporei*). Imperfect active of *diaporeō*, to be thoroughly at a loss, unable to find a way out (*dia*, a privative, *poros*, way), common ancient verb, but only in Luke's writings in the N.T. *Because it was said* (*dia to legesthai*). Neat Greek idiom, the articular passive infinitive after *dia*. Three reports came to the ears of Herod as Luke has it, each introduced by *hoti* (that) in indirect discourse: "By some" (*hupo tinōn*), "by some" (*hupo tinōn de*), "by others" (*allōn de*, *hupo* not here expressed, but carried over). The verbs in the indirect discourse here (verses 7 and 8) are all three aorists (*ēgerthē* first passive; *ephanē* second passive; *anestē* second active), not past perfects as the English has them.

9. *He sought* (*ezētei*). Imperfect active. He keep on seeking to see Jesus. The rumours disturbed Herod because he was sure that he had put him to death ("John I beheaded").

10. *Declared* (*diēgēsanto*). First aorist middle of *diēgeomai*, to carry a narrative through to the end. Jesus listened to it all. *They had done* (*epoiēsan*). Aorist active indicative, they did. *He took them* (*paralabōn autous*). Second aorist active participle of *paralambanō*. Very common verb. *Bethsaida* (*Bēthsaida*). Peculiar to Luke. Bethsaida Julias is the territory of Philip, for it is on the other side of the Sea of Galilee (John 6:1).

11. *Spake* (*elalei*). Imperfect active, he continued speaking. *He healed* (*iāto*). Imperfect middle, he continued healing.

12. *To wear away* (*klinein*). Old verb usually transitive, to bend or bow down. Many compounds as in English decline, incline, recline, clinic (*klinē*, bed), etc. Luke alone in the N.T. uses it intransitively as here. The sun was turning down towards setting. *Lodge* (*katalusōsin*). First aorist active subjunctive of *kataluō*, a common verb, to dissolve, destroy, overthrow, and then of travellers to break a journey, tc lodge (*kataluma*, inn, Luke 2:7). Only here and 19:7

in the N.T. in this sense. *Get victuals* (*heurōsin episitismon*). Ingressive aorist active of *heuriskō*, very common verb. *Victuals* (*episitismon*, from *episitizomai*, to provision oneself, *sitizō*, from *siton*, wheat) only here in the N.T., though common in ancient Greek, especially for provisions for a journey (snack). See on Mark 6:32–44 = Matt. 14:13–21 for discussion of details.

13. *Except we should go and buy food* (*ei mēti poreuthentes hēmeis agorasōmen brōmata*). This is a condition of the third class with the aorist subjunctive (*agorasōmen*), where the conjunction is usually *ean* (with negative *ean mē*), but not always or necessarily so especially in the *Koiné*. So in I Cor. 14:5 *ei mē diermēneuēi* and in Phil. 3:12 *ei kai katalabō*. "Unless" is better here than "except." *Food* (*brōmata*), means eaten pieces from *bibrōskō*, to eat, somewhat like our "edibles" or vernacular "eats."

14. *About* (*hōsei*). Luke as Matt. 14:21 adds this word to the definite statement of Mark 6:44 that there were 5,000 men, a hundred companies of fifty each. *Sit down* (*kataklinate*). First aorist active imperative. Recline, lie down. Only in Luke in the N.T. See also verse 15. *In companies* (*klisias*). Cognate accusative after *kataklinate*. Only here in the N.T. A row of persons reclining at meals (table company). *About fifty each* (*hōsei ana pentēkonta*). Distributive use of *ana* and approximate number again (*hōsei*).

16. *The five . . . the two* (*tous pente . . . tous duo*). Pointing back to verse 13, fine example of the Greek article. *And gave* (*kai edidou*). Imperfect active of *didōmi*, kept on giving. This picturesque imperfect is preceded by the aorist *kateklasen* (brake), a single act. This latter verb in the N.T. only here and the parallel in Mark 6:41, though common enough in ancient Greek. We say "break off" where here the Greek has "break down" (or thoroughly), perfective use of *kata*.

17. *Twelve baskets* (*kophinoi dōdeka*). For discussion of

kophonoi and *sphurides* as well as of *klasmata* (broken pieces) see on Mark 6:43 = Matt. 14:20.

18. *As he was praying (en tōi einai auton proseuchomenon).* Common Lukan idiom of *en* with the articular infinitive for a temporal clause, only here Luke has the periphrastic infinitive (*einai proseuchomenon*) as also in 11:1. This item about Christ's praying alone in Luke. *Alone (kata monas).* In the N.T. only here and Mark 4:10. Perhaps *chōras* (places) is to be supplied with *monas* (lonely places). *Were with him (sunēsan autōi).* This seems like a contradiction unless "alone" is to be taken with *sunēsan.* Westcott and Hort put *sunēntēsan* in the margin. This would mean that as Jesus was praying alone, the disciples fell in with him. At any rate he was praying apart from them.

19. *That I am (me einai).* Accusative and infinitive in indirect assertion, a common Greek idiom. Matt. 16:13 for "I" has "the Son of man" as identical in the consciousness of Christ. The various opinions of men about Jesus here run parallel to the rumours heard by Herod (verses 8 and 9).

20. *But who say ye? (Humeis de tina legete;).* Note the emphatic proleptical position of *humeis:* "But *ye* who do ye say? This is really what mattered now with Jesus. *The Christ of God (Ton christon tou theou).* The accusative though the infinitive is not expressed. The Anointed of God, the Messiah of God. See on 2:26 for "the Anointed of the Lord." See on Matt. 16:17 for discussion of Peter's testimony in full. Mark 6:29 has simply "the Christ." It is clear from the previous narrative that this is not a new discovery from Simon Peter, but simply the settled conviction of the disciples after all the defections of the Galilean masses and the hostility of the Jerusalem ecclesiastics. The disciples still believed in Jesus as the Messiah of Jewish hope and prophecy. It will become plain that they do not grasp the spiritual conception of the Messiah and his kingdom that

Jesus taught, but they are clear that he is the Messiah however faulty their view of the Messiah may be. There was comfort in this for Jesus. They were loyal to him.

21. *To tell this to no man* (*mēdeni legein touto*). Indirect command with the negative infinitive after *commanded* (*parēggeilen*). It had been necessary for Jesus to cease using the word *Messiah* (*Christos*) about himself because of the political meaning to the Jews. Its use by the disciples would lead to revolution as was plain after the feeding of the five thousand (John 6:15).

22. *Rejected* (*apodokimasthēnai*). First aorist passive infinitive of *apodokimazō*, to reject after trial. *The third day* (*tēi tritēi hēmerāi*). Locative case of time as in Matt. 16:21. Here in the parallel passage Mark 8:31 has "after three days" (*meta treis hēmeras*) in precisely the same sense. That is to say, "after three days" is just a free way of saying "on the third day" and cannot mean "on the fourth day" if taken too literally. For discussion of this plain prediction of the death of Christ with various details see discussion on Matt. 16:21 = Mark 8:31. It was a melancholy outlook that depressed the disciples as Mark and Matthew show in the protest of Peter and his rebuke.

23. *He said unto all* (*elegen de pros pantas*). This is like Luke (cf. verse 43). Jesus wanted all (the multitude with his disciples, as Mark 8:34 has it) to understand the lesson of self-sacrifice. They could not yet understand the full meaning of Christ's words as applied to his approaching death of which he had been speaking. But certainly the shadow of the cross is already across the path of Jesus as he is here speaking. For details (soul, life, forfeit, gain, profit, lose, world) see discussion on Matt. 16:24-26 = Mark 8:34-37. The word for lose (*apolesei*, from *apollumi*, a very common verb) is used in the sense of destroy, kill, lose, as here. Note the mercantile terms in this passage (gain, lose, fine or forfeit, exchange). *Daily* (*kath' hēmeran*). Peculiar to Luke

in this incident. Take up the cross (his own cross) daily (aorist tense, *āratō*), but keep on following me (*akoloutheitō*, present tense). The cross was a familiar figure in Palestine. It was rising before Jesus as his destiny. Each man has his own cross to meet and bear.

26. *Whosoever shall be ashamed* (*hos an epaischunthēi*). Rather, *Whosoever is ashamed* as in Mark 8:38. The first aorist passive subjunctive in an indefinite relative clause with *an*. The passive verb is transitive here also. This verb is from *epi* and *aischunē*, shame (in the eyes of men). Jesus endured the shame of the cross (Heb. 12:2). The man at the feast who had to take a lower seat did it with shame (Luke 14:9). Paul is not ashamed of the Gospel (Rom. 1:16). Onesiphorus was not ashamed of Paul (II Tim. 1:16). *In his own glory* (*en tēi doxēi autou*). This item added to what is in Mark 8:38 = Matt. 16:27.

27. *Till they see* (*heōs an idōsin*). Second aorist active subjunctive with *heōs* and *an* referring to the future, an idiomatic construction. So in Mark 9:1 = Matt. 16:28. In all three passages "shall not taste of death" (*ou mē geusōntai thanatou*, double negative with aorist middle subjunctive) occurs also. Rabbinical writings use this figure. Like a physician Christ tasted death that we may see how to die. Jesus referred to the cross as "this cup" (Mark 14:36 = Matt. 26:39 = Luke 22:42). Mark speaks of the kingdom of God as "come" (*elēluthuian*, second perfect active participle). Matthew as "coming" (*erchomenon*) referring to the Son of man, while Luke has neither form. See Matthew and Mark for discussion of the theories of interpretation of this difficult passage. The Transfiguration follows in a week and may be the first fulfilment in the mind of Jesus. It may also symbolically point to the second coming.

28. *About eight days* (*hōsei hēmerai oktō*). A *nominativus pendens* without connexion or construction. Mark 9:2 (=Matt. 17:1) has "after six days" which agrees with the

general statement. *Into the mountain (eis to oros)*. Probably Mount Hermon because we know that Jesus was near Caesarea Philippi when Peter made the confession (Mark 8:27 = Matt. 16:13). Hermon is still the glory of Palestine from whose heights one can view the whole of the land. It was a fit place for the Transfiguration. *To pray (proseuxasthai)*. Peculiar to Luke who so often mentions Christ's habit of prayer (cf. 3:21). See also verse 29 "as he was praying" (*en tōi proseuchesthai*, one of Luke's favourite idioms). *His countenance was altered (egeneto to eidos tou prosōpou autou heteron)*. Literally, "the appearance of his face became different." Matt. 17:2 says that "his face did shine as the sun." Luke does not use the word "transfigured" (*metemorphōthē*) in Mark 9:2 = Matt. 17:2. He may have avoided this word because of the pagan associations with this word as Ovid's *Metamorphoses*. *And his raiment became white and dazzling (kai ho himatismos autou leukos exastraptōn)*. Literally, *And his raiment white radiant*. There is no *and* between "white" and "dazzling." The participle *exastraptōn* is from the compound verb meaning to flash (*astraptō*) out or forth (*ex*). The simple verb is common for lightning flashes and bolts, but the compound in the LXX and here alone in the N.T. See Mark 9:3 "exceeding white" and Matt. 17:2 "white as the light."

31. *There talked with him (sunelaloun autōi)*. Imperfect active, were talking with him. *Who appeared in glory (hoi ophthentes en doxēi)*. First aorist passive participle of *horaō*. This item peculiar to Luke. Compare verse 26. *Spake of his decease (elegon tēn exodon)*. Imperfect active, were talking about his *exodus* (departure from earth to heaven) very much like our English word "decease" (Latin *decessus*, a going away). The glorious light graphically revealed Moses and Elijah talking with Jesus about the very subject concerning which Peter had dared to rebuke Jesus for mentioning (Mark 8:32 = Matt. 16:22). This very

word *exodus* (way out) in the sense of death occurs in II Pet.
1:15 and is followed by a brief description of the Transfiguration glory. Other words for death (*thanatos*) in the N.T.
are *ekbasis*, going out as departure (Heb. 13:7), *aphixis*,
departing (Acts 20:29), *analusis*, loosening anchor (II Tim.
4:6) and *analusai* (Phil. 1:23). *To accomplish* (*plēroun*).
To fulfil. Moses had led the Exodus from Egypt. Jesus
will accomplish the exodus of God's people into the Promised
Land on high. See on Mark and Matthew for discussion of
significance of the appearance of Moses and Elijah as representatives of law and prophecy and with a peculiar death.
The purpose of the Transfiguration was to strengthen the
heart of Jesus as he was praying long about his approaching death and to give these chosen three disciples a glimpse
of his glory for the hour of darkness coming. No one on
earth understood the heart of Jesus and so Moses and
Elijah came. The poor disciples utterly failed to grasp the
significance of it all.

32. *Were heavy with sleep* (*ēsan bebarēmenoi hupnōi*).
Periphrastic past perfect of *bareō*, a late form for the ancient
barunō (not in N.T. save Textus Receptus in Luke 21:34).
This form, rare and only in passive (present, aorist, perfect)
in the N.T., is like *barunō*, from *barus*, and that from *baros*,
weight, burden (Gal. 6:2). *Hupnōi* is in the instrumental
case. They had apparently climbed the mountain in the
early part of the night and were now overcome with sleep
as Jesus prolonged his prayer. Luke alone tells of their
sleep. The same word is used of the eyes of these three disciples in the Garden of Gethsemane (Matt. 26:43) and of the
hearts of many (Luke 21:34). *But when they were fully awake*
(*diagrēgorēsantes de*). First aorist active participle of this
late (Herodian) and rare compound verb (here alone in the
N.T.), *diagrēgoreō* (Luke is fond of compounds with *dia*).
The simple verb *grēgoreō* (from the second perfect active
egrēgora) is also late, but common in the LXX and the N.T.

The effect of *dia* can be either to remain awake in spite of desire to sleep (margin of Revised Version) or to become thoroughly awake (ingressive aorist tense also) as Revised Version has it. This is most likely correct. The Syriac Sinaitic has it "When they awoke." Certainly they had been through a strain. *His glory* (*tēn doxan autou*). See also verse 26 in the words of Jesus.

33. *As they were departing from him* (*en tōi diachōrizesthai autous ap' autou*). Peculiar to Luke and another instance of Luke's common idiom of *en* with the articular infinitive in a temporal clause. This common verb occurs here only in the N.T. The present middle voice means to separate oneself fully (direct middle). This departing of Moses and Elijah apparently accompanied Peter's remark as given in all three Gospels. See for details on Mark and Matthew. *Master* (*Epistata*) here, *Rabbi* (Mark 9:5), Lord (*Kurie*, Matt. 17:4). *Let us make* (*poiēsōmen*, first aorist active subjunctive) as in Mark 9:5, but Matt. 17:4 has "I will make" (*poiēsō*). It was near the time of the feast of the tabernacles. So Peter proposes that they celebrate it up here instead of going to Jerusalem for it as they did a bit later (John 7). *Not knowing what he said* (*mē eidōs ho legei*). Literally, *not understanding what he was saying* (*mē*, regular negative with participle and *legei*, present indicative retained in relative clause in indirect discourse). Luke puts it more bluntly than Mark (Peter's account), "For he wist not what to answer; for they became sore afraid" (Mark 9:6). Peter acted according to his impulsive nature and spoke up even though he did not know what to say or even what he was saying when he spoke. He was only half awake as Luke explains and he was sore afraid as Mark (Peter) explains. He had bewilderment enough beyond a doubt, but it was Peter who spoke, not James and John.

34. *Overshadowed them* (*epeskiazen autous*). Imperfect active (aorist in Matt. 17:5) as present participle in Mark

9:7, inchoative, the shadow began to come upon them. On Hermon as on many high mountains a cloud will swiftly cover the cap. I have seen this very thing at Blue Ridge, North Carolina. This same verb is used of the Holy Spirit upon Mary (Luke 1:35). Nowhere else in the N.T., though an old verb (*epi, skiazō*, from *skia*, shadow). *As they entered into the cloud (en tōi eiselthein autous eis tēn nephelēn)*. Luke's idiom of *en* with the articular infinitive again (aorist active this time, on the entering in as to them). All six "entered into" the cloud, but only Peter, James, and John "became afraid" (*ephobēthēsan*, ingressive first aorist passive).

35. If *ekeinous* be accepted here instead of *autous*, the three disciples would be outside of the cloud. *Out of the cloud (ek tēs nephelēs)*. This voice was the voice of the Father like that at the baptism of Jesus (Luke 3:22 = Mark 1:11 = Matt. 3:17) and like that near the end (John 12:28-30) when the people thought it was a clap of thunder or an angel. *My son, my chosen (Ho huios mou, ho eklelegmenos)*. So the best documents (Aleph B L Syriac Sinaitic). The others make it "My Beloved" as in Mark 9:7 = Matt. 17:5. These disciples are commanded to hear Jesus, God's Son, even when he predicts his death, a pointed rebuke to Simon Peter as to all.

36. *When the voice came (en toi genesthai tēn phōnēn)*. Another example of Luke's idiom, this time with the second aorist middle infinitive. Literally, "on the coming as to the voice" (accusative of general reference). It does not mean that it was "after" the voice was past that Jesus was found alone, but simultaneously with it (ingressive aorist tense). *Alone (monos)*. Same adjective in Mark 9:8 = Matt. 17:8 translated "only." Should be rendered "alone" there also. *They held their peace (esigēsan)*. Ingressive aorist active of common verb *sigaō*, became silent. In Mark 9:9 = Matt. 17:9, Jesus commanded them not to tell till His Resurrection from the dead. Luke notes that they in awe obeyed that

command and it turns out that they finally forgot the lesson of this night's great experience. By and by they will be able to tell them, but not "in those days." *Which they had seen* (*hōn heōrakan*). Attraction of the relative *ha* into the case of the unexpressed antecedent *toutōn*. Perfect active indicative *heōrakan* with *Koiné* (papyri) form for the ancient *heōrakāsin* changed by analogy to the first aorist ending in *-an* instead of *-asin*.

37. *On the next day* (*tēi hexēs hēmerāi*). Alone in Luke. It shows that the Transfiguration took place on the preceding night. *They were come down* (*katelthontōn autōn*). Genitive absolute of second aorist active participle of *katerchomai*, a common enough verb, but in the N.T. only in Luke's writings save James 3:15. *Met him* (*sunēntēsen autōi*). First aorist active of *sunantaō*, common compound verb, to meet with, only in Luke's writings in the N.T. save Heb. 7:1. With associative instrumental case *autōi*.

38. *Master* (*Didaskale*). Teacher as in Mark 9:17. *Lord* (*kurie*, Matt. 17:15). *To look upon* (*epiblepsai*). Aorist active infinitive of *epiblepō* (*epi*, upon, *blepō*, look), common verb, but in the N.T. only here and James 2:3 except Luke 1:48 in quotation from LXX. This compound verb is common in medical writers for examining carefully the patient. *Mine only child* (*monogenēs moi*). Only in Luke as already about an only child in 7:12; 8:42.

39. *Suddenly* (*exephnēs*). Old adverb, but in the N.T. only in Luke's writings save Mark 13:36. Used by medical writers of sudden attacks of disease like epilepsy. *It teareth him that he foameth* (*sparassei auton meta aphrou*). Literally, "It tears him with (accompanied with, *meta*) foam" (old word, *aphros*, only here in the N.T.). From *sparassō*, to convulse, a common verb, but in the N.T. only here and Mark 1:26; 9:26 (and *sunsparassō*, Mark 9:20). See Mark 9:17 and Matt. 17:15 and Luke 9:39 for variations in the symptoms in each Gospel. The use of *meta aphrou* is a medical item.

Hardly (molis). Late word used in place of *mogis*, the old Greek term (in some MSS. here) and alone in Luke's writings in the N.T. save I Pet. 4:18 and Rom. 5:7. *Bruising him sorely (suntribon auton)*. Common verb for rubbing together, crushing together like chains (Mark 5:4) or as a vase (Mark 14:3). See on Matthew and Mark for discussion of details here.

41. *How long shall I be with you and bear with you? (heōs pote esomai pros humās kai anexomai humōn;)*. Here the two questions of Mark 9:19 (only one in Matt. 17:17) are combined in one sentence. *Bear with (anexomai*, direct middle future) is, hold myself from you (ablative case *humōn*). *Faithless (apistos)* is disbelieving and perverse (*diestrammenē*, perfect passive participle of *diastrephō*), is twisted, turned, or torn in two.

42. *As he was yet a coming (eti proserchomenou autou)*. Genitive absolute. While he was yet coming (the boy, that is, not Jesus). Note quaint English "a coming" retained in the Revised Version. *Dashed him (errēxen auton)*. First aorist active indicative of *rēgnumi* or *rēssō*, to rend or convulse, a common verb, used sometimes of boxers giving knockout blows. *Tare grievously (sunesparaxen)*. Rare word as only here and Mark 9:20 in the N.T., which see. *Gave him back to his father (apedōken auton tōi patri autou)*. Tender touch alone in Luke as in 7:15. *They were all astonished (exeplēssonto de pantes)*. Imperfect passive of the common verb *ekplēssō* or *ekplēgnumi*, to strike out, a picturesque description of the amazement of all at the easy victory of Jesus where the nine disciples had failed. *At the majesty of God (epi tēi megaleiotēti tou theou)*. A late word from the adjective *megaleios* and that from *megas* (great). In the N.T. only here and Acts 19:27 of Artemis and in II Pet. 1:16 of the Transfiguration. It came to be used by the emperors like our word "Majesty." *Which he did (hois epoiei)*. This is one of the numerous poor verse divisions. This sentence has nothing

to do with the first part of the verse. The imperfect active *epoiei* covers a good deal not told by Luke (see Mark 9:30 = Matt. 17:22). Note the attraction of the relative *hois* into the case of *pāsin*, its antecedent.

44. *Sink into your ears* (*Thesthe humeis eis ta ōta humōn*). Second aorist imperative middle of *tithēmi*, common verb. "Do you (note emphatic position) yourselves (whatever others do) put into your ears." No word like "sink" here. The same prediction here as in Mark 9:31 = Matt. 17:22 about the Son of man only without mention of death and resurrection as there, which see for discussion.

45. *It was concealed from them* (*ēn parakekalummenon ap' autōn*). Periphrastic past perfect of *parakaluptō*, a common verb, but only here in the N.T., to cover up, to hide from. This item only in Luke. *That they should not perceive it* (*hina mē aisthōntai auto*). Second aorist middle subjunctive of the common verb *aisthanomai* used with *hina mē*, negative purpose. This explanation at least relieves the disciples to some extent of full responsibility for their ignorance about the death of Jesus as Mark 9:32 observes, as does Luke here that they were afraid to ask him. Plummer says, "They were not allowed to understand the saying then, in order that they might remember it afterwards, and see that Jesus had met His sufferings with full knowledge and free will." Perhaps also, if they had fully understood, they might have lacked courage to hold on to the end. But it is a hard problem.

46. *A reasoning* (*dialogismos*). A dispute. The word is from *dialogizomai*, the verb used in Mark 9:33 about this incident. In Luke this dispute follows immediately after the words of Jesus about his death. They were afraid to ask Jesus about that subject, but Matt. 18:1 states that they came to Jesus to settle it. *Which of them should be greatest* (*to tis an eiē meizōn autōn*). Note the article with the indirect question, the clause being in the accusative of general

reference. The optative with *an* is here because it was so in the direct question (potential optative with *an* retained in the indirect). But Luke makes it plain that it was not an abstract problem about greatness in the kingdom of heaven as they put it to Jesus (Matt. 18:1), but a personal problem in their own group. Rivalries and jealousies had already come and now sharp words. By and by James and John will be bold enough to ask for the first places for themselves in this political kingdom which they expect (Mark 10:35 = Matt. 20:20). It is a sad spectacle.

47. *Took a little child* (*epilabomenos paidion*). Second aorist middle participle of the common verb *epilambanō*. Strictly, Taking a little child to himself (indirect middle). Mark 9:36 has merely the active *labōn* of the simple verb *lambanō*. *Set him by his side* (*estēsen auto par' heautōi*). "In his arms" Mark 9:36 has it, "in the midst of them" Matt. 18:3 says. All three attitudes following one another (the disciples probably in a circle around Jesus anyhow) and now the little child (Peter's child?) was slipped down by the side of Jesus as he gave the disciples an object lesson in humility which they sorely needed.

48. *This little child* (*touto to paidion*). As Jesus spoke he probably had his hand upon the head of the child. Matt. 18:5 has "one such little child." The honoured disciple, Jesus holds, is the one who welcomes little children "in my name" (*epi tōi onomati mou*), upon the basis of my name and my authority. It was a home-thrust against the selfish ambition of the Twelve. Ministry to children is a mark of greatness. Have preachers ever yet learned how to win children to Christ? They are allowed to slip away from home, from Sunday school, from church, from Christ. *For he that is least among you all* (*ho gar mikroteros en pasin humin huparchōn*). Note the use of *huparchō* as in 8:41 and 23:50. The comparative *mikroteros* is in accord with the *Koinē* idiom where the superlative is vanishing (nearly gone in modern

Greek). But *great* (*megas*) is positive and very strong. This saying peculiar to Luke here.

49. *And John answered* (*apokritheis de Iōanēs*). As if John wanted to change the subject after the embarrassment of the rebuke for their dispute concerning greatness (Luke 9:46–48). *Master* (*epistata*). Only in Luke in the N.T. as already four times (5:5; 8:24, 45; 9:33). *We forbade him* (*ekōluomen auton*). Conative imperfect as in Mark 9:38, We tried to hinder him. *Because he followeth not with us* (*hoti ouk akolouthei meth hēmōn*). Present tense preserved for vividness where Mark has imperfect *ēkolouthei*. Note also here "with us" (*meth' hēmōn*) where Mark has associative instrumental *hēmin*. It is a pitiful specimen of partisan narrowness and pride even in the Beloved Disciple, one of the Sons of Thunder. The man was doing the Master's work in the Master's name and with the Master's power, but did not run with the group of the Twelve.

50. "*Against you is for you*" (*kath' hūmōn huper hūmōn*). Mark 9:40 has "against us is for us" (*hēmōn . . . hēmōn*). The *Koinē* Greek *ē* and *ū* were often pronounced alike and it was easy to interchange them. So many MSS. here read just as in Mark. The point is precisely the same as it is a proverbial saying. See a similar saying in Luke 11:23: "He that is not with me is against me." The prohibition here as in Mark 9:39 is general: "Stop hindering him" (*mē kōluete*, *mē* and the present imperative, not *mē* and the aorist subjunctive). The lesson of toleration in methods of work for Christ is needed today.

51. *When the days were well-nigh come* (*en tōi sumplērousthai tas hēmeras*). Luke's common idiom *en* with the articular infinitive, "in the being fulfilled as to the days." This common compound occurs in the N.T. only here and Luke 8:23 and Acts 2:1. The language here makes it plain that Jesus was fully conscious of the time of his death as near as already stated (Luke 9:22, 27, 31). *That he should be re-*

ceived up (*tēs analēmpseōs autou*). Literally, "of his taking up." It is an old word (from Hippocrates on), but here alone in the N.T. It is derived from *analambanō* (the verb used of the Ascension, Acts 1:2, 11, 22; I Tim. 3:16) and refers here to the Ascension of Jesus after His Resurrection. Not only in John's Gospel (17:5) does Jesus reveal a yearning for a return to the Father, but it is in the mind of Christ here as evidently at the Transfiguration (9:31) and later in Luke 12:49f. *He steadfastly set his face* (*autos to prosōpon estērisen*). Note emphatic *autos*, *he himself*, with fixedness of purpose in the face of difficulty and danger. This look on Christ's face as he went to his doom is noted later in Mark 10:32. It is a Hebraistic idiom (nine times in Ezekiel), this use of face here, but the verb (effective aorist active) is an old one from *stērizō* (from *stērigx*, a support), to set fast, to fix. *To go to Jerusalem* (*tou poreuesthai eis Ierousalēm*). Genitive infinitive of purpose. Luke three times mentions Christ making his way to Jerusalem (9:51; 13:22; 17:11) and John mentions three journeys to Jerusalem during the later ministry (7:10; 11:17; 12:1). It is natural to take these journeys to be the same in each of these Gospels. Luke does not make definite location of each incident and John merely supplements here and there. But in a broad general way they seem to correspond.

52. *Sent messengers* (*apesteilen aggelous*). As a precaution since he was going to Jerusalem through Samaria. The Samaritans did not object when people went north from Jerusalem through their country. He was repudiating Mount Gerizim by going by it to Jerusalem. This was an unusual precaution by Jesus and we do not know who the messengers (*angels*) were. *To make ready for him* (*hōs hetoimasai autōi*). *Hōs* is correct here, not *hōste*. The only examples of the final use of *hōs* with the infinitive in the N.T. are this one and Heb. 7:9 (absolute use). In Acts 20:24

Westcott and Hort read *hōs teleiōsō* and put *hōs teleiōsai* in
the margin (Robertson, *Grammar*, p. 1091).

53. *And they did not receive him (kai ouk edexanto auton)*.
Adversative use of *kai* = But. *Because his face was going
to Jerusalem (hoti to prosōpon autou ēn poreuomenon eis
Ierousalēm)*. Periphrastic imperfect middle. It was reason
enough to the churlish Samaritans.

54. *Saw this (idontes)*. Second aorist active participle
of *horaō*. Saw the messengers returning. *We bid (theleis
eipōmen)*. Deliberative subjunctive *eipōmen* after *theleis*
without *hina*, probably two questions, Dost thou wish?
Shall we bid? Perhaps the recent appearance of Elijah on
the Mount of Transfiguration reminded James and John
of the incident in II Kings 1:10–12. Some MSS. add here
"as Elijah did." The language of the LXX is quoted by
James and John, these fiery Sons of Thunder. Note the
two aorist active infinitives (*katabēnai, analōsai*, the first
ingressive, the second effective).

55. *But he turned (strapheis de)*. Second aorist passive
participle of *strephō*, common verb, to turn round. Dramatic act. Some ancient MSS. have here: *Ye know not
what manner of spirit ye are of (ouk oidate poiou pneumatos
este)*. This sounds like Christ and may be a genuine saying
though not a part of Luke's Gospel. A smaller number of
MSS. add also: *For the Son of Man came not to destroy
men's lives, but to save them (Ho gar huios tou anthrōpou
ouk ēlthen psuchas anthrōpōn apolesai alla sōsai)*, a saying
reminding us of Matt. 5:17 and Luke 19:10. Certain it is
that here Jesus rebuked the bitterness of James and John
toward Samaritans as he had already chided John for his
narrowness towards a fellow-worker in the kingdom.

57. *A certain man (tis)*. Matt. 8:19 calls him "a scribe."
Luke 9:57–60 = Matt. 8:19–22, but not in Mark and so
from Q or the Logia. *Wherever you go (hopou ean aperchēi)*
is the present middle subjunctive with the indefinite rela-

tive adverb *ean*, common Greek idiom. See on Matthew for
"holes," "nests," "Son of man." The idiom "where to
lay his head" (*pou tēn kephalēn klinēi*) is the same in both,
the deliberative subjunctive retained in the indirect question. "Jesus knows the measure of the scribe's enthusiasm"
(Plummer). The wandering life of Jesus explains this statement.

59. *And he said unto another* (*eipen de pros heteron*).
Matt. 8:21 omits Christ's "Follow me" (*akolouthei moi*)
and makes this man a volunteer instead of responding to
the appeal of Jesus. There is no real opposition, of course.
In Matthew's account the man is apologetic as in Luke.
Plummer calls him "one of the casual disciples" of whom
there are always too many. The scribes knew how to give
plausible reasons for not being active disciples. *First* (*prōton*). One of the problems of life is the relation of duties to
each other, which comes first. The burial of one's father
was a sacred duty (Gen. 25:9), but, as in the case of Tobit
4:3, this scribe's father probably was still alive. What the
scribe apparently meant was that he could not leave his
father while still alive to follow Jesus around over the country.

60. *Leave the dead to bury their own dead* (*aphes tous nekrous thapsai tous heautōn nekrous*). This paradox occurs so
in Matt. 8:22. The explanation is that the spiritually dead
can bury the literally dead. For such a quick change in the
use of the same words see John 5:21–29 (spiritual resurrection from sin in 21–27, bodily resurrection from the grave,
28 and 29) and John 11:25f. The harshness of this proverb
to the scribe probably is due to the fact that he was manifestly using his aged father as an excuse for not giving Christ
active service. *But go thou and publish abroad the kingdom
of God* (*su de apelthōn diaggelle tēn basileian tou theou*). The
scribe's duty is put sharply (*But do thou, su de*). Christ
called him to preach, and he was using pious phrases about

his father as a pretext. Many a preacher has had to face a similar delicate problem of duty to father, mother, brothers, sisters and the call to preach. This was a clear case. Jesus will help any man called to preach to see his duty. Certainly Jesus does not advocate renunciation of family duties on the part of preachers.

61. *And another also said* (*eipen de kai heteros*). A volunteer like the first. This third case is given by Luke alone, though the incident may also come from the same Logia as the other two. *Heteros* does not here mean one of a "different" sort as is sometimes true of this pronoun, but merely another like *allos* (Robertson, *Grammar*, p. 749). *But first* (*prōton de*). He also had something that was to come "first." *To bid farewell to them that are at my house* (*apotaxasthai tois eis ton oikon mou*). In itself that was a good thing to do. This first aorist middle infinitive is from *apotassō*, an old verb, to detach, to separate, to assign as a detachment of soldiers. In the N.T. it only appears in the middle voice with the meaning common in late writers to bid adieu, to separate oneself from others. It is used in Acts 18:18 of Paul taking leave of the believers in Corinth. See also Mark 6:46; II Cor. 2:13. It is thus a formal function and this man meant to go home and set things in order there and then in due time to come and follow Jesus.

62. *Having put his hand to the plough* (*epibalōn tēn cheira ep' arotron*). Second aorist active participle of *epiballō*, an old and common verb, to place upon. Note repetition of preposition *epi* before *arotron* (plough). This agricultural proverb is as old as Hesiod. Pliny observes that the ploughman who does not bend attentively to his work goes crooked. It has always been the ambition of the ploughman to run a straight furrow. The Palestine *fellah* had good success at it. *And looking back* (*kai blepōn eis ta opisō*). Looking to the things behind. To do that is fatal as any ploughman

knows. The call to turn back is often urgent. *Fit* (*euthetos*).
From *eu* and *tithēmi* = well-placed, suited for, adapted to.
"The first case is that of inconsiderate impulse, the second
that of conflicting duti:s, the third that of a divided mind"
(Bruce).

CHAPTER X

1. *Appointed* (*anedeixen*). First aorist active indicative of *anadeiknumi*, an old verb, not only common, but in LXX. In the N.T. only here and Acts 1:24. Cf. *anadeixis* in Luke 1:80. To show forth, display, proclaim, appoint. *Seventy others* (*heterous hebdomēkonta kai*). The "also" (*kai*) and the "others" point back to the mission of the Twelve in Galilee (9:1-6). Some critics think that Luke has confused this report of a mission in Judea with that in Galilee, but needlessly so. What earthly objection can there be to two similar missions? B D Syr. Cur. and Syr. Sin. have "seventy-two." The seventy elders were counted both ways and the Sanhedrin likewise and the nations of the earth. It is an evenly balanced point. *Two and two* (*ana duo*). For companionship as with the Twelve though Mark 6:7 has it *duo duo* (vernacular idiom). B K have here *ana duo duo*, a combination of the idiom in Mark. 6:7 and that here. *He himself was about to come* (*ēmellen autos erchesthai*). Imperfect of *mellō* with present infinitive and note *autos*. Jesus was to follow after and investigate the work done. This was only a temporary appointment and no names are given, but they could cover a deal of territory.

2. *Harvest* (*therismos*). Late word for the older *theros*, summer, harvest. The language in this verse is verbatim what we have in Matt. 9:37 and 38 to the Twelve. Why not? The need is the same and prayer is the answer in each case. Prayer for preachers is Christ's method for increasing the supply.

3. *As lambs* (*hōs arnas*). Here again the same language as that in Matt. 10:16 except that there "sheep" (*probata*) appears instead of "lambs." Pathetic picture of the risks

144

of missionaries for Christ. They take their life in their hands.

4. *Purse* (*ballantion*). Old word for money-bag, sometimes a javelin as if from *ballō*. Only in Luke in the N.T. (10:4; 12:33; 22:35ff.). See Luke 9:3 = Mark. 6:7f. = Matt. 10:9f. for the other similar items. *Salute no man on the way* (*mēdena kata tēn hodon aspasēsthe*). First aorist (ingressive) middle subjunctive with *mēdena*. The peril of such wayside salutations was palaver and delay. The King's business required haste. Elisha's servant was not to tarry for salutations or salaams (II Kings 4:29). These oriental greetings were tedious, complicated, and often meddlesome if others were present or engaged in a bargain.

5. *First say* (*prōton legete*). Say first. The adverb *prōton* can be construed with "enter" (*eiselthēte*), but probably with *legete* is right. The word spoken is the usual oriental salutation.

6. *A son of peace* (*huios eirēnēs*). A Hebraism, though some examples occur in the vernacular *Koinê* papyri. It means one inclined to peace, describing the head of the household. *Shall rest* (*epanapaēsetai*). Second future passive of *epanapauō*, a late double compound (*epi, ana*) of the common verb *pauō*. *It shall turn to you again* (*eph' humās anakampsei*). Common verb *anakamptō*, to bend back, return. The peace in that case will bend back with blessing upon the one who spoke it.

7. *In that same house* (*en autēi tēi oikiāi*). Literally, in the house itself, not "in the same house" (*en tēi autēi oikiāi*), a different construction. A free rendering of the common Lukan idiom is, "in that very house." *Eating* (*esthontes*). An old poetic verb *esthō* for *esthiō* that survives in late Greek. *Such things as they give* (*ta par' autōn*). "The things from them." *For the labourer is worthy of his hire* (*axios gar ho ergatēs tou misthou autou*). In Matt. 10:10 we have *tēs trophēs autou* (his food). I Tim. 5:18 has this saying quoted as

scripture. That is not impossible if Luke wrote by A.D. 62. Paul there however may quote only Deut. 25:4 as scripture and get this quotation either from Luke 10:7 or from a proverbial saying of Jesus. It is certainly not a real objection against the Pauline authorship of First Timothy. *Go not from house to house* (*mē metabainete ex oikias eis oikian*). As a habit, *mē* and the present imperative, and so avoid waste of time with such rounds of invitations as would come.

8. *Such things as are set before you* (*ta paratithemena humin*). The things placed before you from time to time (present passive participle, repetition). Every preacher needs this lesson of common politeness. These directions may seem perfunctory and even commonplace, but every teacher of young preachers knows how necessary they are. Hence they were given both to the Twelve and to the Seventy.

9. *Is come nigh unto you* (*ēggiken eph' humās*). Perfect active indicative of *eggizō* as in Matt. 3:2 of the Baptist and Mark 1:15 of Jesus. Note *eph' humās* here.

10. *Into the streets thereof* (*eis tas plateias autēs*). Out of the inhospitable houses into the broad open streets.

11. *Even the dust* (*kai ton koniorton*). Old word from *konis*, dust, and *ornumi*, to stir up. We have seen it already in Matt. 10:14; Luke 9:5. Dust is a plague in the east. Shake off even that. *Cleaveth* (*kollēthenta*). First aorist passive participle of *kollaō*, to cling as dust and mud do to shoes. Hence the orientals took off the sandals on entering a house. *We wipe off* (*apomassometha*). Middle voice of an old verb *apomassō*, to rub off with the hands. Nowhere else in the N.T. But *ekmassō*, occurs in Luke 7:38, 44. *Against you* (*Humin*). Fine example of the dative of disadvantage (the case of personal interest, the dative).

12. *More tolerable* (*anektoteron*). Comparative of the verbal adjective *anektos* from *anechomai*. An old adjective, but only the comparative in the N.T. and in this phrase (Matt. 10:15; 11:22, 24; Luke 10:12, 14).

13. *Would have repented* (*an metenoēsan*). Conclusion (apodosis) of second-class condition, determined as unfulfilled. *Long ago* (*palai*). Implies a considerable ministry in these cities of which we are not told. Chorazin not mentioned save here and Matt. 11:21. Perhaps *Karāzeh* near Tell Hum (Capernaum). *Sitting in sackcloth and ashes* (*en sakkōi kai spodōi kathēmenoi*). Pictorial and graphic. The *sakkos* (sackcloth) was dark coarse cloth made of goat's hair and worn by penitents, mourners, suppliants. It is a Hebrew word, *sag*. The rough cloth was used for sacks or bags. To cover oneself with ashes was a mode of punishment as well as of voluntary humiliation.

15. *Shalt thou be exalted?* (*mē hupsōthēsei;*). *Mē* expects the answer No. The verb is future passive indicative second singular of *hupsoō*, to lift up, a late verb from *hupsos*, height. It is used by Jesus of the Cross (John 12:32). *Unto Hades* (*heōs Haidou*). See on Matt. 16:18 for this word which is here in contrast to Heaven as in Isa. 14:13-15. Hades is not Gehenna. "The desolation of the whole neighbourhood, and the difficulty of identifying even the site of these flourishing towns, is part of the fulfilment of this prophecy" (Plummer). Ragg notes the omission of Nazareth from this list of cities of neglected privilege and opportunity. "Is it the tender memories of boyhood that keep from His lips the name of the arch-rejector (4:28 sqq.) Nazareth?"

16. *Rejecteth him that sent me* (*athetei ton aposteilanta me*). These solemn words form a fit close for this discourse to the Seventy. The fate of Chorazin, Bethsaida, Capernaum will befall those who set aside (*a* privative and *theteō*, from *ti-thēmi*) the mission and message of these messengers of Christ. See this verb used in 7:30 of the attitude of the scribes and Pharisees toward John and Jesus. It is this thought that makes it so grave a responsibility to be co-workers with Christ, high privilege as it is (John 9:4).

17. *Returned with joy* (*hupestrepsan meta charas*). They

had profited by the directions of Jesus. Joy overflows their faces and their words. *Even the demons* (*kai ta daimonia*). This was a real test. The Twelve had been expressly endowed with this power when they were sent out (Luke 9:1), but the Seventy were only told to heal the sick (10:9). It was better than they expected. The Gospel worked wonders and they were happy. The demons were merely one sign of the conflict between Christ and Satan. Every preacher has to grapple with demons in his work. *Are subject* (*hupotassetai*). Present passive indicative (repetition).

18. *I beheld Satan fallen* (*etheōroun ton Satanān pesonta*). Imperfect active (I was beholding) and second aorist (constative) active participle of *piptō* (not *fallen, peptōkota*, perfect active participle, nor *falling, piptonta*, present active participle, but *fall, pesonta*). As a flash of lightning out of heaven, quick and startling, so the victory of the Seventy over the demons, the agents of Satan, forecast his downfall and Jesus in vision pictured it as a flash of lightning.

19. *And over all the power of the enemy* (*kai epi pāsan tēn dunamin tou echthrou*). This is the heart of "the authority" (*tēn exousian*) here given by Jesus which is far beyond their expectations. The victory over demons was one phase of it. The power to tread upon serpents is repeated in Mark 16:18 (the Appendix) and exemplified in Paul's case in Malta (Acts 28:3–5). But protection from physical harm is not the main point in this struggle with Satan "the enemy" (Matt. 13:25; Rom. 16:20; I Pet. 5:8). *Nothing shall in any wise hurt you* (*ouden humās ou mē adikēsei*). Text has future active indicative, while some MSS. read *adikēsēi*, aorist active subjunctive of *adikeō*, common verb from *adikos* (*a* privative and *dikos*), to suffer wrong, to do wrong. The triple negative here is very strong. Certainly Jesus does not mean this promise to create presumption or foolhardiness for he repelled the enemy's suggestion on the pinnacle of the temple.

20. *Are written* (*engegraptai*). Perfect passive indicative,

state of completion, stand written, enrolled or engraved, from *engraphō*, common verb. "As citizens possessing the full privileges of the commonwealth" (Plummer).

21. *In that same hour* (*en autēi tēi hōrāi*). Literally, "at the hour itself," almost a demonstrative use of *autos* (Robertson, *Grammar*, p. 686) and in Luke alone in the N.T. (2:38; 10:21; 12:12; 20:19). Matt. 11:25 uses the demonstrative here, "at that time" (*en ekeinōi tōi kairōi*). *Rejoiced in the Holy Spirit* (*ēgalliasato tōi pneumati tōi hagiōi*). First aorist middle of the late verb *agalliaō* for *agallō*, to exult. Always in the middle in the N.T. save Luke 1:47 in Mary's *Magnificat*. This holy joy of Jesus was directly due to the Holy Spirit. It is joy in the work of his followers, their victories over Satan, and is akin to the joy felt by Jesus in John 4:32–38 when the vision of the harvest of the world stirred his heart. The rest of this verse is precisely like Matt. 11:25f., a peculiarly Johannine passage in Matthew and Luke, but not in Mark, and so from Q (the Logia of Jesus). It has disturbed critics who are unwilling to admit the Johannine style and type of teaching as genuine, but here it is. See on Matthew for discussion. "That God had proved his independence of the human intellect is a matter for thankfulness. Intellectual gifts, so far from being necessary, are often a hindrance" (Plummer).

22. *Knoweth who the Son is* (*ginōskei tis estin ho huios*). Knows by experience, *ginōskei*. Here Matt. 11:27 has *epiginōskei* (fully knows) and simply *ton huion* (the Son) instead of the "who" (*tis*) clause. So also in "who the Father is" (*tis estin ho pater*). But the same use and contrast of "the Father," "the Son." in both Matthew and Luke, "an aerolite from the Johannean heaven" (Hase). No sane criticism can get rid of this Johannine bit in these Gospels written long before the Fourth Gospel was composed. We are dealing here with the oldest known document about Christ (the Logia) and the picture is that drawn in the

Fourth Gospel (see my *The Christ of the Logia*). It is idle
to try to whittle away by fantastic exegesis the high claims
made by Jesus in this passage.   It is an ecstatic prayer in
the presence of the Seventy under the rapture of the Holy
Spirit on terms of perfect equality and understanding between the Father and the Son in the tone of the priestly
prayer in John 17.   We are justified in saying that this prayer
of supreme Fellowship with the Father in contemplation of
final victory over Satan gives us a glimpse of the prayers
with the Father when the Son spent whole nights on the
mountain alone with the Father.   Here is the Messianic
consciousness in complete control and with perfect confidence
in the outcome.   Here as in Matt. 11:27 by the use of *willeth
to reveal him* (*boulētai apokalupsai*).   The Son claims the
power to reveal the Father "to whomsoever he wills" (*hōi
an boulētai*, indefinite relative and present subjunctive of
boulomai, to will, not the future indicative).   This is divine
sovereignty most assuredly.   Human free agency is also
true, but it is full divine sovereignty in salvation that is here
claimed along with possession (*paredothē*, timeless aorist
passive indicative) of all power from the Father.   Let that
supreme claim stand.

23. *Turning to the disciples* (*strapheis pros tous mathētas*).
Second aorist passive of *strephō* as in 9:55.   The prayer was
a soliloquy though uttered in the presence of the Seventy on
their return.   Now Jesus turned and spoke "privately"
or to the disciples (the Twelve, apparently), whether on this
same occasion or a bit later.   *Blessed* (*makarioi*).   A beatitude, the same adjective as in Matt. 5:3–11.   A beatitude of
privilege very much like that in Matt. 13–16.   Jesus often
repeated his sayings.

24. *Which ye see* (*ha humeis blepete*).   The expression of
humeis makes "ye" very emphatic in contrast with the
prophets and kings of former days.

25. *And tempted him* (*ekpeirazōn auton*).   Present active

participle, conative idea, trying to tempt him. There is no
"and" in the Greek. He "stood up (*aneste*, ingressive second aorist active) trying to tempt him." *Peirazō* is a late
form of *peiraō* and *ekpeirazō* apparently only in the LXX,
and N.T. (quoted by Jesus from Deut. 6:16 in Matt. 4:7 =
Luke 4:12 against Satan). Here and I Cor. 10:9. The spirit
of this lawyer was evil. He wanted to entrap Jesus if possible. *What shall I do to inherit eternal life?* (*Ti poiēsas zōēn
aiōniou klēronomēsō;*). Literally, "By doing what shall I
inherit eternal life?" Note the emphasis on "doing"
(*poiēsas*). The form of his question shows a wrong idea as
to how to get it. *Eternal life* (*zōēn aiōnion*) is endless life
as in John's Gospel (16:9; 18:18, 30) and in Matt. 25:46,
which see.

26. *How readest thou?* (*pōs anaginōskeis;*). As a lawyer
it was his business to know the facts in the law and the proper
interpretation of the law. See on Luke 7:30 about *nomikos*
(lawyer). The rabbis had a formula, "What readest thou?"

27. *And he answering* (*ho de apokritheis*). First aorist
participle, no longer passive in idea. The lawyer's answer
is first from the *Shema'* (Deut. 6:3; 11:13) which was written
on the phylacteries. The second part is from Lev. 19:18
and shows that the lawyer knew the law. At a later time
Jesus himself in the temple gives a like summary of the law
to a lawyer (Mark 12:28-34 = Matt. 22:34-40) who wanted to
catch Jesus by his question. There is no difficulty in the two
incidents. God is to be loved with all of man's four powers
(heart, soul, strength, mind) here as in Mark 12:30.

28. *Thou hast answered right* (*orthōs apekrithēs*). First
aorist passive indicative second singular with the adverb
orthōs. The answer was correct so far as the words went. In
Mark 12:34 Jesus commends the scribe for agreeing to his
interpretation of the first and the second commandments.
That scribe was "not far from the kingdom of God," but this
lawyer was "tempting" Jesus. *Do this and thou shalt live*

(*touto poiei kai zēsēi*).   Present imperative (keep on doing this forever) and the future indicative middle as a natural result. There was only one trouble with the lawyer's answer.   No one ever did or ever can "do" what the law lays down towards God and man always.   To slip once is to fail.   So Jesus put the problem squarely up to the lawyer who wanted to know *by doing what*.   Of course, if he kept the law *perfectly always*, he would inherit eternal life.

29. *Desiring to justify himself* (*thelōn dikaiōsai heauton*). The lawyer saw at once that he had convicted himself of asking a question that he already knew.   In his embarrassment he asks another question to show that he did have some point at first: *And who is my neighbour?* (*kai tis estin mou plēsion;*).   The Jews split hairs over this question and excluded from "neighbour" Gentiles and especially Samaritans. So here was his loop-hole.   A neighbour is a nigh dweller to one, but the Jews made racial exceptions as many, alas, do today.   The word *plēsion* here is an adverb (neuter of the adjective *plēsios*) meaning *ho plēsion ōn* (the one who is near), but *ōn* was usually not expressed and the adverb is here used as if a substantive.

30. *Made answer* (*hupolabōn*).   Second aorist active participle of *hupolambanō* (see 7:43), to take up literally, and then in thought and speech, old verb, but in this sense of interrupting in talk only in the N.T.   *Was going down* (*katebainen*). Imperfect active describing the journey.   *Fell among robbers* (*lēistais periepesen*).   Second aorist ingressive active indicative of *peripiptō*, old verb with associative instrumental case, to fall among and to be encompassed by (*peri*, around), to be surrounded by robbers.   A common experience to this day on the road to Jericho.   The Romans placed a fort on this "red and bloody way."   These were bandits, not petty thieves.   *Stripped* (*ekdusantes*).   Of his clothing as well as of his money, the meanest sort of robbers.   *Beat him* (*plēgas epithentes*).   Second aorist active participle of *epitithēmi*,

a common verb. Literally, "placing strokes or blows" (*plēgas*, plagues) upon him. See Luke 12:48; Acts 16:23; Rev. 15:1, 6, 8 for "plagues." *Half-dead* (*hēmithanē*). Late word from *hēmi*, half, and *thnēskō*, to die. Only here in the N.T. Vivid picture of the robbery.

31. *By chance* (*kata sugkurian*). Here only in the N.T., meaning rather, "by way of coincidence." It is a rare word elsewhere and in late writers like Hippocrates. It is from the verb *sugkureō*, though *sugkurēsis* is more common. *Was going down* (*katebainen*). Imperfect active as in verse 30. *Passed by on the other side* (*antiparēlthen*). Second aorist active indicative of *antiparerchomai*, a late double compound here (verses 31 and 32) only in the N.T., but in the papyri and late writers. It is the ingressive aorist (*ēlthen*), came alongside (*para*), and then he stepped over to the opposite side (*anti*) of the road to avoid ceremonial contamination with a stranger. A vivid and powerful picture of the vice of Jewish ceremonial cleanliness at the cost of moral principle and duty. The Levite in verse 32 behaved precisely as the priest had done and for the same reason.

33. *A certain Samaritan* (*Samareitēs de tis*). Of all men in the world to do a neighbourly act! *As he journeyed* (*hodeuōn*). Making his way. *Came where he was* (*ēlthen kat' auton*). Literally, "came down upon him." He did not sidestep or dodge him, but had compassion on him.

34. *Bound up his wounds* (*katedēsen ta traumata*). First aorist active indicative of *katadeō*, old verb, but here only in the N.T. The verb means "bound down." We say "bind up." Medical detail that interested Luke. The word for "wounds" (*traumata*) here only in the N.T. *Pouring on them oil and wine* (*epicheōn elaion kai oinon*). Old verb again, but here only in the N.T. Oil and wine were household remedies even for wounds (soothing oil, antiseptic alcohol). Hippocrates prescribed for ulcers: "Bind with soft wool, and sprinkle with wine and oil." *Set him* (*epibibasas*). An

old verb *epibibazō* (*epi*, *bibazō*), to cause to mount. In the
N.T. only here and Acts 19:35; 23:24, common in LXX.
Beast (*ktēnos*). Old word from *ktaomai*, to acquire, and so
property (*ktēma*) especially cattle or any beast of burden.
An inn (*pandocheion*). The old Attic form was *pandokeion*
(from *pan*, all, and *dechomai*, to receive). A public place for
receiving all comers and a more pretentious caravanserai
than a *kataluma* like that in Luke 2:7. Here only in the
N.T. There are ruins of two inns about halfway between
Bethany and Jericho.

35. *On the morrow* (*epi tēn aurion*). Towards the morrow
as in Acts 4:5. (Cf. also Acts 3:1). Syriac Sinaitic has it
"at dawn of the day." An unusual use of *epi*. *Took out*
(*ekbalōn*). Second aorist active participle of *ekballō*. It
could mean, "fling out," but probably only means "drew
out." Common verb. *Two pence* (*duo dēnaria*). About
thirty-five cents, but worth more in purchasing power. *To
the host* (*tōi pandochei*). The innkeeper. Here only in the
N.T. *Whatsoever thou spendest more* (*hoti an prosdapanēsēis*).
Indefinite relative clause with *an* and the aorist active subjunctive of *prosdapanaō*, to spend besides (*pros*), a late verb
for the common *prosanaliskō* and here only in the N.T. *I
will repay* (*ego apodōsō*). Emphatic. What he had paid
was merely by way of pledge. He was a man of his word
and known to the innkeeper as reliable. *When I come back
again* (*en tōi epanerchesthai me*). Luke's favourite idiom of
en and the articular infinitive with accusative of general
reference. Double compound verb *epanerchomai*.

36. *Proved neighbour to him that fell* (*plēsion gegonenai tou
empesontos*). Second perfect infinitive of *ginomai* and second
aorist active participle of *empiptō*. Objective genitive, became neighbour to the one, etc. Jesus has changed the lawyer's standpoint and has put it up to him to decide which of
"these three" (*toutōn tōn triōn*, priest, Levite, Samaritan)
acted like a neighbour to the wounded man.

37. *On him (met' autou).* With him, more exactly. The lawyer saw the point and gave the correct answer, but he gulped at the word "Samaritan" and refused to say that. *Do thou (su poiei).* Emphasis on "thou." Would this Jewish lawyer act the neighbour to a Samaritan? This parable of the Good Samaritan has built the world's hospitals and, if understood and practised, will remove race prejudice, national hatred and war, class jealousy.

38. *Now as they went on their way (ēn de tōi poreuesthai autous).* Luke's favourite temporal clause again as in verse 35. *Received him into her house (hupedexato auton eis tēn oikian).* Aorist middle indicative of *hupodechomai,* an old verb to welcome as a guest (in the N.T. only here and Luke 19:6; Acts 17:7; James 2:25). Martha is clearly the mistress of the home and is probably the elder sister. There is no evidence that she was the wife of Simon the leper (John 12:1f.). It is curious that in an old cemetery at Bethany the names of Martha, Eleazar, and Simon have been found.

39. *Which also sat (hē kai parakathestheisa).* First aorist passive participle of *parakathezomai,* an old verb, but only here in the N.T. It means to sit beside (*para*) and *pros* means right in front of the feet of Jesus. It is not clear what the point is in *kai* here. It may mean that Martha loved to sit here also as well as Mary. *Heard (ēkouen).* Imperfect active. She took her seat by the feet of Jesus and went on listening to his talk.

40. *Was cumbered (periespāto).* Imperfect passive of *perispaō,* an old verb with vivid metaphor, to draw around. One has sometimes seen women whose faces are literally drawn round with anxiety, with a permanent twist, distracted in mind and in looks. *She came up to him (epistāsa).* Second aorist active participle of *ephistēmi,* an old verb to place upon, but in the N.T. only in the middle voice or the intransitive tenses of the active (perfect and second aorist as here). It is the ingressive aorist here and really means.

stepping up to or bursting in or upon Jesus. It is an explosive act as is the speech of Martha. *Dost thou not care* (*ou melei soi*). This was a reproach to Jesus for monopolizing Mary to Martha's hurt. *Did leave me* (*me kateleipen*). Imperfect active, she kept on leaving me. *Bid her* (*eipon autēi*). Late form instead of *eipe*, second aorist active imperative, common in the papyri. Martha feels that Jesus is the key to Mary's help. *That she help me* (*hina moi sunantilabētai*). Sub-final use of *hina* with second aorist middle subjunctive of *sunantilambanomai*, a double compound verb (*sun*, with, *anti*, at her end of the line, and *lambanomai*, middle voice of *lambanō*, to take hold), a late compound appearing in the LXX, Diodorus and Josephus. Deissmann (*Light from the Ancient East*, p. 87) finds it in many widely scattered inscriptions "throughout the whole extent of the Hellenistic world of the Mediterranean." It appears only twice in the N.T. (here and Rom. 8:26). It is a beautiful word, to take hold oneself (middle voice) at his end of the task (*anti*) together with (*sun*) one.

41. *Art anxious* (*merimnāis*). An old verb for worry and anxiety from *merizō* (*meris*, part) to be divided, distracted. Jesus had warned against this in the Sermon on the Mount (Matt. 6:25, 28, 31, 34. See also Luke 12:11, 22, 26). *And troubled* (*kai thorubazēi*). From *thorubazomai*, a verb found nowhere else so far. Many MSS. here have the usual form *turbazēi*, from *turbazō*. Apparently from *thorubos*, a common enough word for tumult. Martha had both inward anxiety and outward agitation. *But one thing is needful* (*henos de estin chreia*). This is the reading of A C and may be correct. A few manuscripts have: "There is need of few things." Aleph B L (and Westcott and Hort) have: "There is need of few things or one," which seems like a conflate reading though the readings are all old. See Robertson, *Introduction to Textual Criticism of the N.T.*, p. 190. Jesus seems to say to Martha that only one dish was really necessary for

the meal instead of the "many" about which she was so
anxious.

42. *The good portion* (*tēn agathēn merida*). The best dish
on the table, fellowship with Jesus. This is the spiritual
application of the metaphor of the dishes on the table.
Salvation is not "the good portion" for Martha had that
also. *From her* (*autēs*). Ablative case after *aphairethēsetai*
(future passive indicative). Jesus pointedly takes Mary's
side against Martha's fussiness.

CHAPTER XI

1. *As he was praying in a certain place (en tōi einai auton en topōi tini proseuchomenon)*. Characteristically Lukan idiom: *en* with articular periphrastic infinitive (*einai proseuchomenon*) with accusative of general reference (*auton*). *That*. Not in the Greek, asyndeton (*kai egeneto eipen*). *When he ceased (hōs epausato)*. Supply *proseuchomenos* (praying), complementary or supplementary participle. *Teach us (didaxon hēmas)*. Jesus had taught them by precept (Matt. 6:7–15) and example (Luke 9:29). Somehow the example of Jesus on this occasion stirred them to fresh interest in the subject and to revival of interest in John's teachings (Luke 5:33). So Jesus gave them the substance of the Model Prayer in Matthew, but in shorter form. Some of the MSS. have one or all of the phrases in Matthew, but the oldest documents have it in the simplest form. See on Matt. 6:7–15 for discussion of these details (Father, hallowed, kingdom, daily bread, forgiveness, bringing us into temptation). In Matt. 6:11 "give" is *dos* (second aorist active imperative second singular, a single act) while here Luke 11:3 "give" is *didou* (present active imperative, both from *didōmi*) and means, "keep on giving." So in Luke 11:4 we have "For we ourselves also forgive" (*kai gar autoi aphiomen*), present active indicative of the late *ō* verb *aphiō* while Matt. 6:12 has "as we also forgave" (*hōs kai hēmeis aphēkamen*), first aorist (*k* aorist) active of *aphiēmi*. So also where Matt. 6:12 has "debts" (*ta opheilēmata*) Luke 11:4 has "sins" (*tas hamartias*). But the spirit of each prayer is the same. There is no evidence that Jesus meant either form to be a ritual. In both Matt. 6:13 and Luke 11:4 *mē eisenegkēis* occurs (second aorist subjunctive with

158

mē in prohibition, ingressive aorist). "Bring us not" is a better translation than "lead us not." There is no such thing as God enticing one to sin (James 1:13). Jesus urges us to pray not to be tempted as in Luke 22:40 in Gethsemane.

5. *At midnight (mesonuktiou).* Genitive of time. *And say to him (kai eipēi autōi).* This is the deliberative subjunctive, but it is preceded by two future indicatives that are deliberative also *(hexei, poreusetai).* *Lend me (chrēson moi).* First aorist active imperative second singular. Lend me now. From *kichrēmi,* an old verb, to lend as a matter of friendly interest as opposed to *daneizō,* to lend on interest as a business. Only here in the N.T.

6. *To set before him (ho parathēsō autōi).* *Which I shall place beside him.* Future active of *paratithēmi.* See 9:16 for this same verb.

7. *And he (kàkeinos).* Emphatic. *Shall say (eipēi).* Still the aorist active deliberative subjunctive as in verse 5 (the same long and somewhat involved sentence). *Trouble me not (mē moi kopous pareche).* *Mē* and the present imperative active. Literally, "Stop furnishing troubles to me." On this use of *kopous parechō* see also Matt. 26:10; Mark 14:6; Gal. 6:17 and the singular *kopon,* Luke 18:5. *The door is now shut (ēdē hē thura kekleistai).* Perfect passive indicative, shut to stay shut. Oriental locks are not easy to unlock. From *kleiō,* common verb. *In bed (eis tēn koitēn).* Note use of *eis* in sense of *en.* Often a whole family would sleep in the same room. *I cannot (ou dunamai).* That is, I am not willing.

8. *Though (ei kai).* *Kai ei* would be "Even if," a different idea. *Because he is his friend (dia to einai philon autou).* *Dia* and the accusative articular infinitive with accusative of general reference, a causal clause = "because of the being a friend of his." *Yet because of his importunity (dia ge tēn anaidian autou).* From *anaidēs,* shameless, and that from *a*

privative and *aidōs*, shame, shamelessness, impudence. **An**
old word, but here alone in the N.T. Examples in the
papyri. The use of *ge* here, one of the intensive particles,
is to be noted. It sharpens the contrast to "though" by
"yet." As examples of importunate prayer Vincent notes
Abraham in behalf of Sodom (Gen. 18:23–33) and the Syro-
Phoenician woman in behalf of her daughter (Matt. 15:22–
28).

9. *Shall be opened* (*anoigēsetai*). Second future passive
third singular of *anoignumi* and the later *anoigō*.

11. *Of which of you that is a father* (*tina de ex humōn ton
patera*). There is a decided anacoluthon here. The MSS.
differ a great deal. The text of Westcott and Hort makes
ton patera (the father) in apposition with *tina* (of whom) and
in the accusative the object of *aitēsei* (shall ask) which has
also another accusative (both person and thing) "a loaf."
So far so good. But the rest of the sentence is, *will ye give
him a stone?* (*mē lithon epidōsei autōi;*). *Mē* shows that the
answer No is expected, but the trouble is that the interrogative *tina* in the first clause is in the accusative the object
of *aitēsei* while here the same man (he) is the subject of *epidōsei*. It is a very awkward piece of Greek and yet it is intelligible. Some of the old MSS. do not have the part about
"loaf" and "stone," but only the two remaining parts about
"fish" and "serpent," "egg" and "scorpion." The same
difficult construction is carried over into these questions also.

13. *Know how to give* (*oidate didonai*). See on Matt. 7:11
for this same saying. Only here Jesus adds the Holy Spirit
(*pneuma hagion*) as the great gift (the *summum bonum*) that
the Father is ready to bestow. Jesus is fond of "how much
more" (*posoi māllon*, by how much more, instrumental case).

14. *When* (*tou daimoniou exelthontos*). Genitive absolute
and asyndeton between *kai egeneto* and *elalēsen* as often in
Luke (no *hoti* or *kai*).

15. *Dumb* (*kōphon*). See on Matt. 9:32. *By Beelzebub*

(*en Beezeboul*). Blasphemous accusation here in Judea as in Galilee (Mark 3:22 =Matt. 12:24, 27). See on Matthew for discussion of the form of this name and the various items in the sin against the Holy Spirit involved in the charge. It was useless to deny the fact of the miracles. So they were explained as wrought by Satan himself, a most absurd explanation.

16. *Tempting him* (*peirazontes*). These "others" (*heteroi*) apparently realized the futility of the charge of being in league with Beelzebub. Hence they put up to Jesus the demand for "a sign from heaven" just as had been done in Galilee (Matt. 12:38). By "sign" (*sēmeion*) they meant a great spectacular display of heavenly power such as they expected the Messiah to give and such as the devil suggested to Jesus on the pinnacle of the temple. *Sought* (*ezētoun*). Imperfect active, kept on seeking.

17. *But he* (*autos de*). In contrast with them. *Knowing their thoughts* (*eidōs autōn ta dianoēmata*). From *dianoeō*, to think through or distinguish. This substantive is common in Plato, but occurs nowhere else in the N.T. It means intent, purpose. Jesus knew that they were trying to tempt him. *And a house divided against a house falleth* (*kai oikos epi oikon piptei*). It is not certain that *diameristheisa* (divided) is to be repeated here as in Matt. 12:25 = Mark 3:25. It may mean, *and house falls upon house*, "one tumbling house knocking down its neighbour, a graphic picture of what happens when a kingdom is divided against itself" (Bruce).

18. *Because ye say* (*hoti legete*). Jesus here repeats in indirect discourse (accusative and infinitive) the charge made against him in verse 15. The condition is of the first class, determined as fulfilled.

19. *And if I by Beelzebub* (*ei de egō en Beezeboul*). Also a condition of the first class, determined as fulfilled. A Greek condition deals only with the *statement*, not with the actual

facts. For sake of argument, Jesus here assumes that he casts out demons by Beelzebub. The conclusion is a *reductio ad absurdum*. The Jewish exorcists practiced incantations against demons (Acts 19:13).

20. *By the finger of God* (*en daktuloi theou*). In distinction from the Jewish exorcists. Matt. 12:28 has "by the Spirit of God." *Then is come* (*ara ephthasen*). *Phthano* in late Greek comes to mean simply to come, not to come before. The aorist indicative tense here is timeless. Note *ara* (accordingly) in the conclusion (*apodosis*).

21. *Fully armed* (*kathoplismenos*). Perfect passive participle of *kathoplizo*, an old verb, but here only in the N.T. Note perfective use of *kata* in composition with *hoplizo*, to arm (from *hopla*, arms). Note indefinite temporal clause (*hotan* and present subjunctive *phulassei*). *His own court* (*ten heautou aulen*). His own homestead. Mark 3:27 = Matt. 12:29 has "house" (*oikian*). *Aule* is used in the N.T. in various senses (the court in front of the house, the court around which the house is built, then the house as a whole). *His goods* (*ta huparchonta autou*). "His belongings." Neuter plural present active participle of *huparcho* used as substantive with genitive.

22. *But when* (*epan de*). Note *hotan* in verse 21. *Stronger than he* (*ischuroteros autou*). Comparative of *ischuros* followed by the ablative. *Come upon him and overcome him* (*epelthon nikesei auton*). Second aorist active participle of *eperchomai* and first aorist active subjunctive of *nikao*. Aorist tense here because a single onset while in verse 22 the guarding (*phulassei*, present active subjunctive) is continuous. *His whole armour* (*ten panoplian autou*). An old and common word for all the soldier's outfit (shield, sword, lance, helmet, greaves, breastplate). Tyndale renders it "his harness." In the N.T. only here and Eph. 6:11, 13 where the items are given. *Wherein he trusted* (*eph' hei epepoithei*). Second past perfect active of *peitho*, to persuade.

The second perfect *pepoitha* is intransitive, to trust. Old and common verb. He trusted his weapons which had been so efficacious. *His spoils (ta skula autou)*. It is not clear to what this figure refers. Strong as Satan is Jesus is stronger and wins victories over him as he was doing then. In Col. 2:15 Christ is pictured as triumphing openly over the powers of evil by the Cross.

23. *He that is not with me (ho mē ōn met' emou)*. This verse is just like Matt. 12:30.

24. *And finding none (kai mē heuriskon)*. Here Matt. 12:43 has *kai ouch heuriskei* (present active indicative instead of present active participle). Luke 11:24–26 is almost verbatim like Matt. 12:43–45, which see. Instead of just "taketh" (*paralambanei*) in verse 26, Matthew has "taketh with himself" (*paralambanei meth' heautou*). And Luke omits: "Even so shall it be also unto this evil generation" of Matt. 12:45. *Than the first (tōn prōtōn)*. Ablative case after the comparative *cheirona*. The seven demons brought back remind one of the seven that afflicted Mary Magdalene (Luke 8:2).

27. *As he said these things (en tōi legein auton)*. Luke's common idiom, *en* with articular infinitive. Verses 27 and 28 are peculiar to Luke. His Gospel in a special sense is the Gospel of Woman. This woman "speaks well, but womanly" (Bengel). Her beatitude (*makaria*) reminds us of Elisabeth's words (Luke 1:42, *eulogēmenē*). She is fulfilling Mary's own prophecy in 1:48 (*makariousin me*, shall call me happy).

28. *But he said (autos de eipen)*. Jesus in contrast turns attention to others and gives them a beatitude (*makarioi*). "The originality of Christ's reply guarantees its historical character. Such a comment is beyond the reach of an inventor" (Plummer).

29. *Were gathering together unto him (epathroizomenōn)*. Genitive absolute present middle participle of *epathroizō*,

a rare verb, Plutarch and here only in the N.T., from *epi*
and *athroizō* (a common enough verb). It means to throng
together (*athroos*, in throngs). Vivid picture of the crowds
around Jesus. *But the sign of Jonah* (*ei mē to sēmeion Iōnā*).
Luke does not give here the burial and resurrection of Jesus
of which Jonah's experience in the big fish was a type (Matt.
12:39ff.), but that is really implied (Plummer argues) by the
use here of "shall be given" (*dothēsetai*) and "shall be"
(*estai*), for the resurrection of Jesus is still future. The
preaching of Jesus ought to have been sign enough as in the
case of Jonah, but the resurrection will be given. Luke's report is much briefer and omits what is in Matt. 12:41.

31. *With the men of this generation* (*meta tōn andrōn tēs
geneās tautēs*). Here Matt. 12:42 has simply "with this generation," which see.

32. *At the preaching of Jonah* (*eis to kērugma Iōnā*). Note
this use of *eis* as in Matt. 10:41 and 12:41. Luke inserts the
words about the Queen of the South (31) in between the discussion of Jonah (verses 29f., 32). Both *Solomōnos* (31) and
Iōnā (verse 32) are in the ablative case after the comparative
pleion (more, *something more*).

33. *In a cellar* (*eis kruptēn*). A crypt (same word) or
hidden place from *kruptō*, to hide. Late and rare word and
here only in the N.T. These other words (lamp, *luchnon*,
bushel, *modion*, stand, *luchnian*) have all been discussed previously (Matt. 5:15). Luke 11:33 is like Matt. 6:22f., which
see for details.

35. *Whether not* (*mē*). This use of *mē* in an indirect question is good Greek (Robertson, *Grammar*, p. 1045). It is a
pitiful situation if the very light is darkness. This happens
when the eye of the soul is too diseased to see the light of
Christ.

36. *With its bright shining* (*tēi astrapēi*). Instrumental
case, as if by a flash of lightning the light is revealed in him.
See on 10:18.

37. *Now as he spake* (*en de tōi lalēsai*). Luke's common idiom, *en* with the articular infinitive (aorist active infinitive) but it does not mean "after he had spoken" as Plummer argues, but simply "in the speaking," no time in the aorist infinitive. See 3:21 for similar use of aorist infinitive with *en. Asketh* (*erōtāi*). Present active indicative, dramatic present. Request, not question. *To dine* (*hopōs aristēsēi*). Note *hopōs* rather than the common *hina*. Aorist active subjunctive rather than present, for a single meal. The verb is from *ariston* (breakfast). See distinction between *ariston* and *deipnon* (dinner or supper) in Luke 14:12. It is the morning meal (breakfast or lunch) after the return from morning prayers in the synagogue (Matt. 22:4), not the very early meal called *akratisma*. The verb is, however, used for the early meal on the seashore in John 21:12, 15. *With him* (*par' autōi*). By his side. *Sat down to meat* (*anepesen*). Second aorist active indicative of *anapiptō*, old verb, to recline, to fall back on the sofa or lounge. No word here for "to meat."

38. *That he had not first washed before dinner* (*hoti ou prōton ebaptisthē pro tou aristou*). The verb is first aorist passive indicative of *baptizō*, to dip or to immerse. Here it is applied to the hands. It was the Jewish custom to dip the hands in water before eating and often between courses for ceremonial purification. In Galilee the Pharisees and scribes had sharply criticized the disciples for eating with unwashed hands (Mark 7:1–23 = Matt. 15:1–20) when Jesus had defended their liberty and had opposed making a necessity of such a custom (tradition) in opposition to the command of God. Apparently Jesus on this occasion had himself reclined at the breakfast (not dinner) without this ceremonial dipping of the hands in water. The Greek has "first before" (*prōton pro*), a tautology not preserved in the translation.

39. *The Lord* (*ho kurios*). The Lord Jesus plainly and in the narrative portion of Luke. *Now* (*nun*). Probably refers

to him.   You Pharisees do now what was formerly done.
The platter (*tou pinakos*).   The dish.   Old word, rendered
"the charger" in Matt. 14:8.   Another word for "platter"
(*paropsis*) in Matt. 23:25 means "side-dish."   *But your
inward part* (*to de esōthen humōn*).   The part within you
(Pharisees).   They keep the external regulations, but their
hearts are full of plunder (*harpagēs*, from *harpazō*, to seize)
and wickedness (*ponērias*, from *ponēros*, evil man).   See
Matt. 23:25 for a like indictment of the Pharisees for care
for the outside of the cup but neglect of what is on the
inside.   Both inside and outside should be clean, but the
inside first.

40. *Howbeit* (*plēn*).   See Luke 6:24.   Instead of devoting
so much attention to the outside.   *Those things which are
within* (*ta enonta*).   Articular neuter plural participle from
eneimi, to be in, common verb.   This precise phrase only
here in the N.T. though in the papyri, and it is not clear
what it means.   Probably, give as alms the things within the
dishes, that is have inward righteousness with a brotherly
spirit and the outward becomes "clean" (*kathara*).   Properly
understood, this is not irony and is not Ebionism, but good
Christianity (Plummer).

42. *Tithe* (*apodekatoute*).   Late verb for the more common
dekateuō.   So in Matt. 23:23.   Take a tenth off (*apo-*).   Rue
(*pēganon*).   Botanical term in late writers from *pēgnumi*, to
make fast because of its thick leaves.   Here Matt. 23:23 has
"anise."   *Every herb* (*pān lachanon*).   General term as in
Mark 4:32.   Matthew has "cummin."   *Pass by* (*parerchesthe*).
Present middle indicative of *parerchomai*, common verb, to
go by or beside.   Matt. 23:23 has "ye have left undone"
(*aphēkate*).   Luke here has "love" (*agapēn*), not in Matthew.
Ought (*edei*).   As in Matthew.   Imperfect of a present obligation, not lived up to just like our "ought" (*owed*, not paid).
Pareinai, as in Matthew, the second aorist active infinitive
of *aphiēmi*. to leave off.   Common verb.   Luke does not have

the remark about straining out the gnat and swallowing the camel (Matt. 23:34). It is plain that the terrible exposure of the scribes and Pharisees in Matt. 23 in the temple was simply the culmination of previous conflicts such as this one.

43. *The chief seats in the synagogues (tēn prōtokathedrian en tais sunagōgais).* Singular here, plural in Matt. 23:6. This semi-circular bench faced the congregation. Matt. 23:6 has also the chief place at feasts given by Luke also in that discourse (20:46) as well as in 14:7, a marked characteristic of the Pharisees.

44. *The tombs which appear not (ta mnēneia ta adēla).* These hidden graves would give ceremonial defilement for seven days (Num. 19:16). Hence they were usually white-washed as a warning. So in Matt. 23:27 the Pharisees are called "whited sepulchres." Men do not know how rotten they are. The word *adēlos* (*a* privative and *dēlos*, apparent or plain) occurs in the N.T. only here and I Cor. 14:8, though an old and common word. *Here men walking around (peripatountes)* walk over the tombs without knowing it. These three woes cut to the quick and evidently made the Pharisees wince.

45. *Thou reproachest us also (kai hēmās hubrizeis).* Because the lawyers (scribes) were usually Pharisees. The verb *hubrizō* is an old one and common for outrageous treatment, a positive insult (so Luke 18:32; Matt. 22:6; Acts 14:5; I Thess. 2:2). So Jesus proceeds to give the lawyers three woes as he had done to the Pharisees.

46. *Grievous to be borne (dusbastakta).* A late word in LXX and Plutarch (*dus* and *bastazō*). Here alone in text of West-cott and Hort who reject it in Matt. 23:4 where we have "heavy burdens" (*phortia barea*). In Gal. 6:2 we have *barē* with a distinction drawn. Here we have *phortizete* (here only in the N.T. and Matt. 11:28) for "lade," *phortia* as cognate accusative and then *phortiois* (dative after *ou prospsauete*, touch not). It is a fierce indictment of scribes (lawyers) for

their pettifogging interpretations of the written law in their oral teaching (later written down as *Mishna* and then as *Gemarah*), a terrible load which these lawyers did not pretend to carry themselves, not even "with one of their fingers" to "touch" (*prospsauō*, old verb but only here in the N.T.), touch with the view to remove. Matt. 23:4 has *kinēsai*, to move. A physician would understand the meaning of *prospauō* for feeling gently a sore spot or the pulse.

48. *Consent* (*suneudokeite*). Double compound (*sun, eu, dokeō*), to think well along with others, to give full approval. A late verb, several times in the N.T., in Acts 8:1 of Saul's consenting to and agreeing to Stephen's death. It is a somewhat subtle, but just, argument made here. Outwardly the lawyers build tombs for the prophets whom their fathers (forefathers) killed as if they disapproved what their fathers did. But in reality they neglect and oppose what the prophets teach just as their fathers did. So they are "witnesses" (*martures*) against themselves (Matt. 23:31).

49. *The wisdom of God* (*hē sophia tou theou*). In Matt. 23:34 Jesus uses "I send" (*egō apostellō*) without this phrase "the wisdom of God." There is no book to which it can refer. Jesus is the wisdom of God as Paul shows (I Cor. 1:30), but it is hardly likely that he so describes himself here. Probably he means that God in his wisdom said, but even so "Jesus here speaks with confident knowledge of the Divine counsels" (Plummer). See Luke 10:22; 15:7, 10. Here the future tense occurs, "I will send" (*apostelō*). *Some of them* (*ex autōn*). No "some" (*tinas*) in the Greek, but understood. They will act as their fathers did. They will kill and persecute.

50. *That . . . may be required* (*hina . . . ekzētēthēi*). Divinely ordered sequence, first aorist passive subjunctive of *ekzēteō*, a late and rare verb outside of LXX and N.T., requiring as a debt the blood of the prophets. *Which was shed* (*to ekkechumenon*). Perfect passive participle of *ekcheō* and

ekchunnō (an Aeolic form appearing in the margin of Westcott and Hort here, *ekchunnomenon*, present passive participle). If the present passive is accepted, it means the blood which is perpetually shed from time to time. *From the foundation of the world* (*apo katabolēs kosmou*). See also Matt. 25:34; John 17:24; Eph. 1:4, etc. It is a bold metaphor for the purpose of God.

51. *From the blood of Abel to the blood of Zachariah* (*apo haimatos Abel heōs haimatos Zachariou*). The blood of Abel is the first shed in the Old Testament (Gen. 4:10), that of Zacharias the last in the O.T. canon which ended with Chronicles (II Chron. 24:22). Chronologically the murder of Uriah by Jehoiakim was later (Jer. 26:23), but this climax is from Genesis to II Chronicles (the last book in the canon). See on Matt. 23:35 for discussion of Zachariah as "the son of Barachiah" rather than "the son of Jehoiada." *Between the altar and the sanctuary* (*metaxu tou thusiastēriou kai tou oikou*). Literally, between the altar and the house (Matt. 23:35 has temple, *naou*).

52. *Ye took away the key of knowledge* (*ērate tēn kleida tēs gnōseōs*). First aorist active indicative of *airō*, common verb. But this is a flat charge of obscurantism on the part of these scribes (lawyers), the teachers (rabbis) of the people. They themselves (*autoi*) refused to go into the house of knowledge (beautiful figure) and learn. They then locked the door and hid the key to the house of knowledge and hindered (*ekōlusate*, effective aorist active) those who were trying to enter (*tous eiserchomenous*, present participle, conative action). It is the most pitiful picture imaginable of blind ecclesiastics trying to keep others as blind as they were, blind leaders of the blind, both falling into the pit.

53. *From thence* (*kakeithen*). Out of the Pharisee's house. What became of the breakfast we are not told, but the rage of both Pharisees and lawyers knew no bounds. *To press upon him* (*enechein*). An old Greek verb to hold in, to be

enraged at, to have it in for one. It is the same verb used of the relentless hatred of Herodias for John the Baptist (Mark 6:19). *To provoke him to speak (apostomatizein).* From *apo* and *stoma* (mouth). Plato uses it of repeating to a pupil for him to recite from memory, then to recite by heart (Plutarch). Here (alone in the N.T.) the verb means to ply with questions, to entice to answers, to catechize. *Of many things (peri pleionōn).* "Concerning more (comparative) things." They were stung to the quick by these woes which laid bare their hollow hypocrisy.

54. *Laying wait for him (enedreuontes auton).* An old verb from *en* and *hedra,* a seat, so to lie in ambush for one. Here only and Acts 23:21 in the N.T. Vivid picture of the anger of these rabbis who were treating Jesus as if he were a beast of prey. *To catch something out of his mouth (thēreusai to ek tou stomatos autou).* An old Greek verb, though here only in the N.T., from *thēra* (cf. Rom. 11:9), to ensnare, to catch in hunting, to hunt. These graphic words from the chase show the rage of the rabbis toward Jesus. Luke gives more details here than in 20:45–47 = Matt. 23:1–7, but there is no reason at all why Jesus should not have had this conflict at the Pharisee's breakfast before that in the temple in the great Tuesday debate.

CHAPTER XII

1. *In the meantime (en hois).* It is a classic idiom to start a sentence or even a paragraph as here with a relative, "in which things or circumstances," without any expressed antecedent other than the incidents in 11:53f. In 12:3 Luke actually begins the sentence with two relatives *anth' hōn hosa* (wherefore whatsoever). *Many thousands (muriadōn).* Genitive absolute with *episunachtheisōn* (first aorist passive participle feminine plural because of *muriadōn*), a double compound late verb, *episunagō*, to gather together unto. The word "myriads" is probably hyperbolical as in Acts 21:20, but in the sense of ten thousand, as in Acts 19:19, it means a very large crowd apparently drawn together by the violent attacks of the rabbis against Jesus. *Insomuch that they trode one upon another (hōste katapatein allēlous).* The imagination must complete the picture of this jam. *Unto his disciples first of all (pros tous mathētas autou prōton).* This long discourse in Luke 12 is really a series of separate talks to various groups in the vast crowds around Jesus. This particular talk goes through verse 12. *Beware of (prosechete heautois apo).* Put your mind (*noun* understood) for yourselves (dative) and avoid (*apo* with the ablative). *The leaven of the Pharisees which is hypocrisy (tēs zumēs hētis estin hupocrisis tōn Pharisaiōn).* In Mark 8:15 Jesus had coupled the lesson of the Pharisees with that of Herod, in Matt. 16:6 with that of the Sadducees also. He had long ago called the Pharisees hypocrites (Matt. 6:2, 5, 16). The occasion was ripe here for this crisp saying. In Matt. 13:33 leaven does not have an evil sense as here, which see. See Matt. 23:13 for hypocrites. Hypocrisy was the leading Pharisaic vice (Bruce) and was a mark of sanctity to hide an evil heart.

2. *Covered up* (*sugkekalummenon estin*). Periphrastic perfect passive indicative of *sugkaluptō*, an old verb, but here only in the N.T., to cover up on all sides and so completely. Verses 2 to 9 here are parallel with Matt. 10:26–33 spoken to the Twelve on their tour of Galilee, illustrating again how often Jesus repeated his sayings unless we prefer to say that he never did so and that the Gospels have hopelessly jumbled them as to time and place. See the passage in Matthew for discussion of details.

3. *In the inner chambers* (*en tois tameiois*). Old form *tamieion*, a store chamber (Luke 12:24), secret room (Matt. 6:6; Luke 12:3).

4. *Unto you my friends* (*humin tois philois*). As opposed to the Pharisees and lawyers in 11:43, 46, 53. *Be not afraid of* (*mē phobēthēte apo*). First aorist passive subjunctive with *mē*, ingressive aorist, do not become afraid of, with *apo* and the ablative like the Hebrew *min* and the English "be afraid of," a translation Hebraism as in Matt. 10:28 (Moulton, *Prolegomena*, p. 102). *Have no more that they can do* (*mē echontōn perissoteron ti poiēsai*). Luke often uses the infinitive thus with *echō*, a classic idiom (7:40, 42; 12:4, 50; 14:14; Acts 4:14, etc.).

5. *Whom ye shall fear* (*tina phobēthēte*). First aorist passive subjunctive deliberative retained in the indirect question. *Tina* is the accusative, the direct object of this transitive passive verb (note *apo* in verse 4). *Fear him who* (*phobēthēte ton*). First aorist passive imperative, differing from the preceding form only in the accent and governing the accusative also. *After he hath killed* (*meta to apokteinai*). Preposition *meta* with the articular infinitive. Literally, "After the killing" (first aorist active infinitive of the common verb *apokteinō*, to kill. *Into hell* (*eis tēn geennan*). See on Matt. 5:22. Gehenna is a transliteration of *Ge-Hinnom*, Valley of Hinnon where the children were thrown on to the red-hot arms of Molech. Josiah (II Kings 23:10) abolished

these abominations and then it was a place for all kinds of refuse which burned ceaselessly and became a symbol of punishment in the other world. *This one fear* (*touton phobēthēte*). As above.

6. *Is forgotten* (*estin epilelēsmenon*). Periphrastic perfect passive indicative of *epilanthanomai*, common verb to forget. See Matt. 10:29 for a different construction.

7. *Numbered* (*ērithmēntai*). Perfect passive indicative. Periphrastic form in Matt. 10:30 which see for details about sparrows, etc.

8. *Everyone who shall confess me* (*pas hos an homologēsei en emoi*). Just like Matt. 10:32 except the use of *an* here which adds nothing. The Hebraistic use of *en* after *homologeō* both here and in Matthew is admitted by even Moulton (*Prolegomena*, p. 104). *The Son of man* (*ho huios tou anthrōpou*). Here Matt. 10:32 has *k'agō* (I also) as the equivalent.

9. *Shall be denied* (*aparnēthēsetai*). First future passive of the compound verb *aparneomai*. Here Matt. 10:33 has *arnēsomai* simply. Instead of "in the presence of the angels of God" (*emprosthen tōn aggelōn tou theou*) Matt. 10:33 has "before my Father who is in heaven."

10. *But unto him that blasphemeth against the Holy Spirit* (*tōi de eis to hagion pneuma blasphēmēsanti*). This unpardonable sin is given by Mark 3:28f. = Matt. 12:31f. immediately after the charge that Jesus was in league with Beelzebub. Luke here separates it from the same charge made in Judea (11:15–20). As frequently said, there is no sound reason for saying that Jesus only spoke his memorable sayings once. Luke apparently finds a different environment here. Note the use of *eis* here in the sense of "against."

11. *Be not anxious* (*mē merimnēsēte*). First aorist active subjunctive with *mē* in prohibition. Do not become anxious. See a similar command to the Twelve on their Galilean tour

(Matt. 10:19f.) and in the great discourse on the Mount of Olives at the end (Mark 13:11 = Luke 21:14f.), given twice by Luke as we see. *How or what ye shall answer* (*pōs ē ti apologēsēsthe*). Indirect question and retaining the deliberative subjunctive *apologēsēsthe* and also *eipēte* (say).

12. *What ye ought to say* (*hā dei eipein*). Literally, what things it is necessary (*dei*) to say. This is no excuse for neglect in pulpit preparation. It is simply a word for courage in a crisis to play the man for Christ and to trust the issue with God without fear.

13. *Bid my brother* (*eipe tōi adelphōi mou*). This volunteer from the crowd draws attention to the multitude (verses 13–21). He does not ask for arbitration and there is no evidence that his brother was willing for that. He wants a decision by Jesus against his brother. The law (Deut. 21:17) was two-thirds to the elder, one-third to the younger.

14. *A judge or a divider* (*kritēn ē meristēn*). Jesus repudiates the position of judge or arbiter in this family fuss. The language reminds one of Ex. 2:14. Jesus is rendering unto Caesar the things of Caesar (Luke 20:25) and shows that his kingdom is not of this world (John 18:36). The word for divider or arbiter (*meristēs*) is a late word from *merizomai* (verse 13) and occurs here only in the N.T.

15. *From all covetousness* (*apo pasēs pleonexias*). Ablative case. From every kind of greedy desire for more (*pleon*, more, *hexia*, from *echō*, to have) an old word which we have robbed of its sinful aspects and refined to mean business thrift. *In the abundance of the things which he possesseth* (*en tōi perisseuein tini ek tōn huparchontōn autōi*). A rather awkward Lukan idiom: "In the abounding (articular infinitive) to one out of the things belonging (articular participle) to him."

16. *A parable unto them* (*parabolēn pros autous*). The multitude of verses 13 and 15. A short and pungent parable suggested by the covetousness of the man of verse 13.

Brought forth plentifully (euphorēsen). Late word from *euphoros* (bearing well), in medical writers and Josephus, here only in the N.T.

17. *Reasoned within himself (dielogizeto en hautōi).* Imperfect middle, picturing his continued cogitations over his perplexity. *Where to bestow (pou sunaxō).* Future indicative deliberative, where I shall gather together. *My fruits (tous karpous mou).* So it is with the rich fool: my fruits, my barns, my corn, my goods, just like Nabal whose very name means fool (I Sam. 25:11), whether a direct reference to him or not.

18. *I will pull down (kathelō).* Future active of *kathaireō,* an old verb, the usual future being *kathairēsō.* This second form from the second aorist *katheilon* (from obsolete *helō*) like *aphelei* in Rev. 22:19. *My barns (mou tas apothēkas).* From *apotithēmi,* to lay by, to treasure. So a granary or storehouse, an old word, six times in the N.T. (Matt. 3:12; 6:26; 13:30; Luke 3:17; 12:18, 24). *All my corn (panta ton siton).* Better grain (wheat, barley), not maize or Indian corn. *My goods (ta agatha mou).* Like the English, my good things. So the English speak of goods (freight) train.

19. *Laid up for many years (keimena eis etē polla).* Not in D and some other Latin MSS. The man's apostrophe to his "soul" (*psuchē*) is thoroughly Epicurean, for his soul feeds on his goods. The asyndeton here (take thine ease, eat, drink, be merry) shows his eagerness. Note difference in tenses (*anapauou,* keep on resting, *phage,* eat at once, *pie,* drink thy fill, *euphrainou,* keep on being merry), first and last presents, the other two aorists.

20. *Thou foolish one (aphrōn).* Fool, for lack of sense (*a* privative and *phrēn,* sense) as in 11:40 and II Cor. 11:19. Old word, used by Socrates in Xenophon. Nominative form as vocative. *Is thy soul required of thee (tēn psuchēn sou aitousin apo sou).* Plural active present, not passive: "They are demanding thy soul from thee." The impersonal plural

(aitousin) is common enough (Luke 6:38; 12:11; 16:9; 23:31). The rabbis used "they" to avoid saying "God."

21. *Not rich toward God* (*mē eis theon ploutōn*). The only wealth that matters and that lasts. Cf. 16:9 and Matt. 6:19f. Some MSS. do not have this verse. Westcott and Hort bracket it.

22. *Unto his disciples* (*pros tous mathētas autou*). So Jesus turns from the crowd to the disciples (verses 22 to 40, when Peter interrupts the discourse). From here to the end of the chapter Luke gives material that appears in Matthew, but not in one connection as here. In Matthew part of it is in the charge to the Twelve on their tour in Galilee, part in the eschatological discourse on the Mount of Olives. None of it is in Mark. Hence Q or the Logia seems to be the source of it. The question recurs again whether Jesus repeated on other occasions what is given here or whether Luke has here put together separate discourses as Matthew is held by many to have done in the Sermon on the Mount. We have no way of deciding these points. We can only say again that Jesus would naturally repeat his favourite sayings like other popular preachers and teachers. So Luke 12:22–31 corresponds to Matt. 6:25–33, which see for detailed discussion. The parable of the rich fool was spoken to the crowd, but this exhortation to freedom from care (22–31) is to the disciples. So the language in Luke 12:22 is precisely that in Matt. 6:25. See there for *mē merimnāte* (stop being anxious) and the deliberative subjunctive retained in the indirect question (*phagēte, endusēsthe*). So verse 23 here is the same in Matt. 6:25 except that there it is a question with *ouch* expecting the affirmative answer, whereas here it is given as a reason (*gar*, for) for the preceding command.

24. *The ravens* (*tous korakas*). Nowhere else in the N.T. The name includes the whole crow group of birds (rooks and jackdaws). Like the vultures they are scavengers. Matt. 6:26 has simply "the birds" (*ta peteina*). *Storechamber*

(*tameion*). Not in Matt. 6:26. Means secret chamber in Luke 12:3. *Of how much more* (*posōi māllon*). Matt. 6:26 has question, *ouch māllon*.

25. *A cubit* (*pēchun*). Matt. 6:27 has *pēchun hena* (one cubit, though *hena* is sometimes merely the indefinite article. *Stature* (*hēlikian*) as in Matthew, which see.

26. *Not able to do even that which is least* (*oude elachiston dunasthe*). Negative *oude* in the condition of the first class. Elative superlative, very small. This verse not in Matthew and omitted in D. Verse 27 as in Matt. 6:28, save that the verbs for toil and spin are plural in Matthew and singular here (neuter plural subject, *ta krina*).

28. *Clothe* (*amphiazei*). Late Greek verb in the *Koinê* (papyri) for the older form *amphiennumi* (Matt. 6:30). See Matthew for discussion of details. Matthew has "the grass of the field" instead of "the grass in the field" as here.

29. *Seek not ye* (*humeis mē zēteite*). Note emphatic position of "ye" (*humeis*). Stop seeking (*mē* and present imperative active). Matt. 6:31 has: "Do not become anxious" (*mē merimnēsēte*), *mē* and ingressive subjunctive occur as direct questions (What are we to eat? What are we to drink? What are we to put on?) whereas here they are in the indirect form as in verse 22 save that the problem of clothing is not here mentioned: *Neither be ye of doubtful mind* (*kai mē meteōrizesthe*). *Mē* and present passive imperative (stop being anxious) of *meteōrizō*. An old verb from *meteōros* in midair, high (our meteor), to lift up on high, then to lift oneself up with hopes (false sometimes), to be buoyed up, to be tossed like a ship at sea, to be anxious, to be in doubt as in late writers (Polybius, Josephus). This last meaning is probably true here. In the LXX and Philo, but here only in the N.T.

31. See Matt. 6:33 for this verse. Luke does not have "first" nor "his righteousness" nor "all."

32. *Little flock* (*to mikron poimnion*). Vocative with the

article as used in Hebrew and often in the *Koiné* and so in the N.T. See both *pater* and *ho patēr* in the vocative in Luke 10:21. See Robertson, *Grammar*, pp. 465f. *Poimnion* (flock) is a contraction from *poimenion* from *poimēn* (shepherd) instead of the usual *poimnē* (flock). So it is not a diminutive and *mikron* is not superfluous, though it is pathetic. *For it is your Father's good pleasure* (*hoti eudokēsen ho patēr humōn*). First aorist active indicative of *eudokeō*. Timeless aorist as in Luke 3:22. This verse has no parallel in Matthew.

33. *Sell that ye have* (*Pōlēsate ta huparchonta humōn*). Not in Matthew. Did Jesus mean this literally and always? Luke has been charged with Ebionism, but Jesus does not condemn property as inherently sinful. "The attempt to keep the letter of the rule here given (Acts 2:44, 45) had disastrous effects on the church of Jerusalem, which speedily became a church of paupers, constantly in need of alms (Rom. 15:25, 26; I Cor. 16:3; II Cor. 8:4; 9:1)" (Plummer). *Purses which wax not old* (*ballantia mē palaioumena*). So already *ballantion* in Luke 10:4. Late verb *palaioō* from *palaios*, old, to make old, declare old as in Heb. 8:13, is passive to become old as here and Heb. 1:11. *That faileth not* (*anekleipton*). Verbal from *a* privative and *ekleipō*, to fail. Late word in Diodorus and Plutarch. Only here in the N.T. or LXX, but in papyri. "I prefer to believe that even Luke sees in the words not a mechanical rule, but a law for the spirit" (Bruce). *Draweth near* (*eggizei*). Instead of Matt. 6:19 "dig through and steal." *Destroyeth* (*diaphtheirei*). Instead of "doth consume" in Matt. 6:19.

34. *Will be* (*estai*). Last word in the sentence in Luke. Otherwise like Matt. 6.21. See I Cor. 7:32–34 for similar principle.

35. *Be girded about* (*estōsan periezōsmenai*). Periphrastic perfect passive imperative third plural of the verb *perizōnnumi* or *perizōnnuō* (later form), an old verb, to gird around,

to fasten the garments with a girdle. The long garments of
the orientals made speed difficult. It was important to use
the girdle before starting. Cf. 17:8; Acts 12:8. *Burning*
(*kaiomenoi*). Periphrastic present middle imperative, already burning and continuously burning. The same point
of the Parable of the Ten Virgins (Matt. 25:1–13) is found
here in condensed form. This verse introduces the parable
of the waiting servants (Luke 12:35–40).

36. *When he shall return from the marriage feast* (*pote
analusēi ek tōn gamōn*). The interrogative conjunction *pote*
and the deliberative aorist subjunctive retained in the indirect question. The verb *analuō*, very common Greek verb,
but only twice in the N.T. (here and Phil. 1:23). The figure
is breaking up a camp or loosening the mooring of a ship,
to depart. Perhaps here the figure is from the standpoint of
the wedding feast (plural as used of a single wedding feast in
Luke 14:8), departing from there. See on Matt. 22:2. *When
he cometh and knocketh* (*elthontos kai krousantos*). Genitive
absolute of the aorist active participle without *autou* and in
spite of *autōi* (dative) being used after *anoixōsin* (first aorist
active subjunctive of *anoigō*).

37. *He shall gird himself* (*perizōsetai*). Direct future middle. Jesus did this (John 13:4), not out of gratitude, but to
give the apostles an object lesson in humility. See the usual
course in Luke 17:7–10 with also the direct middle (verse 8)
of *perisōnnuō*.

38. *And if* (*k'an = kai + ean*). Repeated. *Elthēi* and
heurēi, both second aorist subjunctive with *ean*, condition
of the third class, undetermined, but with prospect of
being determined. *Blessed* (*makarioi*). Beatitude here as in
verse 37.

39. *The thief* (*ho kleptēs*). The change here almost makes
a new parable to illustrate the other, the parable of the
housebreaking (verses 39 and 40) to illustrate the parable
of the waiting servants (35–38). This same language appears

in Matt. 24:43f. "The Master returning from a wedding is replaced by a thief whose study it is to come to the house he means to plunder at an unexpected time" (Bruce). The parallel in Matt. 24:43–51 with Luke 12:39–46 does not have the interruption by Peter. *He would have watched* (*egrēgorē-sen an*). Apodosis of second-class condition, determined as unfulfilled, made plain by use of *an* with aorist indicative which is not repeated with *ouk aphēken* (first aorist active indicative of *aphiēmi*, *k* aorist), though it is sometimes repeated (Matt. 24:43).

40. *Be ye* (*ginesthe*). Present middle imperative, keep on becoming. *Cometh* (*erchetai*). Futuristic present indicative. See Matt. 24:43 to 51 for details in the comparison with Luke.

41. *Peter said* (*Eipen de ho Petros*). This whole paragraph from verse 22 to verse 40 had been addressed directly to the disciples. Hence it is not surprising to find Peter putting in a question. This incident confirms also the impression that Luke is giving actual historical data in the environment of these discourses. He is certain that the Twelve are meant, but he desires to know if others are included, for he had spoken to the multitude in verses 13 to 21. Recall Mark 13:37. This interruption is somewhat like that on the Mount of Transfiguration (Luke 9:33) and is characteristic of Peter. Was it the magnificent promise in verse 37 that stirred Peter's impulsiveness? It is certainly more than a literary device of Luke. Peter's question draws out a parabolic reply by Jesus (42–48).

42. *Who then* (*tis ara*). Jesus introduces this parable of the wise steward (42–48) by a rhetorical question that answers itself. Peter is this wise steward, each of the Twelve is, anyone is who acts thus. *The faithful and wise steward* (*ho pistos oikonomos ho phronimos*). The faithful steward, the wise one. A steward is house manager (*oikos*, *nemō*, to manage). Each man is a steward in his own responsibilities.

Household (*therapeias*). Literally, service from *therapeuō*, medical service as in Luke 9:11, by metonymy household (a body of those domestics who serve). *Their portion of food* (*to sitometrion*). Late word from *sitometreō* (Gen. 47:12) for the Attic *ton siton metreō*, to measure the food, the rations. Here only in the N.T. or anywhere else till Deissmann (*Bible Studies*, p. 158) found it in an Egyptian papyrus and then an inscription in Lycia (*Light from the Ancient East*, p. 104).

44. *Over all* (*epi pāsin*). See Matt. 24-47 for *epi* with locative in this sense. Usually with genitive as in verse 42 and sometimes with accusative as in verse 14.

45. *Shall say* (*eipēi*). Second aorist subjunctive, with *ean*, condition of the third class, undetermined, but with prospect of being determined. *Delayeth* (*chronizei*). From *chronos*, time, spends time, lingers. *Shall begin* (*arxētai*). First aorist middle subjunctive with *ean* and the same condition as *eipēi*, above. *The menservants* (*tous paidas*) *and the maidservants* (*kai tas paidiskas*). *Paidiskē* is a diminutive of *pais* for a young female slave and occurs in the papyri, orginally just a damsel. Here *pais* can mean slave also though strictly just a boy.

46. *Shall cut him asunder* (*dichotomēsei*). An old and somewhat rare word from *dichotomos* and that from *dicha* and *temnō*, to cut, to cut in two. Used literally here. In the N.T. only here and Matt. 24:51. *With the unfaithful* (*meta tōn apistōn*). Not here "the unbelieving" though that is a common meaning of *apistos* (*a* privative and *pistos*, from *peithō*), but the unreliable, the untrustworthy. Here Matt. 24:51 has "with the hypocrites," the same point. The parallel with Matt. 24:43-51 ends here. Matt. 24:51 adds the saying about the wailing and the gnashing of teeth. Clearly there Luke places the parable of the wise steward in this context while Matthew has it in the great eschatological discourse. Once again we must either think that Jesus

repeated the parable or that one of the writers has misplaced it. Luke alone preserves what he gives in verses 47 and 48.

47. *Which knew* (*ho gnous*). Articular participle (second aorist active, punctiliar and timeless). The one who knows. So as to *mē hetoimasas ē poiēsas* (does not make ready or do). *Shall be beaten with many stripes* (*darēsetai pollas*). Second future passive of *derō*, to skin, to beat, to flay (see on Matt. 21:35; Mark 12:3, 5). The passive voice retains here the accusative *pollas* (supply *plēgas*, present in Luke 10:30). The same explanation applies to *oligas* in verse 48.

48. *To whomsoever much is given* (*panti de hōi edothē polu*). Here is inverse attraction from *hōi* to *panti* (Robertson, *Grammar*, pp. 767f.). Note *par' autou* (from him) without any regard to *panti*. *They commit* (*parethento*). Second aorist middle indicative, timeless or gnomic aorist. Note the impersonal plural after the passive voice just before.

49. *I came to cast fire* (*Pur ēlthon balein*). Suddenly Jesus lets the volcano in his own heart burst forth. The fire was already burning. "Christ came to set the world on fire, and the conflagration had already begun" (Plummer). The very passion in Christ's heart would set his friends on fire and his foes in opposition as we have just seen (Luke 11: 53f.). It is like the saying of Jesus that he came to bring not peace, but a sword, to bring cleavage among men (Matt. 10:34-36). *And what will I, if it is already kindled?* (*kai ti thelō ei ēdē anēphthē;*). It is not clear what this passage means. Probably *ti* is be taken in the sense of "how" (*pōs*). How I wish. Then *ei* can be taken as equal to *hoti*. How I wish that it were already kindled. *Anēphthē* is first aorist passive of *anaptō*, to set fire to, to kindle, to make blaze. Probably Luke means the conflagration to come by his death on the Cross for he changes the figure and refers to that more plainly.

50. *I have a baptism* (*baptisma de echō*). Once again Jesus will call his baptism the baptism of blood and will

challenge James and John to it (Mark 10:32f. = Matt.
20:22f.). So here. "Having used the metaphor of fire,
Christ now uses the metaphor of water. The one sets forth
the result of his coming as it affects the world, the other as
it affects himself. The world is lit up with flames and Christ
is bathed in blood" (Plummer). *And how I am straitened
(kai pōs sunechomai).* See this same vivid verb *sunechomai*
in Luke 8:37 and in Acts 18:5 and in Phil. 1:23 where Paul
uses it of his desire for death just as Jesus does here. The
urge of the Cross is upon Jesus at the moment of these words.
We catch a glimpse of the tremendous passion in his soul that
drove him on. *Till it be accomplished (heōs hotou telesthēi).*
First aorist passive subjunctive of *teleō* with *heōs hotou*
(until which time), the common construction for the future
with this conjunction.

51. *But rather division (all' ē diamerismon).* Peace at any
price is not the purpose of Christ. It is a pity for family jars
to come, but loyalty to Christ counts more than all else.
These ringing words (Luke 12:51–53) occur in Matt. 10:34–36
in the address to the Twelve for the Galilean tour. See discussion of details there. These family feuds are inevitable
where only part cleave to Christ. In Matthew we have *kata*
with the genitive whereas in Luke it is *epi* with the dative
(and accusative once).

54. *To the multitudes also (kai tois ochlois).* After the
strong and stirring words just before with flash and force
Jesus turns finally in this series of discourses to the multitudes again as in verse 15. There are similar sayings to these
verses 54–59 in Matt. 16:1f. and 5:25f. There is a good deal
of difference in phraseology whether that is due to difference
of source or different use of the same source (Q or Logia) we
do not know. Not all the old MSS. give Matt. 16:2 and 3.
In Matthew the Pharisees and Sadducees were asking for a
sign from heaven as they often did. These signs of the
weather, "a shower" (*ombros*, Luke 12:54) due to clouds

in the west, "a hot wave" (*kausōn*, verse 55) due to a south wind (*noton*) blowing, "fair weather" (*eudia*, Matt. 16:2) when the sky is red, are appealed to today. They have a more or less general application due to atmospheric and climatic conditions.

56. *To interpret this time* (*ton kairon touton dokimazein*). To test *dokimazein* as spiritual chemists. No wonder that Jesus here calls them "hypocrites" because of their blindness when looking at and hearing him. So it is today with those who are willfully blind to the steps of God among men. This ignorance of the signs of the times is colossal.

57. *Even of yourselves* (*kai aph' heautōn*). Without the presence and teaching of Jesus they had light enough to tell what is right (*to dikaion*) and so without excuse as Paul argued in Rom. 1 to 3.

58. *Give diligence to be quit of him* (*dos ergasian apēllachthai ap' autou*). Second aorist active imperative *dos* from *didōmi*. *Apēllachthai*, perfect passive infinitive of *apallassō* an old verb common, but only twice in the N.T. (here and Acts 19:12). Used here in a legal sense and the tense emphasizes a state of completion, to be rid of him for good. *Hale thee* (*katasurēi*). Drag down forcibly, old verb, only here in the N.T. *To the officer* (*tōi praktori*). The doer, the proctor, the exactor of fines, the executor of punishment. Old word, only here in the N.T.

59. *Till thou have paid* (*heōs apodōis*). Second aorist active subjunctive of *apodidōmi*, to pay back in full. *The last mite* (*to eschaton lepton*). From *lepō*, to peel off the bark. Very small brass coin, one-eighth of an ounce. In the N.T. only here and Luke 21:2 = Mark 12:42 (the poor widow's mite) which see.

CHAPTER XIII

1. *At that very season* (*en autōi tōi kairōi*). Luke's frequent idiom, "at the season itself." Apparently in close connexion with the preceding discourses. Probably "were present" (*parēsan*, imperfect of *pareimi*) means "came," "stepped to his side," as often (Matt. 26:50; Acts 12:20; John 11:28). These people had a piece of news for Jesus. *Whose blood Pilate had mingled with their sacrifices* (*hōn to haima Peilatos emixen meta tōn thusiōn autōn*). The verb *emixen* is first aorist active (not past perfect) of *mignumi*, a common verb. The incident is recorded nowhere else, but is in entire harmony with Pilate's record for outrages. These Galileans at a feast in Jerusalem may have been involved in some insurrection against the Roman government, the leaders of whom Pilate had slain right in the temple courts where the sacrifices were going on. Jesus comments on the incident, but not as the reporters had expected. Instead of denunciation of Pilate he turned it into a parable for their own conduct in the uncertainty of life.

2. *Sinners above all* (*hamartōloi para pantas*). *Para* means "beside," placed beside all the Galileans, and so beyond or above (with the accusative). *Have suffered* (*peponthasin*). Second perfect active indicative third plural from *paschō*, common verb, to experience, suffer. The tense notes that it is "an irrevocable fact" (Bruce).

3. *Except ye repent* (*ean mē metanoēte*). Present active subjunctive of *metanoeō*, to change mind and conduct, linear action, keep on changing. Condition of third class, undetermined, but with prospect of determination. *Ye shall perish* (*apoleisthe*). Future middle indicative of *apollumi* and intransitive. Common verb.

4. *The tower in Siloam* (*ho purgos en Silōam*). Few sites have been more clearly located than this. Jesus mentions this accident (only in Luke) of his own accord to illustrate still further the responsibility of his hearers. Jesus makes use of public events in both these incidents to teach spiritual lessons. He gives the "moral" to the massacre of the Galilean pilgrims and the "moral" of the catastrophe at Siloam. *Offenders* (*opheiletai*). Literally, *debtors*, not sinners as in verse 2 and as the Authorized Version renders here. See 7:41; 11:4; Matt. 6:12; 18:24–34.

5. *Except ye repent* (*ean mē metanoēsēte*). First aorist active subjunctive, immediate repentance in contrast to continued repentance, *metanoēte* in verse 3, though Westcott and Hort put *metanoēte* in the margin here. The interpretation of accidents is a difficult matter, but the moral pointed out by Jesus is obvious.

6. *Planted* (*pephuteumenēn*). Perfect passive participle of *phuteuō*, to plant, an old verb, from *phuton*, a plant, and that from *phuō*, to grow. But this participle with *eichen* (imperfect active of *echō*) does not make a periphrastic past perfect like our English "had planted." It means rather, he had a fig tree, one already planted in his vineyard.

7. *The vinedresser* (*ton ampelourgon*). Old word, but here only in the N.T., from *ampelos*, vine, and *ergon*, work. *These three years I come* (*tria etē aph' hou erchomai*). Literally, "three years since (from which time) I come." These three years, of course, have nothing to do with the three years of Christ's public ministry. The three years are counted from the time when the fig tree would normally be expected to bear, not from the time of planting. The Jewish nation is meant by this parable of the barren fig tree. In the withering of the barren fig tree later at Jerusalem we see parable changed to object lesson or fact (Mark 11:12–14 = Matt. 21:18f.). *Cut it down* (*ekkopson*). "Cut it out," the Greek has it, out of the vineyard, perfective use of *ek* with the

effective aorist active imperative of *koptō*, where we prefer "down." *Why?* (*hina ti*). Ellipsis here of *genētai* of which *ti* is subject (Robertson, *Grammar*, pp. 739, 916). *Also* (*kai*). Besides bearing no fruit. *Doth cumber the ground* (*tēn gēn katargei*). Makes the ground completely idle, of no use (*kata, argeō*, from *argos, a* privative and *ergon,* work). Late verb, here only in the N.T. except in Paul's Epistles.

8. *Till I shall dig* (*heōs hotou skapsō*). First aorist active subjunctive like *balō* (second aorist active subjunctive of *ballō*), both common verbs. *Dung it* (*balō kopria*). Cast dung around it, manure it. *Kopria*, late word, here alone in the N.T.

9. *And if it bear fruit thenceforth* (*kàn men poiēsēi karpon eis to mellon*). Aposiopesis, sudden breaking off for effect (Robertson, *Grammar*, p. 1203). See it also in Mark 11:32; Acts 23:9. Trench (*Parables*) tells a story like this of intercession for the fig tree for one year more which is widely current among the Arabs today who say that it will certainly bear fruit this time.

10. *He was teaching* (*ēn didaskōn*). Periphrastic imperfect active.

11. *A spirit of infirmity* (*pneuma astheneias*). A spirit that caused the weakness (*astheneias*, lack of strength) like a spirit of bondage (Rom. 8:15), genitive case. *She was bowed together* (*ēn sunkuptousa*). Periphrastic imperfect active of *sunkuptō*, old verb, here only in the N.T., to bend together, medical word for curvature of the spine. *And could in no wise lift herself up* (*kai mē dunamenē anakupsai eis to panteles*). Negative form of the previous statement. *Anakupsai*, first aorist active infinitive of *anakuptō* (*ana, kuptō*, same verb above compounded with *sun*). Unable to bend herself up or back at all (*eis to panteles*, wholly as in Heb. 7:25 only other passage in the N.T. where it occurs). The poor old woman had to come in all bent over·

12. *He called her* (*prosephōnēsen*). To come to him (*pros*). *Thou art loosed* (*apolelusai*). Perfect passive indicative of *apoluō*, common verb, loosed to stay free. Only N.T. example of use about disease.

13. *He laid his hands upon her* (*epethēken autēi tas cheiras*). First aorist active indicative of *epitithēmi*. As the Great Physician with gentle kindness. *She was made straight* (*anōrthōthē*). First aorist (effective) passive indicative of *anorthoō*, old verb, but only three times in the N.T. (Luke 13:13; Heb. 12:12; Acts 15:16), to make straight again. Here it has the literal sense of making straight the old woman's crooked back. *She glorified God* (*edoxazen ton theon*). Imperfect active. Began it (inchoative) and kept it up.

14. *Answered* (*apokritheis*). First aorist passive participle of *apokrinomai*. No one had spoken to him, but he felt his importance as the ruler of the synagogue and was indignant (*aganaktōn*, from *agan* and *achomai*, to feel much pain). His words have a ludicrous sound as if all the people had to do to get their crooked backs straightened out was to come round to his synagogue during the week. He forgot that this poor old woman had been coming for eighteen years with no result. He was angry with Jesus, but he spoke to the multitude (*tōi ochlōi*). *Ought* (*dei*). Really, must, necessary, a direct hit at Jesus who had "worked" on the sabbath in healing this old woman. *And not* (*kai mē*). Instead of *kai ou*, because in the imperative clause.

15. *The Lord answered him* (*apekrithē de autōi ho Kurios*). Note use of "the Lord" of Jesus again in Luke's narrative. Jesus answered the ruler of the synagogue who had spoken to the crowd, but about Jesus. It was a crushing and overwhelming reply. *Hypocrites* (*hupokritai*). This pretentious faultfinder and all who agree with him. *Each of you* (*hekastos humōn*). An *argumentum ad hominen*. These very critics of Jesus cared too much for an ox or an ass to leave

it all the sabbath without water. *Stall (phatnēs)*. Old word, in the N.T. only here and Luke 2:7, 12, 16 the manger where the infant Jesus was placed. *To watering (potizei)*. Old verb, causative, to give to drink.

16. *Daughter of Abraham (thugatera Abraam)*. Triple argument, human being and not an ox or ass, woman, daughter of Abraham (Jewess), besides being old and ill. *Ought not (ouk edei)*. Imperfect active. Of necessity. Jesus simply had to heal her even if on the sabbath. *Whom Sātan bound (hēn edēsen ho Satanas)*. Definite statement that her disease was due to Satan.

17. *Were put to shame (kateischunonto)*. Imperfect passive of *kataischunō*, old verb, to make ashamed, make one feel ashamed. Passive here, to blush with shame at their predicament. *Rejoiced (echairen)*. Imperfect active. Sharp contrast in the emotions of the two groups. *Were done (ginomenois)*. Present middle participle, were continually being done.

18. *He said therefore (elegen oun)*. It is not clear to what to refer "therefore," whether to the case of the woman in verse 11, the enthusiasm of the crowd in verse 17, or to something not recorded by Luke.

19. *A grain of mustard seed (kokkōi sinapeōs)*. Either the *sinapis nigra* or the *salvadora persica*, both of which have small seeds and grow to twelve feet at times. The Jews had a proverb: "Small as a mustard seed." Given by Mark 4:30–32 and Matt. 13:31f. in the first great group of parables, but just the sort to be repeated. *Cast into his own garden (ebalen eis kēpon heautou)*. Different from "earth" (Mark) or "field" (Matthew.)" *Kēpos*, old word for garden, only here in the N.T. and John 19:1, 26; 19:41. *Became a tree (egeneto eis dendron)*. Common Hebraism, very frequent in LXX, only in Luke in the N.T., but does appear in *Koiné* though rare in papyri; this use of *eis* after words like *ginomai*. It is a translation Hebraism in Luke.

Lodged (*kateskēnōsen*). Mark and Matthew have *kata-skēnoin* infinitive of the same verb, to make tent (or nest).

20. *Whereunto shall I liken?* (*Tini homoiōsō;*). This question alone in Luke here as in verse 18. But the parable is precisely like that in Matt. 13:33, which see for details.

22. *Journeying on unto Jerusalem* (*poreian poioumenos eis Ierosoluma*). Making his way to Jerusalem. Note tenses here of continued action, and distributive use of *kata* with cities and villages. This is the second of the journeys to Jerusalem in this later ministry corresponding to that in John 11.

23. *Are they few that be saved?* (*ei oligoi hoi sōzomenoi;*). Note use of *ei* as an interrogative which can be explained as ellipsis or as *ei* = *ē* (Robertson, *Grammar*, p. 1024). This was an academic theological problem with the rabbis, the number of the elect.

24. *Strive* (*agōnizesthe*). Jesus makes short shrift of the question. He includes others (present middle plural of *agōnizomai*, common verb, our agonize). Originally it was to contend for a prize in the games. The kindred word *agōnia* occurs of Christ's struggle in Gethsemane (Luke 22:44). The narrow gate appears also in Matt. 7:13, only there it is an outside gate (*pulēs*) while here it is the entrance to the house, "the narrow door" (*thuras*).

25. *When once* (*aph' hou an*). Possibly to be connected without break with the preceding verse (so Westcott and Hort), though Bruce argues for two parables here, the former (verse 24) about being in earnest, while this one (verses 25–30) about not being too late. The two points are here undoubtedly. It is an awkward construction, *aph' hou* = *apo toutou hote* with *an* and the aorist subjunctive (*egerthēi* and *apokleisēi*). See Robertson, *Grammar*, p. 978. *Hath shut to* (*apokleisēi*), first aorist active subjunctive of *apokleiō*, old verb, but only here in the N.T. Note effective aorist tense and perfective use of *apo*, slammed the door fast.

And ye begin (kai arxēsthe). First aorist middle subjunctive of *archomai* with *aph' hou an* like *egerthēi* and *apokleisēi.* *To stand (hestanai).* Second perfect active infinitive of *histēmi,* intransitive tense *and to knock (kai krouein).* Present active infinitive, to keep on knocking. *Open to us (anoixon hēmin).* First aorist active imperative, at once and urgent. *He shall say (erei).* Future active of *eipon* (defective verb). This is probably the apodosis of the *aph' hou* clause.

26. *Shall ye begin (arxesthe).* Future middle, though Westcott and Hort put *arxēsthe* (aorist middle subjunctive of *archomai*) and in that case a continuation of the *aph' hou* construction. It is a difficult passage and the copyists had trouble with it. *In thy presence (enōpion sou).* As guests or hosts or neighbours some claim, or the master of the house. It is grotesque to claim credit because Christ taught in their streets, but they are hard run for excuses and claims.

27. *I know not whence ye are (ouk oida pothen este).* This blunt statement cuts the matter short and sweeps away the flimsy cobwebs. Acquaintance with Christ in the flesh does not open the door. Jesus quotes Psa. 8:9 as in Matt. 7:23, there as in the LXX, here with *pantes ergatai adikias,* there with *hoi ergazomenoi tēn anomian.* But *apostēte* (second aorist active imperative) here, and there *apochōreite* (present active imperative).

28. *There (ekei).* Out there, outside the house whence they are driven. *When ye shall see (hotan opsēsthe).* First aorist middle subjunctive (of a late aorist *ōpsamēn*) of *horaō,* though *opsesthe* (future middle) in margin of Westcott and Hort, unless we admit here a "future" subjunctive like Byzantine Greek (after Latin). *And yourselves cast forth without (humās de ekballomenous exō).* Present passive participle, continuous action, "you being cast out" with the door shut. See on Matt. 8:11f. for this same picture.

29. *Shall sit down (anaklithēsontai).* Future passive indicative third plural. Recline, of course, is the figure of this

heavenly banquet. Jesus does not mean that these will be
saved in different ways, but only that many will come from
all the four quarters of the earth.

30. *Last (eschatoi)*. This saying was repeated many times
(Matt. 19:30 = Mark 10:31; Matt. 20:16).

31. *In that very hour (en autēi tēi hōrāi)*. Luke's favourite
notation of time. Pharisees *(Pharisaioi)*. Here we see the
Pharisees in a new rôle, warning Jesus against the machina-
tions of Herod, when they are plotting themselves.

32. *That fox (tēi alōpeki tautēi)*. This epithet for the cunning and cowardice of Herod shows clearly that Jesus understood the real attitude and character of the man who had
put John the Baptist to death and evidently wanted to get
Jesus into his power in spite of his superstitious fears that
he might be John the Baptist *redivivus*. The message of
Jesus means that he is independent of the plots and schemes
of both Herod and the Pharisees. The preacher is often put
in a tight place by politicians who are quite willing to see him
shorn of all real power. *Cures (iaseis)*. Old word, but in the
N.T. only here and Acts 4:22, 30. *I am perfected (teleioumai)*.
Present passive indicative of *teleioō*, old verb from *teleios*, to
bring to perfection, frequent in the N.T. Used in Heb. 2: 10
of the Father's purpose in the humanity of Christ. Perfect
humanity is a process and Jesus was passing through that,
without sin, but not without temptation and suffering. It
is the prophetic present with the sense of the future.

33. *The day following (tēi echomenēi)*. See Acts 20:15.
The same as the third day in verse 32. A proverb. *It cannot
be (ouk endechetai)*. It is not accepted, it is inadmissible.
A severely ironical indictment of Jerusalem. The shadow
of the Cross reaches Perea where Jesus now is as he starts
toward Jerusalem.

34. *O Jerusalem, Jerusalem (Ierousalēm, Ierousalēm)*.
In Matt. 23:37f. Jesus utters a similar lament over Jerusalem. The connection suits both there and here, but Plummer

considers it "rather a violent hypothesis" to suppose that
Jesus spoke these words twice. It is possible, of course,
though not like Luke's usual method, that he put the words
here because of the mention of Jerusalem. In itself it is not
easy to see why Jesus could not have made the lament both
here and in Jerusalem. The language of the apostrophe is
almost identical in both places (Luke 13:34f. = Matt. 23:
37-39). For details see on Matthew. In Luke we have
episunaxai (late first aorist active infinitive) and in Matthew
episunagagein (second aorist active infinitive), both from
episunagō, a double compound of late Greek (Polybius).
Both have "How often would I" (*posakis ēthelēsa*). How
often did I wish. Clearly showing that Jesus made repeated
visits to Jerusalem as we know otherwise only from John's
Gospel. *Even as* (*hon tropon*). Accusative of general reference and in Matt. 23:37 also. Incorporation of antecedent
into the relative clause. *Brood* (*nossian*) is in Luke while
Matthew has *chickens* (*nossia*), both late forms for the older
neossia. The adjective *desolate* (*erēmos*) is wanting in Luke
13:35 and is doubtful in Matt. 23:39.

CHAPTER XIV

1. *When he went (en tōi elthein auton)*. Luke's favourite temporal clause = "on the going as to him." *That (kai)*. Another common Lukan idiom, *kai = hoti* after *egeneto*, like Hebrew *wav*. *They (autoi)*. Emphatic. *Were watching (ēsan paratēroumenoi)*. Periphrastic imperfect middle. Note force of *autoi*, middle voice, and *para-*. They were themselves watching on the side (on the sly), watching insidiously, with evil intent as in Mark 3:2 (active).

2. *Which had the dropsy (hudrōpikos)*. Late and medical word from *hudōr* (water), one who has internal water (*hudrōps*). Here only in the N.T. and only example of the disease healed by Jesus and recorded.

3. *Answering (apokritheis)*. First aorist passive participle without the passive meaning. Jesus answered the thoughts of those mentioned in verse 1. Here "lawyers and Pharisees" are treated as one class with one article (*tous*) whereas in 7:30 they are treated as two classes with separate articles. *Or not (ē ou)*. The dilemma forestalled any question by them. *They held their peace (hēsuchasan)*. Ingressive aorist active of old verb *hēsuchazō*. They became silent, more so than before.

4. *Took him (epilabomenos)*. Second aorist middle participle of *epilambanō*, an old verb, only in the middle in the N.T. It is not redundant use, "took and healed," but "took hold of him and healed him." Only instance in the N.T. of its use in a case of healing. *Let him go (apelusen)*. Probably, dismissed from the company to get him away from these critics.

5. *An ass or an ox (onos ē bous)*. But Westcott and Hort *huios ē bous (a son or an ox)*. The manuscripts are much

divided between *huios* (son) and *onos* (ass) which in the ab-
breviated uncials looked much alike (TC, OC) and were
much alike. The sentence in the Greek reads literally thus:
Whose ox or ass of you shall fall (*peseitai*, future middle of
pipto) into a well and he (the man) will not straightway draw
him up (*anaspasei*, future active of *anaspaō*) on the sabbath
day? The very form of the question is a powerful argument
and puts the lawyers and the Pharisees hopelessly on the
defensive.

6. *Could not answer again* (*ouk ischusan antapokrithēnai*).
Did not have strength to answer back or in turn (*anti-*) as
in Rom. 9:20. They could not take up the argument and
were helpless. They hated to admit that they cared more
for an ox or ass or even a son than for this poor dropsical
man.

7. *A parable for those which were bidden* (*pros tous keklē-
menous parabolēn*). Perfect passive participle of *kaleō*, to
call, to invite. This parable is for the guests who were there
and who had been watching Jesus. *When he marked* (*epe-
chōn*). Present active participle of *epechō* with *ton noun*
understood, holding the mind upon them, old verb and
common. *They chose out* (*exelegonto*). Imperfect middle,
were picking out for themselves. *The chief seats* (*tas prōto-
klisias*). The first reclining places at the table. Jesus condemned the Pharisees later for this very thing (Matt. 23:6 =
Mark 12:39 = Luke 20:46). On a couch holding three the
middle place was the chief one. At banquets today the name
of the guests are usually placed at the plates. The place
next to the host on the right was then, as now, the post of
honour.

8. *Sit not down* (*mē kataklithēis*). First aorist (ingressive)
passive subjunctive of *kataklinō*, to recline. Old verb, but
peculiar to Luke in the N.T. (7:36; 9:14; 14:8; 24:30). *Be
bidden* (*ei keklēmenos*). Periphrastic perfect passive subjunctive of *kaleō* after *mē pote*.

9. *And say* (*kai erei*). Changes to future indicative with *mē pote* as in 12:58. *Shalt begin with shame* (*arxēi meta aischunēs*). The moment of embarrassment. *To take the lowest place* (*ton eschaton topon katechein*). To hold down the lowest place, all the intermediate ones being taken.

10. *Sit down* (*anapese*). Second aorist active imperative of *anapiptō*, to fall up or back, to lie back or down. Late Greek word for *anaklinō* (cf. *kataklinō* in verse 8). *He that hath bidden thee* (*ho keklēkōs se*). Perfect active participle as in verse 12 (*tōi keklēkoti*) with which compare *ho kalesas* in verse 9 (first aorist active participle). *He may say* (*erei*). The future indicative with *hina* does occur in the *Koinē* (papyri) and so in the N.T. (Robertson, *Grammar*, p. 984). *Go up higher* (*prosanabēthi*). Second aorist active imperative second singular of *prosanabainō*, an old double compound verb, but here cnly in the N.T. Probably, "Come up higher," because the call comes from the host and because of *pros*.

11. *Shall be humbled* (*tapeinōthēsetai*). First future passive. One of the repeated sayings of Jesus (18:14; Matt. 23:12).

12. *A dinner or a supper* (*ariston ē deipnon*). More exactly, a breakfast or a dinner with distinction between them as already shown. This is a parable for the host as one had just been given for the guests, though Luke does not term this a parable. *Call not* (*mē phōnei*). *Mē* and the present imperative active, prohibiting the habit of inviting only friends. It is the *exclusive* invitation of such guests that Jesus condemns. There is a striking parallel to this in Plato's *Phaedrus* 233. *Recompense* (*antapodoma*). In the form of a return invitation. Like *anti* in "bid thee again" (*antikalesōsin*).

13. *When thou makest a feast* (*hotan dochēn poiēis*). *Hotan* and the present subjunctive in an indefinite temporal clause. *Dochē* means reception as in Luke 5:29, late word, only in

these two passages in the N.T. Note absence of article with these adjectives in the Greek (poor people, maimed folks, lame people, blind people).

14. *To recompense thee* (*antapodounai soi*). Second aorist active infinitive of this old and common double compound verb, to give back in return. The reward will come at the resurrection if not before and thou shalt be happy.

15. *Blessed* (*makarios*). Happy, same word in the Beatitudes of Jesus (Matt. 5:3ff.). This pious platitude whether due to ignorance or hypocrisy was called forth by Christ's words about the resurrection. It was a common figure among the rabbis, the use of a banquet for the bliss of heaven. This man may mean that this is a prerogative of the Pharisees. He assumed complacently that he will be among the number of the blest. Jesus himself uses this same figure of the spiritual banquet for heavenly bliss (Luke 22:29). *Shall eat* (*phagetai*). Future middle from *esthiō*, defective verb, from stem of the aorist (*ephagon*) like *edomai* of the old Greek.

16. *Made* (*epoiei*). Imperfect active, was on the point of making (inchoative). *Great supper* (*deipnon*). Or dinner, a formal feast. Jesus takes up the conventional remark of the guest and by this parable shows that such an attitude was no guarantee of godliness (Bruce). This parable of the marriage of the King's son (Luke 14:15–24) has many points of likeness to the parable of the wedding garment (Matt. 22:1–14) and as many differences also. The occasions are very different, that in Matthew grows out of the attempt to arrest Jesus while this one is due to the pious comment of a guest at the feast and the wording is also quite different. Hence we conclude that they are distinct parables. *And he bade many* (*kai ekalesen pollous*). Aorist active, a distinct and definite act following the imperfect *epoiei*.

17. *His servant* (*ton doulon autou*). His bondservant. *Vocator* or Summoner (Esth. 5:8; 6:14). This second summons was the custom then as now with wealthy Arabs.

Tristram (*Eastern Customs*, p. 82) says: "To refuse the second summons would be an insult, which is equivalent among the Arab tribes to a declaration of war."

18. *With one consent* (*apo mias*). Some feminine substantive like *gnōmēs* or *psuchēs* has to be supplied. This precise idiom occurs nowhere else. It looked like a conspiracy for each one in his turn did the same thing. *To make excuse* (*paraiteisthai*). This common Greek verb is used in various ways, to ask something from one (Mark 15:6), to deprecate or ask to avert (Heb. 12:19), to refuse or decline (Acts 25:11), to shun or to avoid (II Tim. 2:23), to beg pardon or to make excuses for not doing or to beg (Luke 14:18ff.). All these ideas are variations of *aiteō*, to ask in the middle voice with *para* in composition. *The first* (*ho prōtos*). In order of time. There are three of the "many" ("all"), whose excuses are given, each more flimsy than the other. *I must needs* (*echō anagkēn*). I have necessity. The land would still be there, a strange "necessity." *Have me excused* (*eche me pareitēmenon*). An unusual idiom somewhat like the English perfect with the auxiliary "have" and the modern Greek idiom with *echō*, but certainly not here a Greek periphrasis for *pareitēso*. This perfect passive participle is predicate and agrees with *me*. See a like idiom in Mark 3:1; Luke 12:19 (Robertson, *Grammar*, pp. 902f.). The Latin had a similar idiom, *habe me excusatum*. Same language in verse 19.

19. *To prove them* (*dokimasai auta*). He could have tested them before buying. The oxen would not run away or be stolen.

20. *I cannot come* (*ou dunamai elthein*). Less polite than the others but a more plausible pretence if he wanted to make it so. The law excused a newly married man from war (Deut. 24:5), "but not from social courtesy" (Ragg). The new wife would probably have been glad to go with him to the feast if asked. But see I Cor. 7:33. There is here as

often a sharp difference between the excuses offered and the reasons behind them.

21. *Being angry* (*orgistheis*). First aorist (ingressive) passive, becoming angry. *Quickly* (*tacheōs*). The dinner is ready and no time is to be lost. The invitation goes still to those in the city. *Streets and lanes* (*tas plateias kai rhumas*). Broadways and runways (broad streets and narrow lanes). *Maimed* (*anapeirous*). So Westcott and Hort for the old word *anapērous*, due to itacism (*ei = ē* in pronunciation). The word is compounded of *ana* and *pēros*, lame all the way up.

22. *And yet there is room* (*kai eti topos estin*). The Master had invited "many" (verse 16) who had all declined. The servant knew the Master wished the places to be filled.

23. *The highways and hedges* (*tas hodous kai phragmous*). The public roads outside the city of Judaism just as the streets and lanes were inside the city. The heathen are to be invited this time. *Hedges* is fenced in places from *phrassō*, to fence in (Rom. 3:19). *Compel* (*anagkason*). First aorist active imperative of *anagkazō*, from *anagkē* (verse 18). By persuasion of course. There is no thought of compulsory salvation. "Not to use force, but to constrain them against the reluctance which such poor creatures would feel at accepting the invitation of a great lord" (Vincent). As examples of such "constraint" in this verb see Matt. 14:22; Acts 26:11; Gal. 6:12. *That my house may be filled* (*hina gemisthēi mou ho oikos*). First aorist passive subjunctive of *gemizō*, to fill full, old verb from *gemō*, to be full. Effective aorist. Subjunctive with *hina* in final clause. The Gentiles are to take the place that the Jews might have had (Rom. 11:25). Bengel says: *Nec natura nec gratia patitur vacuum.*

24. *My supper* (*mou tou deipnou*). Here it is still the Master of the feast who is summing up his reasons for his conduct. We do not have to say that Jesus shuts the door now in the face of the Jews who may turn to him.

25. *And he turned* (*kai strapheis*). Second aorist passive participle of *strephō*, common verb. It is a dramatic act on the part of Jesus, a deliberate effort to check the wild and unthinking enthusiasm of the crowds who followed just to be following. Note "many multitudes" (*ochloi polloi*) and the imperfect tense *suneporeuonto*, were going along with him.

26. *Hateth not* (*ou misei*). An old and very strong verb *miseō*, to hate, detest. The orientals use strong language where cooler spirits would speak of preference or indifference. But even so Jesus does not here mean that one must hate his father or mother of necessity or as such, for Matt. 15:4 proves the opposite. It is only where the element of choice comes in (cf. Matt. 6:24) as it sometimes does, when father or mother opposes Christ. Then one must not hesitate. The language here is more sharply put than in Matt. 10:37. The *ou* here coalesces with the verb *misei* in this conditional clause of the first class determined as fulfilled. It is the language of exaggerated contrast, it is true, but it must not be watered down till the point is gone. In mentioning "and wife" Jesus has really made a comment on the excuse given in verse 20 (I married a wife and so I am not able to come). *And his own life also* (*eti te kai tēn psuchēn heautou*). Note *te kai*, both—and. "The *te* (B L) binds all the particulars into one bundle of *renuncianda*" (Bruce). Note this same triple group of conjunctions (*eti te kai*) in Acts 21:28, "And moreover also," "even going as far as his own life." Martyrdom should be an ever-present possibility to the Christian, not to be courted, but not to be shunned. Love for Christ takes precedence "over even the elemental instinct of self-preservation" (Ragg).

27. *His own cross* (*ton stauron heautou*). This familiar figure we have had already (Luke 9:23; Mark 8:34; Matt. 10:38; 16:24). Each follower has a cross which he must bear as Jesus did his. *Bastazō* is used of cross bearing in the N.T.

only here (figuratively) and John 19:17 literally of Jesus. Crucifixion was common enough in Palestine since the days of Antiochus Epiphanes and Alexander Jannaeus.

28. *Build a tower* (*purgon oikodomēsai*). A common metaphor, either a tower in the city wall like that by the Pool of Siloam (Luke 13:4) or a watchtower in a vineyard (Matt. 21:33) or a tower-shaped building for refuge or ornament as here. This parable of the rash builder has the lesson of counting the cost. *Sit down* (*kathisas*). Attitude of deliberation. *First* (*prōton*). First things first. So in verse 31. *Count* (*psēphizei*). Common verb in late writers, but only here and Rev. 13:18 in the N.T. The verb is from *psēphos*, a stone, which was used in voting and so counting. Calculate is from the Latin *calculus*, a pebble. To vote was to cast a pebble (*tithēmi psēphon*). Luke has Paul using "deposit a pebble" for casting his vote (Acts 26:10). *The cost* (*tēn dapanēn*). Old and common word, but here only in the N.T. from *daptō*, to tear, consume, devour. Expense is something which eats up one's resources. *Whether he hath wherewith to complete it* (*ei echei eis apartismon*). If he has anything for completion of it. *Apartismon* is a rare and late word (in the papyri and only here in the N.T.). It is from *apartizō*, to finish off (*ap-* and *artizō* like our articulate), to make even or square. Cf. *exērtismenos* in II *Tim.* 3:17.

29. *Lest haply* (*hina mēpote*). Double final particles (positive and negative with addition of *pote*). Used here with aorist middle subjunctive in *arxōntai* (begin). *When he hath laid . . . and was not able* (*thentos autou . . . kai mē ischuontos*) *to finish* (*ektelesai*). First aorist active infinitive. Note perfective use of *ek*, to finish out to the end. Two genitive absolutes, first, second aorist active participle *thentos;* second, present active participle *ischuontos*. *To mock him* (*autōi empaizein*). An old verb, *em-paizō*, to play like a child (*pais*), at or with, to mock, scoff at, to trifle with like Latin *illudere*.

30. *This man* (*houtos ho anthrōpos*). This fellow, contemptuous or sarcastic use of *houtos*.

31. *To encounter* (*sunbalein*). Second aorist active infinitive of *sunballō*, old and common verb, to throw or bring together, to dispute, to clash in war as here. *Another king* (*heterōi basilei*), to grapple with another king in war or for war (*eis polemon*). Associative instrumental case. *Take counsel* (*bouleusetai*). Future middle indicative of old and common verb *bouleuō*, from *boulē*, will, counsel. The middle means to take counsel with oneself, to deliberate, to ponder. *With ten thousand* (*en deka chiliasin*). Literally, in ten thousand. See this so-called instrumental use of *en* in Jude 14. Equipped in or with ten thousand. See Luke 1:17. Note *meta eikosi chiliadōn* just below (midst of twenty thousand). *To meet* (*hupantēsai*). Common verb (like *apantaō*) from *antaō* (*anta*, end, face to face, from which *anti*) with preposition *hupo* (or *apo*), to go to meet. Here it has a military meaning.

32. *Or else* (*ei de mēge*). Same idiom in 5:36. Luke is fond of this formula. *An ambassage* (*presbeian*). Old and common word for the office of ambassador, composed of old men (*presbeis*) like Japanese Elder Statesmen who are supposed to possess wisdom. In the N.T. only here and Luke 19:14. *Asketh conditions of peace* (*erōtāi pros eirēnēn*). The use of *erōtaō* in this sense of beg or petition is common in the papyri and *Koiné* generally. The original use of asking a question survives also. The text is uncertain concerning *pros eirēnēn* which means with *erōtaō*, to ask negotiations for peace. In B we have *eis* instead of *pros* like verse 28. Most MSS. have *ta* before *pros* or *eis*, but not in Aleph and B. It is possible that the *ta* was omitted because of preceding *tai* (*homoeoteleuton*), but the sense is the same. See Rom. 14:19 *ta tēs eirēnēs*, the things of peace, which concern or look towards peace, the preliminaries of peace.

33. *Renounceth not* (*ouk apotassetai*). Old Greek word to

set apart as in a military camp, then in the middle voice to
separate oneself from, say good-bye to (Luke 9:61), to re-
nounce, forsake, as here. *All that he hath (pasin tois heautou
huparchousin)*. Dative case, says good-bye to all his property, "all his own belongings" (neuter plural participle used
as substantive) as named in verse 26. This verse gives the
principle in the two parables of the rash builder and of the
rash king. The minor details do not matter. The spirit of
self-sacrifice is the point.

35. *Dunghill (koprian)*. Later word in the *Koiné* vernacular. Here only in the N.T., though in the LXX. *Men cast
it out (exō ballousin auto)*. Impersonal plural. This saying
about salt is another of Christ's repeated sayings (Matt.
5:13; Mark 9:50). Another repeated saying is the one here
about having ears to hear (Luke 8:8; 14:35, Matt. 11:15,
13:43).

CHAPTER XV

1. *All the publicans and sinners* (*pantes hoi telōnai kai hoi hamartōloi*). The two articles separate the two classes (all the publicans and the sinners). They are sometimes grouped together (5:30; Matt. 9:11), but not here. The publicans are put on the same level with the outcasts or sinners. So in verse 2 the repeated article separates Pharisees and scribes as not quite one. The use of "all" here may be hyperbole for very many or the reference may be to these two classes in the particular place where Jesus was from time to time. *Were drawing near unto him* (*ēsan autōi eggizontes*). Periphrastic imperfect of *eggizō*, from *eggus* (near), late verb. *For to hear* (*akouein*). Just the present active infinitive of purpose.

2. *Both . . . and* (*te . . . kai*). United in the complaint. *Murmured* (*diegogguzon*). Imperfect active of *diagogguzō*, late Greek compound in the LXX and Byzantine writers. In the N.T. only here and Luke 19:7. The force of *dia* here is probably between or among themselves. It spread (imperfect tense) whenever these two classes came in contact with Jesus. As the publicans and the sinners were drawing near to Jesus just in that proportion the Pharisees and the scribes increased their murmurings. The social breach is here an open yawning chasm. *This man* (*houtos*). A contemptuous sneer in the use of the pronoun. They spoke out openly and probably pointed at Jesus. *Receiveth* (*prosdechetai*). Present middle indicative of the common verb *prosdechomai*. In 12:36 we had it for expecting, here it is to give access to oneself, to welcome like *hupedexato* of Martha's welcome to Jesus (Luke 10:38). The charge here is that this is the habit of Jesus. He shows no sense of social superiority to these outcasts (like the Hindu "untouchables" in India). *And*

eateth with them (kai sunesthiei autois). Associative instrumental case (*autois*) after *sun-* in composition. This is an
old charge (Luke 5:30) and a much more serious breach from
the standpoint of the Pharisees. The implication is that
Jesus prefers these outcasts to the respectable classes (the
Pharisees and the scribes) because he is like them in character
and tastes, even with the harlots. There was a sting in the
charge that he was the "friend" (*philos*) of publicans and
sinners (Luke 7:34).

3. *This parable (tēn parabolēn tautēn).* The Parable of the
Lost Sheep (15:3-7). This is Christ's way of answering the
cavilling of these chronic complainers. Jesus gave this same
parable for another purpose in another connection (Matt.
18:12-14). The figure of the Good Shepherd appears also in
John 10:1-18. "No simile has taken more hold upon the
mind of Christendom" (Plummer). Jesus champions the lost
and accepts the challenge and justifies his conduct by these
superb stories. "The three Episodes form a climax: The
Pasture—the House—the Home; the Herdsman—the House-
wife—the Father; the Sheep—the Treasure—the Beloved
Son" (Ragg).

4. *In the wilderness (en tēi erēmōi).* Their usual pasturage,
not a place of danger or peril. It is the owner of the hundred
sheep who cares so much for the one that is lost. He knows
each one of the sheep and loves each one. *Go after that which
is lost (poreuetai epi to apolōlos).* The one lost sheep (*apolōlos*,
second perfect active participle of *apollumi*, to destroy, but
intransitive, to be lost). There is nothing more helpless than
a lost sheep except a lost sinner. The sheep went off by its
own ignorance and folly. The use of *epi* for the goal occurs
also in Matt. 22:9; Acts 8:26; 9:11. *Until he find it (heōs
heurēi auto).* Second aorist active subjunctive of *heuriskō*,
common verb, with *heōs*, common Greek idiom. He keeps on
going (*poreuetai*, linear present middle indicative) until success comes (effective aorist, *heurēi*).

5. *On his shoulders* (*epi tous ōmous autou*). He does it himself in exuberant affection and of necessity as the poor lost sheep is helpless. Note the plural shoulders showing that the sheep was just back of the shepherd's neck and drawn around by both hands. The word for shoulder (*ōmos*) is old and common, but in the N.T. only here and Matt. 23:4. *Rejoicing* (*chairōn*). "There is no upbraiding of the wandering sheep, nor murmuring at the trouble" (Plummer).

6. *Rejoice with me* (*suncharēte moi*). Second aorist passive of *sunchairō,* an old and common verb for mutual joy as in Phil. 2:17f. Joy demands fellowship. Same form in verse 9. So the shepherd *calls together* (*sunkalei*, note *sun* again) both his friends and his neighbours. This picture of the Good Shepherd has captured the eye of many artists through the ages.

7. *Over one sinner that repenteth* (*epi heni hamartōlōi metanoounti*). The word sinner points to verse 1. Repenting is what these sinners were doing, these lost sheep brought to the fold. The joy in heaven is in contrast with the grumbling Pharisees and scribes. *More than over* (*ē epi*). There is no comparative in the Greek. It is only implied by a common idiom like our "rather than." *Which need no repentance* (*hoitines ou chreian echousin metanoias*). Jesus does not mean to say that the Pharisees and the scribes do not need repentance or are perfect. He for the sake of argument accepts their claims about themselves and by their own words condemns them for their criticism of his efforts to save the lost sheep. It is the same point that he made against them when they criticized Jesus and the disciples for being at Levi's feast (Luke 5:31f.). They posed as "righteous." Very well, then. That shuts their mouths on the point of Christ's saving the publicans and sinners.

8. *Ten pieces of silver* (*drachmas deka*). The only instance in the N.T. of this old word for a coin of 65.5 grains about the value of the common *dēnarius* (about eighteen cents),

a quarter of a Jewish shekel. The double drachma (*didrachmon*) occurs in the N.T. only in Matt. 17:24. The root is from *drassomai*, to grasp with the hand (I Cor. 3:19), and so a handful of coin. Ten drachmas would be equal to nearly two dollars, but in purchasing power much more. *Sweep* (*saroi*). A late colloquial verb *saroō* for the earlier *sairō*, to clear by sweeping. Three times in the N.T. (Luke 11:25; 15:8; Matt. 12:44). The house was probably without windows (only the door for light and hence the lamp lit) and probably also a dirt floor. Hence Bengel says: *non sine pulvere*. This parable is peculiar to Luke.

9. *Her friends and neighbours* (*tas philas kai geitonas*). Note single article and female friends (feminine article and *philas*). *Heōs hou eurēi* here as in verse 4, only *hou* added after *heōs* (until which time) as often. *Which I lost* (*hēn apōlesa*). First aorist active indicative of *apollumi*. She lost the coin (note article). The shepherd did not lose the one sheep.

10. *There is joy* (*ginetai chara*). More exactly, joy arises. Futuristic present of *ginomai* (cf. *estai* in verse 7). *In the presence of the angels of God* (*enōpion tōn aggelōn tou theou*). That is to say, the joy of God himself. The angels are in a sense the neighbours of God.

11. *Had* (*eichen*). Imperfect active. Note *echōn* (verse 4), *echousa* (verse 8), and now *eichen*. The self-sacrificing care is that of the owner in each case. Here (verses 11 to 32) we have the most famous of all the parables of Jesus, the Prodigal Son, which is in Luke alone. We have had the Lost Sheep, the Lost Coin, and now the Lost Son. Bruce notes that in the moral sphere there must be self-recovery to give ethical value to the rescue of the son who wandered away. That comes out beautifully in this allegory.

12. *The portion* (*to meros*). The Jewish law alloted one-half as much to the younger son as to the elder, that is to say one-third of the estate (Deut. 21:17) at the death of the father. The father did not have to abdicate in favour of the

sons, but "this very human parable here depicts the impatience of home restraints and the optimistic ambition of youth" (Ragg). *And he divided* (*ho de dieilen*). The second aorist active indicative of *diaireō*, an old and common verb to part in two, cut asunder, divide, but in the N.T. only here and I Cor. 12:11. The elder son got his share also of the "substance" or property or estate (*tēs ousias*), "the living" (*ton bion*) as in Mark 12:44, not "life" as in Luke 8:14.

13. *Not many days after* (*met' ou pollas hēmeras*). Literally, after not many days. Luke is fond of this idiom (7:6; Acts 1:5). *Took his journey* (*apedēmēsen*). First aorist active indicative of *apodēmeō* (from *apodēmos*, away from home). Common verb. In the N.T. here and Matt. 21:33; 25:14; Mark 12:1; Luke 20:9. He burned all his bridges behind him, gathering together all that he had. *Wasted* (*dieskorpisen*). First aorist active indicative of *diaskorpizō*, a somewhat rare verb, the very opposite of "gathered together" (*sunagogōn*). More exactly he scattered his property. It is the word used of winnowing grain (Matt. 25:24). *With riotous living* (*zōn asōtōs*). Living dissolutely or profligately. The late adverb *asōtōs* (only here in the N.T.) from the common adjective *asōtos* (*a* privative and *sōzō*), one that cannot be saved, one who does not save, a spendthrift, an abandoned man, a profligate, a prodigal. He went the limit of sinful excesses. It makes sense taken actively or passively (*prodigus* or *perditus*), active probably here.

14. *When he had spent* (*dapanēsantos autou*). Genitive absolute. The verb is here used in a bad sense as in James 4:3. See on *dapanē* Luke 14:28. *He* (*autos*). Emphasis. *To be in want* (*hustereisthai*). The verb is from *husteros*, behind or later (comparative). We use "fall behind" (Vincent) of one in straitened circumstances. Plummer notes the coincidences of Providence. The very land was in a famine when the boy had spent all.

15. *Joined himself* (*ekollēthē*). First aorist passive of

kollaō, an old verb to glue together, to cleave to. In the N.T. only the passive occurs. He was glued to, was joined to. It is not necessary to take this passive in the middle reflexive sense. *The citizens* (*tōn politōn*). Curiously enough this common word citizen (*politēs* from *polis*, city) is found in the N.T. only in Luke's writings (15:15; 19:14; Acts 21:39) except in Heb. 8:11 where it is quoted from Jer. 38:34. *To feed swine* (*boskein choirous*). A most degrading occupation for anyone and for a Jew an unspeakable degradation.

16. *He would fain have been filled* (*epethumei chortasthēnai*). Literally, he was desiring (longing) to be filled. Imperfect indicative and first aorist passive infinitive. *Chortasthēnai* is from *chortazō* and that from *chortos* (grass), and so to feed with grass or with anything. Westcott and Hort put *gemisai tēn koilian autou* in the margin (the Textus Receptus). *With the husks* (*ek tōn keratiōn*). The word occurs here alone in the N.T. and is a diminutive of *keras* (horn) and so means little horn. It is used in various senses, but here refers to the pods of the carob tree or locust tree still common in Palestine and around the Mediterannean, so called from the shape of the pods like little horns, *Bockshornbaum* in German or goat's-horn tree. The gelatinous substance inside has a sweetish taste and is used for feeding swine and even for food by the lower classes. It is sometimes called Saint John's Bread from the notion that the Baptist ate it in the wilderness. *No man gave unto him* (*oudeis edidou autōi*). Imperfect active. Continued refusal of anyone to allow him even the food of the hogs.

17. *But when he came to himself* (*eis heauton de elthōn*). As if he had been far from himself as he was from home. As a matter of fact he had been away, out of his head, and now began to see things as they really were. Plato is quoted by Ackerman (*Christian Element in Plato*) as thinking of redemption as coming to oneself. *Hired servants* (*misthioi*). A late word from *misthos* (hire). In the N.T. only in this

chapter. The use of "many" here suggests a wealthy and luxurious home. *Have bread enough and to spare* (*perisseuontai artōn*). Old verb from *perissos* and that from *peri* (around). Present passive here, "are surrounded by loaves" like a flood. *I perish* (*egō de limōi hōde apollumai*). Every word here counts: While I on the other hand am here perishing with hunger. It is the linear present middle of *apollumi*. Note *egō* expressed and *de* of contrast.

18. *I will arise and go* (*anastas proreusomai*). This determination is the act of the will after he comes to himself and sees his real condition. *I did sin* (*hēmarton*). That is the hard word to say and he will say it first. The word means to miss the mark. I shot my bolt and I missed my aim (compare the high-handed demand in verse 12).

19. *No longer worthy* (*ouketi axios*). Confession of the facts. He sees his own pitiful plight and is humble. *As one* (*hōs hena*). The hired servants in his father's house are high above him now.

20. *To his father* (*pros ton patera heautou*). Literally, to his own father. He acted at once on his decision. *Yet afar off* (*eti autou makran apechontos*). Genitive absolute. *Makran* agrees with *hodon* understood: While he was yet holding off a distant way. This shows that the father had been looking for him to come back and was even looking at this very moment as he came in sight. *Ran* (*dramōn*). Second aorist active participle of the defective verb *trechō*. The eager look and longing of the father. *Kissed* (*katephilēsen*). Note perfective use of *kata* kissed him much, kissed him again and again. The verb occurs so in the older Greek.

21. The son made his speech of confession as planned, but it is not certain that he was able to finish as a number of early manuscripts do not have "Make me as one of the hired servants," though Aleph B D do have them. It is probable that the father interrupted him at this point before he could finish.

22. *The best robe* (*stolēn tēn prōtēn*). *Stolē* is an old word for a fine stately garment that comes down to the feet (from *stello*, to prepare, equip), the kind worn by kings (Mark 16:5; Luke 22:46). Literally, "a robe the first." But not the first that you find, but the first in rank and value, the finest in the house. This in contrast with his shabby clothes. *A ring* (*daktulion*). Common in classical writers and the LXX, but here only in the N.T. From *daktulos*, finger. See *chrusodaktulios* in James 2:2. *Shoes* (*hupodēmata*). Sandals, "bound under." Both sandals and ring are marks of the freeman as slaves were barefooted.

23. *The fatted calf* (*ton moschon ton siteuton*). The calf the fatted one. *Siteuton* is the verbal adjective of *siteuō*, to feed with wheat (*sitos*). The calf was kept fat for festive occasions, possibly in the hope of the son's return. *Kill* (*thusate*). Not as a sacrifice, but for the feast. *Make merry* (*euphranthōmen*). First aorist passive subjunctive (volitive). From *euphrainō*, an old verb from *eu* (well) and *phrēn* (mind).

24. *And is alive* (*kai anezēsen*). First aorist active indicative of *anazaō*, to live again. Literally, he was dead and he came back to life. *He was lost* (*ēn apololōs*, periphrastic past perfect active of *apollumi* and intransitive, in a lost state) and he was found (*heurethē*). He was found, we have to say, but this aorist passive is really timeless, he is found after long waiting (effective aorist) The artists have vied with each other in picturing various items connected with this wonderful parable.

25. *As he came and drew nigh* (*hōs erchomenos ēggisen*). More exactly, "As, coming, he drew nigh," for *erchomenos* is present middle participle and *ēggisen* is aorist active indicative. *Music* (*sumphōnias*). Our word "symphony." An old Greek word from *sumphōnos* (*sun*, together, and *phōnē*, voice or sound), *harmony*, *concord*, by a band of musicians. Here alone in the N.T. *And dancing* (*kai chorōn*). An old word again, but here alone in the N.T. Origin uncertain,

possibly from *orchos* by metathesis (*orcheomai*, to dance). A circular dance on the green.

26. *Servants* (*paidōn*). Not *douloi* (bondslaves) as in verse 22. The Greeks often used *pais* for servant like the Latin *puer*. It could be either a hired servant (*misthios*, verse 17) or slave (*doulos*). *He inquired* (*epunthaneto*). Imperfect middle, inquired repeatedly and eagerly. *What these things might be* (*ti an eiē tauta*). Not "poor" Greek as Easton holds, but simply the form of the direct question retained in the indirect. See the direct form as the apodosis of a condition of the fourth class in Acts 17:18. In Acts 10:17 we have the construction with *an eiē* of the direct retained in the indirect question. So also in Luke 1:62: See Robertson, *Grammar*, p. 1044.

27. *Is come* (*hēkei*). Present indicative active, but a stem with perfect sense, old verb *hēkō* retaining this use after perfect tenses came into use (Robertson, *Grammar*, p. 893). *Hath killed* (*ethusen*). Aorist active indicative and literally means, *did kill*. Difficult to handle in English for our tenses do not correspond with the Greek. *Hath received* (*apelaben*). Second aorist active indicative with similar difficulty of translation. Note *apo* in compositions, like *re-* in "receive," hath gotten him back (*ap-*). *Safe and sound* (*hugiainonta*). Present active participle of *hugiainō* from *hugiēs*, to be in good health. In spite of all that he has gone through and in spite of the father's fears.

28. *But he was angry* (*ōrgisthē*). First aorist (ingressive) passive indicative. But he became angry, he flew into a rage (*orgē*). This was the explosion as the result of long resentment towards the wayward brother and suspicion of the father's partiality for the erring son. *Would not go in* (*ouk ēthelen eiselthein*). Imperfect tense (was not willing, refused) and aorist active (ingressive) infinitive. *Entreated* (*parekalei*). Imperfect tense, he kept on beseeching him.

29. *Do I serve thee* (*douleuō soi*). Progressive present tense

of this old verb from *doulos* (slave) which the elder son uses
to picture his virtual slavery in staying at home and perhaps
with longings to follow the younger son (Robertson, *Grammar*, p. 879). *Transgressed* (*parēlthon*). Second aorist active indicative of *parerchomai*, to pass by. Not even once
(aorist) in contrast with so many years of service (linear
present). *A kid* (*eriphon*). Some MSS. have *eriphion*,
diminutive, a little kid. So margin of Westcott and Hort.
B has it also in Matt. 25:32, the only other N.T. passage
where the word occurs. *That I might make merry* (*hina
euphranthō*). Final clause, first aorist passive subjunctive
of the same verb used in verses 23, 25.

30. *This thy son* (*ho huios sou houtos*). Contempt and
sarcasm. He does not say: "This my brother." *Came*
(*ēlthen*). He does not even say, came back or came home.
Devoured (*kataphagōn*). We say, "eaten up," but the Greek
has, "eaten down" (perfective use of *kata-*). Suggested
by the feasting going on. *With harlots* (*meta pornōn*). This
may be true (verse 13), but the elder son did not know it to
be true. He may reflect what he would have done in like
case.

31. *Son* (*Teknon*). Child. *Thou* (*su*). Expressed and in
emphatic position in the sentence. He had not appreciated
his privileges at home with his father.

32. *It was meet* (*edei*). Imperfect tense. It expressed a
necessity in the father's heart and in the joy of the return
that justifies the feasting. *Euphranthēnai* is used again
(first aorist passive infinitive) and *charēnai* (second aorist
passive infinitive) is more than mere hilarity, deep-seated joy.
The father repeats to the elder son the language of his heart
used in verse 24 to his servants. A real father could do no
less. One can well imagine how completely the Pharisees
and scribes (verse 2) were put to silence by these three marvellous parables. The third does it with a graphic picture of
their own attitude in the case of the surly elder brother.

Luke was called a painter by the ancients.   Certainly he has produced a graphic pen picture here of God's love for the lost that justifies forever the coming of Christ to the world to seek and to save the lost.   It glorifies also soul-saving on the part of his followers who are willing to go with Jesus after the lost in city and country, in every land and of every race.

CHAPTER XVI

1. *Unto the disciples* (*kai pros tous mathētas*). The three preceding parables in chapter 15 exposed the special faults of the Pharisees, "their hard exclusiveness, self-righteousness, and contempt for others" (Plummer). This parable is given by Luke alone. The "*kai*" (also) is not translated in the Revised Version. It seems to mean that at this same time, after speaking to the Pharisees (chapter 15), Jesus proceeds to speak a parable to the disciples (16:1–13), the parable of the Unjust Steward. It is a hard parable to explain, but Jesus opens the door by the key in verse 9. *Which had a steward* (*hos eichen oikonomon*). Imperfect active, continued to have. Steward is house-manager or overseer of an estate as already seen in Luke 12:42. *Was accused* (*dieblēthē*). First aorist indicative passive, of *diaballō*, an old verb, but here only in the N.T. It means to throw across or back and forth, rocks or words and so to slander by gossip. The word implies malice even if the thing said is true. The word *diabolos* (slanderer) is this same root and it is used even of women, she-devils (I Tim. 3:11). *That he was wasting* (*hōs diaskorpizōn*). For the verb see on 15:13. The use of *hōs* with the participle is a fine Greek idiom for giving the alleged ground of a charge against one. *His goods* (*ta huparchonta autou*). "His belongings," a Lukan idiom.

2. *What is this that I hear?* (*ti touto akouō;*). There are several ways of understanding this terse Greek idiom. The Revised Version (above) takes *ti* to be equal to *ti estin touto ho akouō;* That is a possible use of the predicate *touto*. Another way is to take *ti* to be exclamatory, which is less likely. Still another view is that *ti* is "Why": "Why do I hear this about thee?" See Acts 14:15 where

that is the idiom employed. *Render (apodos)*. Second aorist active imperative of *apodidōmi*, Give back (and at once). *The account (ton logon)*. The reckoning or report. Common use of *logos*. *Stewardship (oikonomias)*. Same root as *oikonomos* (steward). This demand does not necessarily mean dismissal if investigation proved him innocent of the charges. But the reason given implies that he is to be dismissed: *Thou canst no longer (ou gar dunēi)*.

3. *Within himself (en heautōi)*. As soon as he had time to think the thing over carefully. He knew that he was guilty of embezzlement of the Master's funds. *Taketh away (aphaireitai)*. Present (linear) middle indicative of *aphaireō*, old verb to take away. Here the middle present means, He is taking away for himself. *To beg I am not ashamed (epaitein aischunomai)*. The infinitive with *aischunomai* means ashamed to begin to beg. The participle, *epaitōn aischunomai* would mean, ashamed while begging, ashamed of begging while doing it.

4. *I am resolved (egnōn)*. Second aorist active indicative of *ginōskō*. A difficult tense to reproduce in English. I knew, I know, I have known, all miss it a bit. It is a burst of daylight to the puzzled, darkened man: I've got it, I see into it now, a sudden solution. *What to do (ti poiēsō)*. Either deliberative first aorist active subjunctive or deliberative future active indicative. *When I am put out (hotan metastathō)*. First aorist passive subjunctive of *methistēmi*, (*meta, histēmi*), old verb, to transpose, transfer, remove. He is expecting to be put out. *They may receive me (dexōntai)*. First aorist middle subjunctive of *dechomai*, common verb. Subjunctive with final particle *hina*. He wishes to put the debtors under obligation to himself. *Debtors (tōn chreophiletōn)*. A late word. In the N.T. only here and Luke 7:41 from *chreos*, loan, and *opheiletēs*, debtor. It is probable that he dealt with "each one" separately.

6. *Measures (batous)*. Transliterated word for Hebrew

bath, between eight and nine gallons. Here alone in the
N.T. Not the same word as *batos* (*bush*) in Luke 6:44.
Thy bond (*sou ta grammata*). Thy writings, thy contracts,
thy note. *Quickly* (*tacheōs*). It was a secret arrangement
and speed was essential.

7. *Measures* (*korous*). Another Hebrew word for dry
measure. The Hebrew *cor* was about ten bushels. Data
are not clear about the Hebrew measures whether liquid
(*bath*) or dry (*cor*).

8. *His lord commended* (*epēinesen ho kurios*). The steward's lord praised him though he himself had been wronged
again (see verse 1 "wasting his goods"). *The unrighteous
steward* (*ton oikonomon tēs adikias*). Literally, the steward
of unrighteousness. The genitive is the case of genus,
species, the steward distinguished by unrighteousness as
his characteristic. See "the mammon of unrighteousness"
in verse 9. See "the forgetful hearer" in James 1:25. It
is a vernacular idiom common to Hebrew, Aramaic, and the
Koiné. *Wisely* (*phronimōs*). An old adverb, though here
alone in the N.T. But the adjective *phronimos* from which
it comes occurs a dozen times as in Matt. 10:16. It is from
phroneō and that from *phrēn*, the mind (I Cor. 14:20), the
discerning intellect. Perhaps "shrewdly" or "discreetly"
is better here than "wisely." The lord does not absolve
the steward from guilt and he was apparently dismissed
from his service. His shrewdness consisted in finding a place
to go by his shrewdness. He remained the steward of unrighteousness even though his shrewdness was commended.
For (*hoti*). Probably by this second *hoti* Jesus means to
say that he cites this example of shrewdness because it
illustrates the point. "This is the moral of the whole parable. Men of the world in their dealings with men like themselves are more prudent than the children of light in their
intercourse with one another" (Plummer). We all know
how stupid Christians can be in their co-operative work

in the kingdom of God, to go no further. *Wiser than*
(*phronimōteroi huper*). Shrewder beyond, a common Greek
idiom.

9. *By the mammon of unrighteousness* (*ek tou mamōnā tēs
adikias*). By the use of what is so often evil (money).
In Matt. 6:24 mammon is set over against God as in Luke
16:13 below. Jesus knows the evil power in money, but
servants of God have to use it for the kingdom of God.
They should use it discreetly and it is proper to make friends
by the use of it. *When it shall fail* (*hotan eklipēi*). Second
aorist active subjunctive with *hotan*, future time. The
mammon is sure to fail. *That they may receive you into the
eternal tabernacles* (*hina dexōntai humas eis tas aiōnious
skēnas*). This is the purpose of Christ in giving the advice
about their making friends by the use of money. The purpose is that those who have been blessed and helped by the
money may give a welcome to their benefactors when they
reach heaven. There is no thought here of purchasing an
entrance into heaven by the use of money. That idea is
wholly foreign to the context. These friends will give a
hearty welcome when one gives him mammon here. The
wise way to lay up treasure in heaven is to use one's money
for God here on earth. That will give a cash account there
of joyful welcome, not of purchased entrance.

10. *Faithful in a very little* (*pistos en elachistōi*). Elative
superlative. One of the profoundest sayings of Christ. We
see it in business life. The man who can be trusted in a
very small thing will be promoted to large responsibilities.
That is the way men climb to the top. Men who embezzle
in large sums began with small sums. Verses 10 to 13 here
explain the point of the preceding parables.

11. *Faithful in the unrighteous mammon* (*en tōi adikōi
mamōnāi*). In the use of what is considered "unrighteous"
as it so often is. Condition of the first class, "if ye did not
prove to be" (*ei ouk egenesthe*). Failure here forfeits confi-

dence in "the true riches" (*to alēthinon*). There is no sadder story than to see a preacher go down by the wrong use of money, caught in this snare of the devil.

12. *That which is your own* (*to hūmeteron*). But Westcott and Hort read *to hēmeteron* (our own) because of B L Origen. The difference is due to itacism in the pronunciation of *hū* and *hē* alike (long *i*). But the point in the passage calls for "yours" as correct. Earthly wealth is ours as a loan, a trust, withdrawn at any moment. It belongs to another (*en tōi allotriōi*). If you did not prove faithful in this, who will give you what is really yours forever? Compare "rich toward God" (Luke 12:21).

13. *Servant* (*oiketēs*). Household (*oikos*) servant. This is the only addition to Matt. 6:24 where otherwise the language is precisely the same, which see. Either Matthew or Luke has put the *logion* in the wrong place or Jesus spoke it twice. It suits perfectly each context. There is no real reason for objecting to repetition of favourite sayings by Jesus.

14. *Who were lovers of money* (*philarguroi huparchontes*). Literally, being lovers of money. *Philarguroi* is an old word, but in the N.T. only here and II Tim. 3:2. It is from *philos* and *arguros*. *Heard* (*ēkouon*). Imperfect active, were listening (all the while Jesus was talking to the disciples (verses 1-13). *And they scoffed at him* (*kai exemuktērizon*). Imperfect active again of *ekmuktērizō*. LXX where late writers use simple verb. In the N.T. only here and Luke 23:35. It means to turn out or up the nose at one, to sneer, to scoff. The Romans had a phrase, *naso adunco suspendere*, to hang on the hooked nose (the subject of ridicule). These money-loving Pharisees were quick to see that the words of Jesus about the wise use of money applied to them. They had stood without comment the three parables aimed directly at them (the lost sheep, the lost coin, the lost son). But now they do not remain quiet while they hear the fourth

parable spoken to the disciples. No words were apparently spoken, but their eyes, noses, faces were eloquent with a fine disdain.

15. *That justify yourselves* (*hoi dikaiountes heautous*). They were past-masters at that and were doing it now by upturned noses. *An abomination in the sight of God* (*bdelugma enōpion tou theou*). See on Matt. 24:15=Mark 13:14 for this LXX word for a detestable thing as when Antiochus Epiphanes set up an altar to Zeus in place of that to Jehovah. There is withering scorn in the use of this phrase by Jesus to these pious pretenders.

16. *Entereth violently into it* (*eis autēn biazetai*). A corresponding saying occurs in Matt. 11:12 in a very different context. In both the verb *biazetai*, occurs also, but nowhere else in the N.T. It is present middle here and can be middle or passive in Matthew, which see. It is rare in late prose. Deissmann (*Bible Studies*, p. 258) cites an inscription where *biazomai* is reflexive middle and used absolutely. Here the meaning clearly is that everyone forces his way into the kingdom of God, a plea for moral enthusiasm and spiritual passion and energy that some today affect to despise.

17. *One tittle* (*mian kerean*). See on Matt. 5:18.

18. *Committeth adultery* (*moicheuei*). Another repeated saying of Christ (Matt. 5:32; Mark 10:11f.=Matt. 19:9f.). Adultery remains adultery, divorce or no divorce, remarriage or no marriage.

19. *He was clothed* (*enedidusketo*). Imperfect middle of *endiduskō*, a late intensive form of *enduō*. He clothed himself in or with. It was his habit. *Purple* (*porphuran*). This purple dye was obtained from the purple fish, a species of mussel or *murex* (I Macc. 4:23). It was very costly and was used for the upper garment by the wealthy and princes (royal purple). They had three shades of purple (deep violet, deep scarlet or crimson, deep blue). See also Mark 15:17, 20; Rev. 18:12. *Fine linen* (*busson*). *Byssus* or Egyptian flax

(India and Achaia also). It is a yellowed flax from which
fine linen was made for undergarments. It was used for
wrapping mummies. "Some of the Egyptian linen was so
fine that it was called *woven air*" (Vincent). Here only in
the N.T. for the adjective *bussinos* occurs in Rev. 18:12;
19:8, 14. *Faring sumptuously (euphrainomenos lamprōs).*
Making merry brilliantly. The verb *euphrainomai* we have
already had in 12:19; 15:23, 25, 32. *Lamprōs* is an old adverb from *lampros*, brilliant, shining, splendid, magnificent.
It occurs here only in the N.T. This parable apparently
was meant for the Pharisees (verse 14) who were lovers of
money. It shows the wrong use of money and opportunity.

20. *Beggar (ptōchos).* Original meaning of this old word.
See on Matt. 5:3. The name Lazarus is from *Eleazaros*,
"God a help," and was a common one. *Lazar* in English
means one afflicted with a pestilential disease. *Was laid*
(*ebeblēto*). Past perfect passive of the common verb *ballō*.
He had been flung there and was still there, "as if contemptuous roughness is implied" (Plummer). *At his gate (pros
ton pulōna autou).* Right in front of the large portico or
gateway, not necessarily a part of the grand house, porch
in Matt. 26:71. *Full of sores (heilkōmenos).* Perfect passive
participle of *helkoō*, to make sore, to ulcerate, from *helkos*,
ulcer (Latin *ulcus*). See use of *helkos* in verse 21. Common
in Hippocrates and other medical writers. Here only in the
N.T.

21. *With the crumbs that fell (apo tōn piptontōn).* From
the things that fell from time to time. The language reminds
one of Luke 15:16 (the prodigal son) and the Syro-Phoenician
woman (Mark 7:28). Only it does not follow that this beggar
did not get the scraps from the rich man's table. Probably
he did, though nothing more. Even the wild street dogs
would get them also. *Yea, even the dogs (alla kai hoi kunes).*
For *alla kai* see also 12:7, 24:22. *Alla* can mean "yea,"
though it often means "but." Here it depends on how one

construes Luke's meaning. If he means that he was dependent on casual scraps and it was so bad that even the wild dogs moreover were his companions in misery, the climax came that he was able to drive away the dogs. The other view is that his hunger was unsatisfied, but even the dogs increased his misery. *Licked his sores (epeleichon ta helkē autou)*. Imperfect active of *epileichō*, a late vernacular *Koiné* verb, to lick over the surface. It is not clear whether the licking of the sores by the dogs added to the misery of Lazarus or gave a measure of comfort, as he lay in his helpless condition. "Furrer speaks of witnessing dogs and lepers waiting together for the refuse" (Bruce). It was a scramble between the dogs and Lazarus.

22. *Was borne (apenechthēnai)*. First aorist passive infinitive from *apopherō*, a common compound defective verb. The accusative case of general reference (*auton*) is common with the infinitive in such clauses after *egeneto*, like indirect discourse. It is his soul, of course, that was so borne by the angels, not his body. *Into Abraham's bosom (eis ton holpon Abraam)*. To be in Abraham's bosom is to the Jew to be in Paradise. In John 1:18 the Logos is in the bosom of the Father. Abraham, Isaac, and Jacob are in heaven and welcome those who come (Matt. 8:11; IV Macc. 14:17). The beloved disciple reclined on the bosom of Jesus at the last passover (John 13:23) and this fact indicates special favour. So the welcome to Lazarus was unusual. *Was buried (etaphē)*. Second aorist (effective) passive of the common verb *thaptō*. Apparently in contrast with the angelic visitation to the beggar.

23. *In Hades (en tōi Hāidēi)*. See on Matt. 16:18 for discussion of this word. Lazarus was in Hades also for both Paradise (Abraham's bosom) and Gehenna are in the unseen world beyond the grave. *In torments (en basanois)*. The touchstone by which gold and other metals were tested, then the rack for torturing people. Old word, but in the N.T.

only here, Luke 16:28, and Matt. 4:24. *Sees (horāi)*. Dramatic present indicative. The Jews believed that Gehenna and Paradise were close together. This detail in the parable does not demand that we believe it. The picture calls for it. *From afar (apo makrothen)*. Pleonastic use of *apo* as *makrothen* means *from afar*.

24. *That he may dip (hina bapsēi)*. First aorist active subjunctive of *baptō*, common verb, to dip. *In water (hudatos)*. Genitive, the specifying case, water and not something else. *Cool (katapsuxēi)*. First aorist active subjunctive of *katapsuchō*, a late Greek compound, to cool off, to make cool. Only here in the N.T. but common in medical books. Note perfective use of *kata-* (down). A small service that will be welcome. *For I am in anguish (hoti odunōmai)*. The active has a causative sense to cause intense pain, the middle to torment oneself (Luke 2:48; Acts 20:38), the passive to be translated as here. Common verb, but no other examples in the N.T.

25. *Receivedst (apelabes)*. Second aorist indicative of *apolambanō*, old verb to get back what is promised and in full. See also Luke 6:34; 18:30; 23:41. *Evil things (ta kaka)*. Not "his," but "the evil things" that came upon him. *Thou art in anguish (odunāsai)*. Like *kauchāsai* in Rom. 2:17. They contracted *-aesai* without the loss of *s*. Common in the *Koiné*.

26. *Beside all this (en pāsi toutois)*. In all these things (or regions). *Gulf (chasma)*. An old word from *chainō*, to yawn, our chasm, a gaping opening. Only here in the N.T. *Is fixed (estēriktai)*. Perfect passive indicative of *stērizō*, old verb (see on Luke 9:51). Permanent chasm. *May not be able (mē dunōntai)*. Present middle subjunctive of *dunamai*. The chasm is there on purpose (*that not, hopōs mē*) to prevent communication.

27. *That you send him (hina pempsēis auton)*. As if he had not had a fair warning and opportunity. The Roman Cath-

olics probably justify prayer to saints from this petition from the Rich Man to Abraham, but both are in Hades (the other world). It is to be observed besides, that Abraham makes no effort to communicate with the five brothers. But heavenly recognition is clearly assumed. Dante has a famous description of his visit to the damned (*Purg.* iii, 114).

28. *That he may testify* (*hopōs diamarturētai*). An old verb for solemn and thorough (*dia-*) witness. The Rich Man labours under the delusion that his five brothers will believe the testimony of Lazarus as a man from the dead.

29. *Let them hear them* (*akousatōsan autōn*). Even the heathen have the evidence of nature to show the existence of God as Paul argues in Romans so that they are without excuse (Rom. 1:20f.).

30. *They will repent* (*metanoēsousin*). The Rich Man had failed to do this and he now sees that it is the one thing lacking. It is not wealth, not poverty, not alms, not influence, but repentance that is needed. He had thought repentance was for others, not for all.

31. *Neither will they be persuaded* (*oud' peisthēsontai*). First future passive of *peithō*. Gressmann calls attention to the fact that Jesus is saying this in the conclusion of the parable. It is a sharp discouragement against efforts today to communicate with the dead. "Saul was not led to repentance when he saw Samuel at Endor nor were the Pharisees when they saw Lazarus come forth from the tomb. The Pharisees tried to put Lazarus to death and to explain away the resurrection of Jesus" (Plummer). Alford comments on the curious fact that Lazarus was the name of the one who did rise from the dead but whose return from the dead "was the immediate exciting cause of their (Pharisees) crowning act of unbelief."

CHAPTER XVII

1. *It is impossible* (*anendekton estin*). See *ouk endechetai* in 13:33. Alpha privative (*an-*) and *endektos*, verbal adjective, from *endechomai*. The word occurs only in late Greek and only here in the N.T. The meaning is inadmissible, unallowable. *But that occasions of stumbling should come* (*tou ta skandala mē elthein*). This genitive articular infinitive is not easy to explain. In Acts 10:25 there is another example where the genitive articular infinitive seems to be used as a nominative (Robertson, *Grammar*, p. 1040). The loose Hebrew infinitive construction may have a bearing here, but one may recall that the original infinitives were either locatives (*-eni*) or datives (*-ai*). *Ta skandala* is simply the accusative of general reference. Literally, the not coming as to occasions of stumbling. For *skandalon* (a trap) see on Matt. 5:29; 16:23. It is here only in Luke. The positive form of this saying appears in Matt. 18:7, which see.

2. *It were well for him* (*lusitelei autōi*). An old word, but only here in the N.T., from *lusitelēs* and this from *luō*, to pay, and *ta telē*, the taxes. So it pays the taxes, it returns expenses, it is profitable. Literally here, "It is profitable for him" (dative case, *autōi*). Matthew has *sumpherei* (it is advantageous, bears together for). *If a millstone were hanged* (*ei lithos mulikos perikeitai*). Literally, "if a millstone is hanged." Present passive indicative from *perikeimai* (to lie or be placed around). It is used as a perfect passive of *perititēmi*. So it is a first-class condition, determined as fulfilled, not second-class as the English translations imply. *Mulikos* is simply a stone (*lithos*), belonging to a mill. Here only in the text of Westcott and Hort, not in Mark 9:42 which is like Matt. 18:6 *mulos onikos* where

the upper millstone is turned by an ass, which see. *Were thrown* (*erriptai*). Perfect passive indicative from *rhiptō*, old verb. Literally, is thrown or has been thrown or cast or hurled. Mark has *beblētai* and Matthew *katapontisthēi*, which see, all three verbs vivid and expressive. *Rather than* (*ē*). The comparative is not here expressed before *ē* as one would expect. It is implied in *lusitelei*. See the same idiom in Luke 15:7.

3. *If thy brother sin* (*ean hamartēi*). Second aorist (ingressive) subjunctive in condition of third class.

4. *Seven times in a day* (*heptakis tēs hēmeras*). Seven times within the day. On another occasion Peter's question (Matt. 18:21) brought Christ's answer "seventy times seven" (verse 22), which see. Seven times during the day would be hard enough for the same offender.

5. *Increase* (*prosthes*). Second aorist active imperative of *prostithēmi*, to add to. Bruce thinks that this sounds much like the stereotyped petition in church prayers. A little reflection will show that they should answer the prayer themselves.

6. *If ye have* (*ei echete*). Condition of the first class, assumed to be true. *Ye would say* (*elegete an*). Imperfect active with *an* and so a conclusion (apodosis) of the second class, determined as unfulfilled, a mixed condition therefore. *Sycamine tree* (*sukaminōi*). At the present time both the black mulberry (sycamine) and the white mulberry (sycamore) exist in Palestine. Luke alone in the N.T. uses either word, the sycamine here, the sycamore in 19:4. The distinction is not observed in the LXX, but it is observed in the late Greek medical writers for both trees have medicinal properties. Hence it may be assumed that Luke, as a physician, makes the distinction. Both trees differ from the English sycamore. In Matt. 17:20 we have "mountain" in place of "sycamine tree." *Be thou rooted up* (*ekrizōthēti*). First aorist passive imperative as is *phuteuthēti*. *Would*

have obeyed (hupēkousen an). First aorist active indicative with *an*, apodosis of a second-class condition (note aorist tense here, imperfect *elegete*).

7. *Sit down to meat (anapese)*. Recline (for the meal). Literally, fall up (or back).

8. *And will not rather say (all' ouk erei)*. But will not say? *Ouk* in a question expects the affirmative answer. *Gird thyself (perizōsamenos)*. Direct middle first aorist participle of *perizōnnumi*, to gird around. *Till I have eaten and drunken (heōs phagō kai piō)*. More exactly, till I eat and drink. The second aorist subjunctives are not future perfects in any sense, simply punctiliar action, effective aorist. *Thou shalt eat and drink (phagesai kai piesai)*. Future middle indicative second person singular, the uncontracted forms -*esai* as often in the *Koinē*. These futures are from the aorist stems *ephagon* and *epion* without *sigma*.

9. *Does he thank?* (*mē echei charin;*). *Mē* expects the negative answer. *Echō charin*, to have gratitude toward one, is an old Greek idiom (I Tim. 1:12; II Tim. 1:3; Heb. 12:28).

10. *Unprofitable (achreioi)*. The Syriac Sinaitic omits "unprofitable." The word is common in Greek literature, but in the N.T. only here and Matt. 25:30 where it means "useless" (*a* privative and *chreios* from *chraomai*, to use). The slave who only does what he is commanded by his master to do has gained no merit or credit. "In point of fact it is not commands, but demands we have to deal with, arising out of special emergencies" (Bruce). The slavish spirit gains no promotion in business life or in the kingdom of God.

11. *Through the midst of Samaria and Galilee (dia meson Samarias kai Galilaias)*. This is the only instance in the N.T. of *dia* with the accusative in the local sense of "through." Xenophon and Plato use *dia mesou* (genitive). Jesus was going from Ephraim (John 11:54) north through

the midst of Samaria and Galilee so as to cross over the Jordan near Bethshean and join the Galilean caravan down through Perea to Jerusalem. The Samaritans did not object to people going north away from Jerusalem, but did not like to see them going south towards the city (Luke 9:51–56).

12. *Which stood afar off* (*hoi anestēsan porrōthen*). The margin of Westcott and Hort reads simply *estēsan*. The compound read by B means "rose up," but they stood at a distance (Lev. 13:45f.). The first healing of a leper (5:12–16) like this is given by Luke only.

13. *Lifted up* (*ēran*). First aorist active of the liquid verb *airō*.

14. *As they went* (*en tōi hupagein autous*). Favourite Lukan idiom of *en* with articular infinitive as in 17:11 and often.

16. *And he was a Samaritan* (*kai autos ēn Samareitēs*). This touch colours the whole incident. The one man who felt grateful enough to come back and thank Jesus for the blessing was a despised Samaritan. The *autos* has point here.

18. *Save this stranger* (*ei mē ho allogenēs*). The old word was *allophulos* (Acts 10:28), but *allogenēs* occurs in the LXX, Josephus, and inscriptions. Deissmann (*Light from the Ancient East*, p. 80) gives the inscription from the limestone block from the Temple of Israel in Jerusalem which uses this very word which may have been read by Jesus: *Let no foreigner enter within the screen and enclosure surrounding the sanctuary* (*Mēthena allogenē eisporeuesthai entos tou peri to hieron truphaktou kai peribolou*).

20. *With observation* (*meta paratēseōs*). Late Greek word from *paratēreō*, to watch closely. Only here in the N.T. Medical writers use it of watching the symptoms of disease. It is used also of close astronomical observations. But close watching of external phenomena will not reveal the signs of the kingdom of God.

21. *Within you (entos humōn)*. This is the obvious, and, as I think, the necessary meaning of *entos*. The examples cited of the use of *entos* in Xenophon and Plato where *entos* means "among" do not bear that out when investigated. Field (*Ot. Norv.*) "contends that there is no clear instance of *entos* in the sense of among" (Bruce), and rightly so. What Jesus says to the Pharisees is that they, as others, are to look for the kingdom of God within themselves, not in outward displays and supernatural manifestations. It is not a localized display "Here" or "There." It is in this sense that in Luke 11:20 Jesus spoke of the kingdom of God as "come upon you" (*ephthasen eph' humās*), speaking to Pharisees. The only other instance of *entos* in the N.T. (Matt. 23:26) necessarily means "within" ("the inside of the cup"). There is, beside, the use of *entos* meaning "within" in the Oxyrhynchus Papyrus saying of Jesus of the Third Century (Deissmann, *Light from the Ancient East*, p. 426) which is interesting: "The kingdom of heaven is within you" (*entos humōn* as here in Luke 17:21).

23. *Go not away nor follow after them (mē apelthēte mēde diōxēte)*. Westcott and Hort bracket *apelthēte mēde*. Note aorist subjunctive with *mē* in prohibition, ingressive aorist. Do not rush after those who set times and places for the second advent. The Messiah was already present in the first advent (verse 21) though the Pharisees did not know it.

24. *Lighteneth (astraptousa)*. An old and common verb, though only here and 24:4 in the N.T. The second coming will be sudden and universally visible. There are still some poor souls who are waiting in Jerusalem under the delusion that Jesus will come there and nowhere else.

25. *But first (prōton de)*. The second coming will be only after the Cross.

27. *They ate, they drank, they married, they were given in marriage (ēsthion, epinon, egamoun, egamizonto)*. Imperfects all of them vividly picturing the life of the time of

Noah.   But the other tenses are aorists (Noah entered *eisēlthen*, the flood came *ēlthen*, destroyed *apōlesen*).

28. Note the same sharp contrast between the imperfects here (*ate ēsthion, drank epinon, bought ēgorazon, sold epōloun, planted ephuteuon, builded ōikodomoun*) and the aorists in verse 29 (*went out exēlthen, rained ebrexen, destroyed apōlesen*).

30. *Is revealed* (*apokaluptetai*).   Prophetic and futuristic present passive indicative.

31. *Let him not go down* (*mē katabatō*).   Second aorist active imperative of *katabainō* with *mē* in a prohibition in the third person singular.   The usual idiom here would be *mē* and the aorist subjunctive.   See Mark 13:15f. = Matt. 24:17f. when these words occur in the great eschatological discussion concerning flight before the destruction of Jerusalem.   Here the application is "absolute indifference to all worldly interests as the attitude of readiness for the Son of Man" (Plummer).

32. *Remember Lot's wife* (*mnēmoneuete tēs gunaikos Lōt*). Here only in the N.T.   A pertinent illustration to warn against looking back with yearning after what has been left behind (Gen. 19:26).

33. *Shall preserve it* (*zōogonēsei autēn*).   Or save it alive. Here only in the N.T. except I Tim. 6:13 and Acts 7:19. It is a late word and common in medical writers, to bring forth alive (*zōos, genō*) and here to keep alive.

34. *In that night* (*tautēi tēi nukti*).   More vivid still, "on this night," when Christ comes.

35. *Shall be grinding* (*esontai alēthousai*).   Periphrastic future active indicative of *alēthō*, an old verb only in the N.T. here and Matt. 24:41.   *Together* (*epi to auto*).   In the same place, near together as in Acts 2:1.

37. *The eagles* (*hoi aetoi*).   Or the vultures attracted by the carcass.   This proverb is quoted also in Matt. 24:28. See Job 39:27–30; Heb. 1:8; Hos. 8:1.   Double compound (*epi-sun-*) in *epi-sun-achthēsontai* completes the picture.

CHAPTER XVIII

1. *To the end that (pros to dein)*. *With a view to the being necessary, pros* and the articular infinitive. The impersonal verb *dei* here is in the infinitive and has another infinitive loosely connected with it *proseuchesthai,* to pray. *Not to faint (mē enkakein)*. Literally, not to give in to evil (*en, kakeō,* from *kakos,* bad or evil), to turn coward, lose heart, behave badly. A late verb used several times in the N.T. (II Cor. 4:1, 16, etc.).

2. *Regarded not (mē entrepomenos)*. Present middle participle of *entrepō,* old verb, to turn one on himself, to shame one, to reverence one. This was a "hard-boiled" judge who knew no one as his superior. See on Matt. 21:37.

3. *Came oft (ērcheto)*. Imperfect tense denotes repetitions, no adverb for "oft" in the Greek. *Avenge me of (ekdikēson me apo)*. A late verb for doing justice, protecting one from another (note both *ek* and *apo,* here). Deissmann (*Light from the Ancient East,* pp. 420ff.) quotes a *stēlē* of the second century B.C. with a prayer for vengeance for a Jewish girl that had been murdered which has this very verb *ekdikeō.*

4. *He would not (ouk ēthelen)*. Imperfect tense of continued refusal. *Though (ei kai)*. Concerning sentence, not *kai ei* (even if).

5. *Yet (ge)*. Delicate intensive particle of deep feeling as here. *Because this widow troubleth me (dia to parechein moi kopon tēn chēran tautēn)*. Literally, because of the furnishing me trouble as to this widow (accusative of general reference with the articular infinitive). *Lest she wear me out (hina mē hupōpiazēi me)*. Some take it that the judge is actually afraid that the widow may come and assault him, literally

beat him under the eye. That idea would be best expressed
here by the aorist tense.

6. *The unrighteous judge* (*ho kritēs tēs adikias*). The judge
of unrighteousness (marked by unrighteousness), as in 16:8
we have "the steward of unrighteousness," the same idiom.

7. *And he is longsuffering* (*makrothumei*). This present
active indicative comes in awkwardly after the aorist subjunctive *poiēsei* after *ou mē*, but this part of the question is
positive. Probably *kai* here means "and yet" as so often
(John 9:30; 16:32, etc.). God delays taking vengeance on
behalf of his people, not through indifference, but through
patient forbearance.

8. *Howbeit* (*plēn*). It is not clear whether this sentence is
also a question or a positive statement. There is no way to
decide. Either will make sense though not quite the same
sense. The use of *āra* before *heurēsei* seems to indicate a
question expecting a negative answer as in Acts 8:30 and
Rom. 14:19. But here *āra* comes in the middle of the sentence instead of near the beginning, an unusual position for
either inferential *ara* or interrogative *āra*. On the whole the
interrogative *āra* is probably correct, meaning to question
if the Son will find a persistence of faith like that of the
widow.

9. *Set all others at naught* (*exouthenountas tous loipous*).
A late verb *exoutheneō*, like *oudeneō*, from *outhen* (*ouden*), to
consider or treat as nothing. In LXX and chiefly in Luke
and Paul in the N.T.

10. *Stood* (*statheis*). First aorist passive participle of
histēmi. Struck an attitude ostentatiously where he could
be seen. Standing was the common Jewish posture in prayer
(Matt. 6:5; Mark 11:25). *Prayed thus* (*tauta proseucheto*).
Imperfect middle, was praying these things (given following).
With himself (*pros heauton*). A soliloquy with his own soul,
a complacent recital of his own virtues for his own self-satis-
faction, not fellowship with God, though he addresses God.

I thank thee (eucharistō soi). But his gratitude to God is for his own virtues, not for God's mercies to him. One of the rabbis offers a prayer like this of gratitude that he was in a class by himself because he was a Jew and not a Gentile, because he was a Pharisee and not of the *am-haaretz* or common people, because he was a man and not a woman. *Extortioners (harpages).* An old word, *harpax* from same root as *harpazō,* to plunder. An adjective of only one gender, used of robbers and plunderers, grafters, like the publicans (Luke 3:13), whether wolves (Matt. 7:15) or men (I Cor. 5:19f.). The Pharisee cites the crimes of which he is not guilty. *Or even (ē kai).* As the climax of iniquity (Bruce), he points to "this publican." Zaccheus will admit robbery (Luke 19:8). *God (ho theos).* Nominative form with the article as common with the vocative use of *theos* (so verse 13; and John 20:28).

12. *Twice in the week (dis tou sabbatou).* One fast a year was required by the law (Lev. 16:29; Num. 29:7). The Pharisees added others, twice a week between passover and pentecost, and between tabernacles and dedication of the temple. *I get (ktōmai).* Present middle indicative, not perfect middle *kektēmai* (I possess). He gave a tithe of his income, not of his property.

13. *Standing afar off (makrothen hestōs).* Second perfect active participle of *histēmi,* intransitive like *statheis* above. But no ostentation as with the Pharisee in verse 11. At a distance from the Pharisee, not from the sanctuary. *Would not lift (ouk ēthelen oude eparai).* Negatives (double) imperfect of *thelō,* was not willing even to lift up, refused to lift (*eparai,* first aorist active infinitive of the liquid compound verb, *ep-airō).* *Smote (etupte).* Imperfect active of *tuptō,* old verb, kept on smiting or beating. Worshippers usually lifted up their closed eyes to God. *Be merciful (hilasthēti).* First aorist passive imperative of *hilaskomai,* an old verb, found also in LXX and inscriptions (*exhilaskomai,* Deissmann, *Bible Studies,* p. 224). *A sinner (tōi hamartōlōi).* The sinner,

not a sinner. It is curious how modern scholars ignore this Greek article. The main point in the contrast lies in this article. The Pharisee thought of others as sinners. The publican thinks of himself alone as the sinner, not of others at all.

14. *This man* (*houtos*). This despised publican referred to contemptuously in verse 11 as "this" (*houtos*) publican. *Rather than the other* (*par' ekeinon*). In comparison with (placed beside) that one. A neat Greek idiom after the perfect passive participle *dedikaiomenos*. *For* (*hoti*). This moral maxim Christ had already used in 14:11. Plummer pertinently asks: "Why is it assumed that Jesus did not repeat his sayings?"

15. *They brought* (*prosepheron*). Imperfect active, they were bringing. So Mark 10:13. *Their babes* (*ta brephē*). Old word for *infants*. Here Mark 10:13 and Matt. 19:13 have *paidia* (little children). Note "also" (*kai*) in Luke, not in Mark and Matthew. *That he should touch them* (*hina autōn haptētai*). Present middle subjunctive (linear action, repeatedly touch or one after the other), where Mark 10:13 has aorist middle subjunctive (*hapsētai*). *Rebuked* (*epetimōn*). Imperfect indicative active. Either inchoative began to rebuke, or continued, kept on rebuking. Matthew and Mark have the aorist *epetimēsan*.

16. *Called* (*prosekalesato*). Indirect middle aorist indicative, called the children with their parents to himself and then rebuked the disciples for their rebuke of the parents. The language of Jesus is precisely that of Mark 10:14 which see, and nearly that of Matt. 19:14 which see also. The plea of Jesus that children be allowed to come to him is one that many parents need to heed. It is a tragedy to think of parents "forbidding" their children or of preachers doing the same or of both being stumbling-blocks to children.

17. *As a little child* (*hōs paidion*). Jesus makes the child the model for those who seek entrance into the kingdom of

God, not the adult the model for the child. He does not say
that the child is already in the kingdom without coming to
him. Jesus has made the child's world by understanding the
child and opening the door for him.

18. *Ruler* (*archōn*). Not in Mark 10:17 or Matt. 19:16.
What shall I do to inherit? (*Ti poiēsas klēronomēsō;*). "By
doing what shall I inherit?" Aorist active participle and
future active indicative. Precisely the same question is asked
by the lawyer in Luke 10:25. This young man probably
thought that by some one act he could obtain eternal life.
He was ready to make a large expenditure for it. *Good*
(*agathon*). See on Mark 10:17 and Matt. 19:16 for discussion
of this adjective for absolute goodness. Plummer observes
that no Jewish rabbi was called "good" in direct address.
The question of Jesus will show whether it was merely ful-
some flattery on the part of the young man or whether he
really put Jesus on a par with God. He must at any rate
define his attitude towards Christ.

22. *One thing thou lackest yet* (*eti hen soi leipei*). Literally,
one thing still fails thee or is wanting to thee. An old verb
with the dative of personal interest. Mark 10:21 has here
husterei se, which see. It was an amazing compliment for
one who was aiming at perfection (Matt. 19:21). The youth
evidently had great charm and was sincere in his claims.
Distribute (*diados*). Second aorist active imperative of
diadidōmi (give to various ones, *dia-*). Here Mark and
Matthew simply have *dos* (give). The rest the same in all
three Gospels.

23. *Became* (*egenēthē*). First aorist passive indicative of
ginomai. Like his countenance fell (*stugnasas*), in Mark
10:22. *Exceedingly sorrowful* (*perilupos*). Old adjective
(*peri, lupē*) with perfective use of *peri*. *Very rich* (*plousios
sphodra*). Rich exceedingly. Today, a multimillionaire.

24. *Shall they enter* (*eisporeuontai*). Present middle indicative, futuristic present.

25. *Through a needle's eye* (*dia trēmatos belonēs*). Both words are old. *Trēma* means a perforation or hole or eye and in the N.T. only here and Matt. 19:24. *Belonē* means originally the point of a spear and then a surgeon's needle. Here only in the N.T. Mark 10:25 and Matt. 19:24 have *rhaphidos* for needle. This is probably a current proverb for the impossible. The Talmud twice speaks of an elephant passing through the eye of a needle as being impossible.

26. *Then who* (*kai tis*). Literally, *and who*. The *kai* calls attention to what has just been said. Wealth was assumed to be mark of divine favour, not a hindrance to salvation.

27. *The impossible with men possible with God* (*ta adunata para anthrōpois dunata para tōi theōi*). Paradoxical, but true. Take your stand "beside" (*para*) God and the impossible becomes possible. Clearly then Jesus meant the humanly impossible by the parabolic proverb about the camel going through the needle's eye. God can break the grip of gold on a man's life, but even Jesus failed with this young ruler.

28. *Our own* (*ta idia*). Our own things (home, business, etc.). Right here is where so many fail. Peter speaks here not in a spirit of boastfulness, but rather with his reactions from their consternation at what has happened and at the words of Jesus (Plummer).

30. *Shall not receive* (*ouchi mē labēi*). Very strong double negative with aorist active subjunctive of *lambanō*. *Manifold more* (*pollaplasiona*). Late Greek word, here alone in the N.T. save Matt. 19:29 where Westcott and Hort have it though many MSS. there read *hekatonplasiona* (a hundred-fold) as in Mark 10:30.

31. *Took unto him* (*paralabōn*). Second aorist active participle of *paralambanō*. *Taking along with himself*. So Mark 10:32. Matt. 20:17 adds *kat' idian* (apart). Jesus is making a special point of explaining his death to the Twelve. *We go up* (*anabainomen*). Present active indicative, we are

going up. *Unto the Son of man (tōi huiōi tou anthrōpou).*
Dative case of personal interest. The position is amphibolous and the construction makes sense either with "shall be
accomplished" *(telesthēsetai)* or "that are written" *(ta
gegrammena),* probably the former. Compare these minute
details of the prophecy here (verses 32f.) with the words in
Mark 10:33f. = Matt. 20:18f., which see.

33. *The third day (tēi hēmerāi tēi tritēi).* The day the
third. In Matt. 20:19 it is "the third day" while in Mark
10:34 "after three days" occurs in the same sense, which see.

34. *And they perceived not (kai ouk eginōskon).* Imperfect
active. They kept on not perceiving. Twice already Luke
has said this in the same sentence. *They understood none
of these things (ouden toutōn sunēkan).* First aorist active
indicative, a summary statement. *This saying was hid from
them (ēn to rhēma touto kekrummenon ap' autōn).* Past perfect passive indicative (periphrastic), state of completion.
It was a puzzling experience. No wonder that Luke tries
three times to explain the continued failure of the apostles
to understand Jesus. The words of Christ about his death
ran counter to all their hopes and beliefs.

35. *Unto Jericho (eis Iereichō).* See on Matt. 20:29 =
Mark 10:46, for discussion of the two Jerichos in Mark and
Matt. (the old and the new as here). *Begging (epaitōn).*
Asking for something. He probably was by the wayside
between the old Jericho and the new Roman Jericho. Mark
gives his name Bartimaeus (10:46). Matt. 20:30 mentions
two.

36. *Inquired (epunthaneto).* Imperfect middle. Repeatedly inquired as he heard the tramp of the passing crowd
going by *(diaporeuomenou). What this meant (Ti eiē touto).*
Literally, What it was. Without *an* the optative is due to
indirect discourse, changed from *estin.* With *an* (margin of
Westcott and Hort) the potential optative of the direct discourse is simply retained.

37. *Passeth by* (*parerchetai*).   Present middle indicative retained in indirect discourse as *paragei* is in Matt. 20:30. No reason for differences of English tenses in the two passages (was passing by, passeth by).

38. *He cried* (*eboēsen*).   Old verb, *boaō*, to shout, as in 9:38. *Son of David* (*huie Daueid*).   Shows that he recognizes Jesus as the Messiah.

39. *That he should hold his peace* (*hina sigēsēi*).   Ingressive aorist subjunctive.   That he should become silent, as with *hina siōpēsēi* in Mark 10:48.   *The more a great deal* (*polloi mallon*).   By much more as in Mark 10:48.

40. *Stood* (*statheis*).   First aorist passive where Mark 10:49 and Matt. 20:32 have *stas* (second aorist active) translated "stood still."   One is as "still" as the other.   The first is that Jesus "stopped."   *Be brought* (*achthēnai*).   First aorist infinitive in indirect command.

41. *What wilt thou that I should do unto thee?* (*Ti soi theleis poiēsō;*).   Same idiom in Mark 10:51 = Matt. 20:32 which see, the use of *thelō* without *hina* with aorist subjunctive (or future indicative).   See same references also for *hina anablepsō* "that I may see again" without verb before *hina*.   Three uses of *anablepō* here (verses 41, 42, 43).

43. *Followed* (*ēkolouthei*).   Imperfect active as in Mark 10:52.   Either inchoative he began to follow, or descriptive, he was following.

CHAPTER XIX

1. *Was passing through (diērcheto).* Imperfect middle. Now Jesus was inside the Roman Jericho with the procession.

2. *Chief publican (architelōnēs).* The word occurs nowhere else apparently but the meaning is clear from the other words with *archi-* like *archiereus* (chief priest) *archipoimēn* (chief shepherd). Jericho was an important trading point for balsam and other things and so Zacchaeus was the head of the tax collections in this region, a sort of commissioner of taxes who probably had other publicans serving under him.

3. *He sought (ezētei).* Imperfect active. He was seeking, conative idea. *Jesus who he was (Iēsoun tis estin).* Prolepsis, to see who Jesus was. He had heard so much about him. He wanted to see which one of the crowd was Jesus. *For the crowd (apo tou ochlou).* He was short and the crowd was thick and close. *Stature (tēi hēlikiāi).* No doubt of that meaning here and possibly so in 2:52. Elsewhere "age" except Luke 12:25; Matt. 6:27 where it is probably "stature" also.

4. *Ran on before (prodramōn eis to emprosthen).* Second aorist active participle of *protrechō* (defective verb). "Before" occurs twice (*pro-* and *eis to emprosthen*). *Into a sycamore tree (epi sukomorean).* From *sukon*, fig, and *moron*, mulberry. The fig-mulberry and quite a different tree from the sycamine tree in 17:6, which see. It bore a poor fruit which poor people ate (Amos 7:14). It was a wide open tree with low branches so that Zacchaeus could easily climb into it. *That way (ekeinēs).* Feminine for *hodos* (way) is understood. Genitive case with *di* in composition (*dierchesthai*) or as an adverbial use.

5. *Make haste and come down* (*speusas katabēthi*). Simultaneous aorist active participle (*speusas*) with the second aorist active imperative. "Come down in a hurry."

6. *He made haste and came down* (*speusas katebē*). Luke repeats the very words of Jesus with the same idiom. *Received him joyfully* (*hupedexato auton chairōn*). The very verb used of Martha's welcome to Jesus (10:38). "Joyfully" is the present active participle, "rejoicing" (*chairōn*).

7. *Murmured* (*diegogguzonto*). Imperfect middle of this compound onomatopoetic word *dia-gogguzō*. In Luke 5:30 we have the simple *gogguzō*, a late word like the cooing doves or the hum of bees. This compound with *dia-* is still rarer, but more expressive. *To lodge* (*katalusai*). Jesus was the hero of this crowd from Galilee on their way to the passover. But here he had shocked their sensibilities and those of the people of Jericho by inviting himself to be the guest of this chief publican and notorious sinner who had robbed nearly everybody in the city by exorbitant taxes.

8. *Stood* (*statheis*). Apparently Jesus and Zacchaeus had come to the house of Zacchaeus and were about to enter when the murmur became such a roar that Zacchaeus turned round and faced the crowd. *If I have wrongfully exacted aught of any man* (*ei tinos ti esukophantēsa*). A most significant admission and confession. It is a condition of the first class (*ei* and the aorist active indicative) that assumes it to be true. His own conscience was at work. He may have heard audible murmurs from the crowd. For the verb *sukophantein*, see discussion on 3:14, the only two instances in the N.T. He had extorted money wrongfully as they all knew. *I return fourfold* (*apodidōmi tetraploun*). I offer to do it here and now on this spot. This was the Mosaic law (Ex. 22:1; Num. 5:6f.). Restitution is good proof of a change of heart. D. L. Moody used to preach it with great power. Without this the offer of Zacchaeus to give half his goods to the poor would be less effective. "It is an odd

coincidence, nothing more, that the fig-mulberry (sycamore) should occur in connexion with the *fig*-shewer (sycophant)."

10. *The lost (to apolōlos)*. The neuter as a collective whole, second perfect active participle of *apollumi*, to destroy. See Luke 15 for the idea of the lost.

11. *He added and spake (prostheis eipen)*. Second aorist active participle of *prostithēmi* with *eipen*. It is a Hebrew idiom seen also in Luke 20:1f. he added to send (*prosetheto pempsai*) and in Acts 12:3 "he added to seize" (*prosetheto sullabein*). This undoubted Hebraism occurs in the N.T. in Luke only, probably due to the influence of the LXX on Luke the Greek Christian. *To appear (anaphainesthai)*. Present passive infinitive of an old verb to be made manifest, to be shown up. In the N.T. only here and Acts 21:3.

12. *To take to himself a kingdom (labein heautōi basileian)*. Second aorist active infinitive of *lambanō* with the dative reflexive *heautōi* where the middle voice could have been used. Apparently this parable has the historical basis of Archelaus who actually went from Jerusalem to Rome on this very errand to get a kingdom in Palestine and to come back to it. This happened while Jesus was a boy in Nazareth and it was a matter of common knowledge.

13. *Trade ye herewith till I come (pragmateusasthe en hōi erchomai)*. First aorist middle imperative of *pragmateuomai*, an old verb from *prāgma*, business. Here only in the N.T. Westcott and Hort in their text read *pragmateusasthai*, first aorist middle infinitive (*-ai* and *-e* were pronounced alike). The infinitive makes it indirect discourse, the imperative direct. *While I am coming* is what *en hōi erchomai* really means.

14. *His citizens (hoi politai autou)*. That actually happened with Archelaus.

15. *When he was come back again (en tōi epanelthein auton)*. "On the coming back again as to him." Luke's favourite idiom of the articular infinitive after *en* and with the accusa-

tive of general reference. *Had given* (*dedōkei*). Past perfect active indicative without augment of *didōmi*. *That he might know* (*hina gnoi*). Second aorist active subjunctive of *ginoskō*. The optative would be *gnoiē*.

16. *Hath made* (*prosērgasato*). Only here in the N.T. Note *pros-* in addition, besides, more.

17. *Have thou authority* (*isthi exousian echōn*). Periphrastic present active imperative. Keep on having authority.

19. *Be thou also over* (*kai su epano ginou*). Present middle imperative. Keep on becoming over. There is no real reason for identifying this parable of the pounds with the parable of the talents in Matt. 25. The versatility of Jesus needs to be remembered by those who seek to flatten out everything.

20. *I kept* (*eichon*). Imperfect active of *echō*. I kept on keeping. *Laid up* (*apokeimenēn*). Present passive participle agreeing with *hēn* (which), used often as perfect passive of *tithēmi* as here, laid away or off (*apo*). It is not the periphrastic construction, but two separate verbs, each with its own force. *In a napkin* (*en soudariōi*). A Latin word *sudarium* from *sudor* (sweat) transliterated into Greek, a sweatcloth handkerchief or napkin. Found in papyrus marriage contracts as part of the dowry (second and third centuries A.D., Deissmann, *Bible Studies*, p. 223). Used also for swathing the head of the dead (John 11:44; 20:7).

21. *I feared* (*ephoboumēn*). Imperfect middle, I continued to fear. *Austere* (*austēros*). Old Greek word from *auō*, to dry up. Reproduced in Latin *austeros* and English *austere*. It means rough to the taste, stringent. Here only in the N.T. Compare *sklēros* (hard) in Matt. 25:24. "Harsh in flavour, then in disposition" (Bruce). *Thou layedst not down* (*ouk ethēkas*). Probably a proverb for a grasping profiteer.

22. *Thou knewest* (*ēideis*). Second past perfect of *horaō*, to see, used as imperfect of *oida*, to know. Either it must be taken as a question as Westcott and Hort do or be understood

as sarcasm as the Revised Version has it. The words of the wicked (*poneros*) slave are turned to his own condemnation.

23. *Then wherefore* (*kai dia ti*). Note this inferential use of *kai-* in that case. *Into the bank* (*epi trapezan*). Literally, *upon a table*. This old word *trapeza*, from *tetrapeza* (*tetra*, four, *pous*, foot). It means then any table (Mark 7:28), food on the table (Acts 16:34), feast or banquet (Rom. 11:9), table of the money-changers (John 2:15; Mark 11:15; Matt. 21:12), or bank as here. Our word bank is from Old English *bench*. *With interest* (*sun tokōi*). Not usury, but proper and legal interest. Old word from *tiktō*, to bring forth. In the N.T. only here and Matt. 25:27. *Should have required it* (*an auto epraxa*). Conclusion of second-class condition the condition or apodosis being implied in the participle "coming" (*elthōn*), and the previous question. On this technical use of *prassō* (*epraxa*) see Luke 3:13.

25. *And they said unto him* (*kai eipan autōi*). Probably the eager audience who had been listening to this wonderful parable interrupted Jesus at this point because of this sudden turn when the one pound is given to the man who has ten pounds. If so, it shows plainly how keenly they followed the story which Jesus was giving because of their excitement about the kingdom (Luke 19:11).

26. *That hath not* (*tou mē echontos*). The present tense of *echō* here, that keeps on not having, probably approaches the idea of acquiring or getting, the one who keeps on not acquiring. This is the law of nature and of grace.

27. *Reign* (*basileusai*). First aorist active infinitive, ingressive aorist, come to rule. *Slay* (*katasphaxate*). First aorist active imperative of *katasphazō*, to slaughter, an old verb, but only here in the N.T.

28. *Went on before* (*eporeueto emprosthen*). Imperfect middle. Jesus left the parable to do its work and slowly went on his way up the hill to Jerusalem.

29. *Unto Bethphage and Bethany* (*eis Bēthphagē kai Bētha-nia*). Both indeclinable forms of the Hebrew or Aramaic names. In Mark 11:1 "Bethany" is inflected regularly, which see. *Of Olives* (*Elaiōn*). As in Mark 11:1 and Matt. 21:1, though some editors take it to be, not the genitive plural of *elaia* (olive tree), but the name of the place Olivet. In the Greek it is just a matter of accent (circumflex or acute) Olivet is correct in Acts 1:12. See on Matt. 21:1ff. and Mark 11:1ff. for details.

30. *Whereon no man ever yet sat* (*eph' hon oudeis pōpote anthrōpōn ekathisen*). Plummer holds that this fact indicated to the disciples a royal progress into the city of a piece with the Virgin Birth of Jesus and the burial in a new tomb.

32. *As he had said unto them* (*kathōs eipen autois*). Luke alone notes this item.

33. *As they were loosing* (*luontōn autōn*). Genitive absolute. *The owners thereof* (*hoi kurioi autou*). The same word *kurios* used of the Lord Jesus in verse 31 (and 34) and which these "owners" would understand. See on Matt. 21:3 = Mark 11:3 for *kurios* used by Jesus about himself with the expectation that these disciples would recognize him by that title as they did. The word in common use for the Roman emperor and in the LXX to translate the Hebrew *Elohim* (God).

35. *Set Jesus thereon* (*epebibasan ton Iēsoun*). First aorist active. Old verb, to cause to mount, causative verb from *bainō*, to go. In the N.T. only here and Luke 10:34; Acts 23:24.

36. *They spread* (*hupestrōnnuon*). Imperfect active describing the continued spreading as they went on. *Hupostrōnnuō* is a late form of the old verb *hupostorennumi*. Here only in the N.T.

37. *At the descent* (*pros tēi katabasei*). Epexegetic of "drawing nigh." They were going by the southern slope of the Mount of Olives. As they turned down to the city,

the grand view stirred the crowd to rapturous enthusiasm. This was the first sight of the city on this route which is soon obscured in the descent. The second view bursts out again (verse 41). It was a shout of triumph from the multitude with their long pent-up enthusiasm (verse 11), restrained no longer by the parable of the pounds. *For all the mighty works which they had seen (peri pasōn eidon dunameōn).* Neat Greek idiom, incorporation of the antecedent (*dunameōn*) into the relative clause and attraction of the case of the relative from the accusative *has* to the genitive *hōn.* And note "all." The climax had come, Lazarus, Bartimaeus, and the rest.

38. *The king cometh (ho erchomenos, ho basileus).* The Messianic hopes of the people were now all ablaze with expectation of immediate realization. A year ago in Galilee he had frustrated their plans for a revolutionary movement "to take him by force to make him king" (John 6:15). The phrase "the coming king" like "the coming prophet" (John 6:14; Deut. 18:15) expressed the hope of the long-looked-for Messiah. They are singing from the Hallel in their joy that Jesus at last is making public proclamation of his Messiahship. *Peace in heaven, and glory in the highest (en ouranōi eirēnē kai doxa en hupsistois).* This language reminds one strongly of the song of the angels at the birth of Jesus (Luke 2:14). Mark 11:10 and Matt. 21:9 have "Hosannah in the highest."

39. *Some of the Pharisees (tines tōn Pharisaiōn).* Luke seems to imply by "from the multitude" (*apo tou ochlou*) that these Pharisees were in the procession, perhaps half-hearted followers of the mob. But John 12:19 speaks of Pharisees who stood off from the procession and blamed each other for their failure and the triumph of Jesus. These may represent the bolder spirits of their same group who dared to demand of Jesus that he rebuke his disciples.

40. *If these shall hold their peace (ean houtoi siōpēsousin).*

A condition of the first class, determined as fulfilled. The use of *ean* rather than *ei* cuts no figure in the case (see Acts 8:31; I Thess. 3:8; I John 5:15). The kind of condition is determined by the mode which is here indicative. The future tense by its very nature does approximate the aorist subjunctive, but after all it is the indicative. *The stones will cry out* (*hoi lithoi kraxousin*). A proverb for the impossible happening.

41. *Wept* (*eklausen*). Ingressive aorist active indicative, burst into tears. Probably audible weeping.

42. *If thou hadst known* (*ei egnōs*). Second aorist active indicative of *ginōskō*. Second-class condition, determined as unfulfilled. *Even thou* (*kai su*). Emphatic position of the subject. *But now* (*nun de*). Aposiopesis. The conclusion is not expressed and the sudden breaking off and change of structure is most impressive. *They are hid* (*ekrubē*). Second aorist passive indicative of *kruptō*, common verb, to hide.

43. *Shall cast up a bank* (*parembalousin charaka*). Future active indicative of *paremballō*, a double compound (*para, en, ballō*) of long usage, finally in a military sense of line of battle or in camp. Here alone in the N.T. So also the word *charaka* (*charax*) for bank, stake, palisade, rampart, is here alone in the N.T., though common enough in the old Greek. *Compass thee round* (*perikuklōsousin se*). Future active indicative. Another common compound to make a circle (*kuklos*) around (*peri*), though here only in the N.T. *Keep thee in* (*sunexousin se*). Shall hold thee together on every side (*pantothen*). See about *sunechō* on 4:38.

44. *Shall dash to the ground* (*edaphiousin*). Attic future of *edaphizō*, to beat level, to raze to the ground, a rare verb from *edaphos*, bottom, base, ground (Acts 22:7), here alone in the N.T. *Because* (*anth' hōn*). "In return for which things." *Thou knewest not* (*ouk egnōs*). Applying the very words of the lament in the condition in verse 42. This

vivid prophecy of the destruction of Jerusalem is used by those who deny predictive prophecy even for Jesus as proof that Luke wrote the Gospel after the destruction of Jerusalem. But it is no proof at all to those who concede to Jesus adequate knowledge of his mission and claims.

45. *Began to cast out* (*ērxato ekballein*). So Mark 11:15 whereas Matt. 21:12 has simply "he cast out." See Mark and Matthew for discussion of this second cleansing of the temple at the close of the public ministry in relation to the one at the beginning in John 2:14–22. There is nothing gained by accusing John or the Synoptics of a gross chronological blunder. There was abundant time in these three years for all the abuses to be revived.

47. *He was teaching* (*ēn didaskōn*). Periphrastic imperfect. *Daily* (*to kath' hēmeran*). Note the accusative neuter article, "as to the according to the day," very awkward English surely, but perfectly good Greek. The same idiom occurs in 11:3. *Sought* (*ezētoun*). Imperfect active, conative imperfect, were seeking, trying to seek. *The principal men of the people* (*hoi prōtoi tou laou*). The first men of the people. The position after the verb and apart from the chief priests and the scribes calls special attention to them. Some of these "first men" were chief priests or scribes, but not all of them. The lights and leaders of Jerusalem were bent on the destruction (*apolesai*) of Jesus. The raising of Lazarus from the dead brought them together for this action (John 11:47–53; 12:9–11).

48. *They could not find* (*ouch hēuriskon*). Imperfect active. They kept on not finding. *What they might do* (*to ti poiēsōsin*). First aorist active deliberative subjunctive in a direct question retained in the indirect. Note the article *to* (neuter accusative) with the question. *Hung upon him* (*exekremeto autou*). Imperfect middle of *ekkremamai*, an old verb (*mi* form) to hang from, here only in the N.T. The form is an *omega* form from *ekkremomai*, a constant

tendency to the *omega* form in the *Koinê*. It pictures the
whole nation (save the leaders in verse 47) hanging upon
the words of Jesus as if in suspense in mid-air, rapt attention that angered these same leaders. Tyndal renders it
"stuck by him."

CHAPTER XX

1. *On one of the days* (*en miāi tōn hēmerōn*). Luke's favourite way of indicating time. It was the last day of the temple teaching (Tuesday). Luke 20:1–19 is to be compared with Mark 27–12:12 and Matt. 21:23–46. *There came upon him* (*epestēsan*). Second aorist active indicative, ingressive aorist of *ephistēmi*, old and common verb, stood up against him, with the notion of sudden appearance. These leaders (cf. 19:47) had determined to attack Jesus on this morning, both Sadducees (chief priests) and Pharisees (scribes), a formal delegation from the Sanhedrin.

2. *Tell us* (*eipon hēmin*). Luke adds these words to what Mark and Matthew have. Second aorist active imperative for the old form *eipe* and with ending -*on* of the first aorist active. Westcott and Hort punctuate the rest of the sentence as an indirect question after *eipon*, but the Revised Version puts a semicolon after "us" and retains the direct question. The Greek manuscripts have no punctuation.

3. *Question* (*logon*). Literally, word. So in Mark 11:29 = Matt. 21:24.

5. *They reasoned with themselves* (*sunelogisanto*). First aorist middle of *sullogizomai*, to bring together accounts, an old word, only here in the N.T. Mark and Matthew have *dielogizonto* (imperfect middle of *dialogizomai*, a kindred verb, to reckon between one another, confer). This form (*dielogizonto*) in verse 14 below. *If we shall say* (*ean eipōmen*). Third-class condition with second aorist active subjunctive. Suppose we say! So in verse 6.

6. *Will stone us* (*katalithasei*). Late verb and here only in the N.T. Literally, will throw stones down on us, stone us down, overwhelm us with stones. *They be persuaded*

249

(*pepeismenos estin*). Periphrastic perfect passive indicative of *peithō*, to persuade, a settled state of persuasion, "is persuaded" (no reason for use of "be" here). *That John was a prophet* (*Iōanēn prophētēn einai*). Accusative and infinitive in indirect assertion.

7. *That they knew not* (*mē eidenai*). Accusative and infinitive in indirect assertion again with the negative *mē* rather than *ou*.

9. *Vineyard* (*ampelōna*). Late word from *ampelos* (vine), place of vines. So in Mark 12:1 = Matt. 21:33. *Let it out* (*exedeto*). Second aorist middle of *ekdidōmi*, but with variable vowel *e* in place of *o* of the stem *do* (*exedoto*). Same form in Mark and Matthew. *For a long time* (*chronous hikanous*). Accusative of extent of time, considerable times or periods of time. Not in Mark and Matthew, though all three have *apedēmēsen* (went off from home). See on Luke 7:6 for *hikanos*.

10. *At the season* (*kairōi*). The definite season for the fruit like *ho kairos tōn karpōn* (Matt. 21:34). *That they should give* (*hina dōsousin*). Future indicative with *hina* for purpose like the aorist subjunctive, though not so frequent.

11. *He sent yet another* (*prosetheto heteron pempsai*). Literally, *he added to send another*. A clear Hebraism repeated in verse 12 and also in 19:11.

12. *They wounded* (*traumatisantes*). First aorist active participle of *traumatizō*. An old verb, from *trauma*, a wound, but in the N.T. only here and Acts 19:16.

13. *What shall I do?* (*Ti poiēsō;*). Deliberative future indicative or aorist subjunctive (same form). This detail only in Luke. Note the variations in all three Gospels. All three have "will reverence" (*entrapēsontai*) for which see Matthew and Mark. *It may be* (*isōs*). Perhaps, from *isos*, equal. Old adverb, but only here in the N.T.

14. *That the inheritance may be ours* (*hina hēmōn genētai*

hē klēronomia). That the inheritance may become (*genētai*, second aorist middle subjunctive of *ginomai*). Here Matt. 21:39 has *schōmen* "let us get, ingressive aorist active subjunctive." Cf. *echōmen*, present subjunctive of the same verb *echō* in Rom. 5:1; Mark 12:7 has "and it will be ours" (*estai*).

16. *God forbid* (*mē genoito*). Optative of wish about the future with *mē*. Literally, *may it not happen*. No word "God" in the Greek. This was the pious protest of the defeated members of the Sanhedrin who began to see the turn of the parable against themselves.

17. *He looked upon them* (*emblepsas autois*). Not in Mark and Matthew. First aorist active participle of *emblepō*, to look on. It was a piercing glance. The scripture quoted is from Psa. 118:22 and is in Mark 11:10 = Matt. 21:42, which see for the inverted attraction of the case *lithon* (stone) to that of the relative *hon* (which).

18. *Shall be broken to pieces* (*sunthlasthēsetai*). Future passive indicative of *sunthlaō*, a rather late compound, only here in the N.T. unless verse 44 in Matt. 21 is genuine. It means to shatter. *Will scatter him as dust* (*likmēsei*). From *likmaō*, an old verb to winnow and then to grind to powder. Only here in the N.T. unless verse 44 in Matt. 21 is genuine, which see.

19. *To lay hands on him* (*epibalein ep' auton tas cheiras*). Second aorist active infinitive of *epiballō*, an old verb and either transitively as here or intransitively as in Mark 4:37. Vivid picture here where Mark 12:12 = Matt. 21:46 has "to seize" (*kratēsai*). *In that very hour* (*en autēi tēi hōrāi*). Luke's favourite idiom, in the hour itself. Not in Mark or Matthew and shows that the Sanhedrin were angry enough to force the climax then. *And they feared* (*kai ephobēthēsan*). Adversative use of *kai* = but they feared. Hence they refrained. *For they perceived* (*egnōsan gar*). The reason for their rage. Second aorist active indicative of *ginōskō*.

Against them (*pros autous*). As in Mark 12:12. The cap fitted them and they saw it.

20. *They watched him* (*paratērēsantes*). First aorist active participle of *paratēreō*, a common Greek verb to watch on the side or insidiously or with evil intent as in Luke 6:7 (*paretērounto*) of the scribes and Pharisees. See on Mark 3:2. There is no "him" in the Greek. They were watching their chance. *Spies* (*enkathetous*). An old verbal adjective from *enkathiēmi*, to send down in or secretly. It means liers in wait who are suborned to spy out, one who is hired to trap one by crafty words. Only here in the N.T. *Feigned themselves* (*hupokrinomenous heautous*). Hypocritically professing to be "righteous" (*dikaious*). "They posed as scrupulous persons with a difficulty of conscience" (Plummer). *That they might take hold of his speech* (*hina epilabōntai autou logou*). Second aorist middle of *epilambanō*, an old verb for seizing hold with the hands and uses as here the genitive case. These spies are for the purpose of (*hina*) catching hold of the talk of Jesus if they can get a grip anywhere. This is their direct purpose and the ultimate purpose or result is also stated, "so as to deliver him up" (*hōste paradounai auton*). Second aorist active infinitive of *paradidōmi*, to hand over, to give from one's side to another. The trap is all set now and ready to be sprung by these "spies." *Of the governor* (*tou hēgemonos*). The Sanhedrin knew that Pilate would have to condemn Jesus if he were put to death. So then all their plans focus on this point as the goal. Luke alone mentions this item here.

21. *Rightly* (*orthōs*). Matthew (22:16) notes that these "spies" were "disciples" (students) of the Pharisees and Mark (12:13) adds that the Herodians are also involved in the plot. These bright theologues are full of palaver and flattery and openly endorse the teaching of Jesus as part of their scheme. *Acceptest not the person of any* (*ou lambaneis prosōpon*). Dost not take the face (or personal appearance)

as the test. It is a Hebraism from which the word *prosōpo-lempsia* (James 2:1) comes. Originally it meant to lift the face, to lift the countenance, to regard the face, to accept the face value. See Mark 12:13–17 and Matt. 22:15–22 for discussion of details here. They both have *blepeis* here.

22. *Tribute* (*phoron*). Old word for the annual tax on land, houses, etc. Mark and Matthew have *kēnson*, which see for this Latin word in Greek letters. The picture on the coin may have been that of Tiberius.

23. *Perceived* (*katanoēsas*). From *katanoeō*, to put the mind down on. Mark has *eidōs*, "knowing," and Matthew *gnous*, coming to know or grasping (second aorist active participle of *ginōskō*). *Craftiness* (*panourgian*). Old word for doing any deed. Matthew has "wickedness" (*ponērian*) and Mark "hypocrisy" (*hupokrisin*). Unscrupulous they certainly were. They would stoop to any trick and go the limit.

26. *They were not able* (*ouk ischusan*). They did not have strength. An old verb *ischuō* from *ischus* (strength). They failed "to take hold (cf. verse 20) of the saying before the people." These "crack" students had made an ignominious failure and were not able to make a case for the surrender of Jesus to Pilate. He had slipped through their net with the utmost ease. *Held their peace* (*esigēsan*). Ingressive aorist active of *sigaō*. They became silent as they went back with the "dry grins."

27. *There is no resurrection* (*anastasin mē einai*). Accusative and infinitive with negative *mē* in indirect assertion. The Sadducees rally after the complete discomfiture of the Pharisees and Herodians. They had a stock conundrum with which they had often gotten a laugh on the Pharisees. So they volunteer to try it on Jesus. For discussion of details here see on Matt. 22:23–33 and Mark 12:18–27. Only a few striking items remain for Luke.

33. *Had her* (*eschon*). Constative second aorist indicative of *echō* including all seven seriatim. So Matt. 22:28 = Mark

12:33. *To wife* (*gunaika*). As wife, accusative in apposition with "her."

36. *Equal unto the angels* (*isaggeloi*). A rare and late word from *isos*, equal, and *aggelos*. Only here in the N.T. Mark and Matthew have "as angels" (*hōs aggeloi*). Angels do not marry, there is no marriage in heaven. *Sons of God, being sons of the resurrection* (*huioi theou tēs anastaseōs huioi ontes*). This Hebraistic phrase, "sons of the resurrection" defines "sons of God" and is a direct answer to the Sadducees.

37. *Even Moses* (*kai Mōusēs*). Moses was used by the Sadducees to support their denial of the resurrection. This passage (Ex. 3:6) Jesus skilfully uses as a proof of the resurrection. See discussion on Matt. 22:32 = Mark 12:26f.

39. *Certain of the scribes* (*tines tōn grammateōn*). Pharisees who greatly enjoyed this use by Jesus of a portion of the Pentateuch against the position of the Sadducees. So they praise the reply of Jesus, hostile though they are to him.

40. *They durst not any more* (*ouketi etolmōn ouden*). Double negative and imperfect active of *tolmaō*. The courage of Pharisees, Sadducees, Herodians vanished.

41. *How say they?* (*Pōs legousin;*). The Pharisees had rallied in glee and one of their number, a lawyer, had made a feeble contribution to the controversy which resulted in his agreement with Jesus and in praise from Jesus (Mark 12:28–34 = Matt. 27:34–40). Luke does not give this incident which makes it plain that by "they say" (*legousin*) Jesus refers to the Pharisees (rabbis, lawyers), carrying on the discussion and turning the tables on them while the Pharisees are still gathered together (Matt. 22:41). The construction with *legousin* is the usual infinitive and the accusative in indirect discourse. By "the Christ" (*ton Christon*) "the Messiah" is meant.

42. *For David himself* (*autos gar Daueid*). This language of Jesus clearly means that he treats David as the author of Psalm 110. The inspiration of this Psalm is expressly stated

in Mark 12:36 = Matt. 22:43 (which see) and the Messianic
character of the Psalm in all three Synoptics who all quote
the LXX practically alike.   Modern criticism that denies
the Davidic authorship of this Psalm has to say either that
Jesus was ignorant of the fact about it or that he declined to
disturb the current acceptation of the Davidic authorship.
Certainly modern scholars are not agreed on the authorship
of Psalm 110.   Meanwhile one can certainly be excused for
accepting the natural implication of the words of Jesus here,
"David himself."   *In the book of the Psalms (en biblōi Psal-
mōn)*.   Compare 3:4 "in the book of the words of Isaiah the
prophet."

44. *David therefore (Daueid oun)*.   Without *ei* as in Matthew 22:45.   On the basis of this definite piece of exegesis
(*oun*, therefore) Jesus presses the problem (*pōs*, how) for an
explanation.   The deity and the humanity of the Messiah in
Psalm 110 are thus set forth, the very problems that disturbed the rabbis then and that upset many critics today.

45. *In the hearing of all the people (akouontos pantos tou
laou)*.   Genitive absolute, "while all the people were listening" (present active participle).   That is the time to speak.
The details in this verse and verse 47 are precisely those
given in Mark 12:38f., which see for discussion of details.
Matt. 23:1–39 has a very full and rich description of this
last phase of the debate in the temple where Jesus drew a
full-length portrait of the hypocrisy of the Pharisees and
scribes in their presence.   It was a solemn climax to this
last public appearance of Christ in the temple when Jesus
poured out the vials of his indignation as he had done before
(Matt. 6:12; Luke 11:12, 15–18).

CHAPTER XXI

1. *And he looked up* (*Anablepsas de*). He had taken his seat, after the debate was over and the Sanhedrin had slunk away in sheer defeat, "over against the treasury" (Mark 12:41). The word for "treasury" (*gazophulakion*) is a compound of *gaza* (Persian word for royal treasury) and *phulakē* guard or protection. It is common in the LXX, but in the N.T. only here and Mark 12:41, 43 and John 8:20. Jesus was watching (Mark 12:41) the rich put in their gifts as a slight diversion from the intense strain of the hours before.

2. *Poor* (*penichran*). A rare word from *penēs* (*penomai*, to work for one's living). Latin *penuria* and Greek *peinaō*, to be hungry are kin to it. Here only in the N.T. Mark 12:42 has *ptōchē*, a more common word from *ptōssō*, to be frightened, to strike and hide from fear, to be in beggary. And Luke uses this adjective also of her in verse 3.

3. *More than they all* (*pleion pantōn*). Ablative case after the comparative *pleion*.

4. *All these did cast* (*pantes houtoi ebalon*). Constative second aorist active indicative covering the whole crowd except the widow. *Living* (*bion*). Livelihood as in Mark 12:44, not *zōēn*, principle of life.

5. *As some spake* (*tinōn legontōn*). Genitive absolute. The disciples we know from Mark 13:1 = Matt. 24:1. *How* (*hoti*). Literally, "that." *It was adorned* (*kekosmētai*). Perfect passive indicative, state of completion, stands adorned, tense retained in indirect discourse, though English has to change it. *Kosmeō*, old and common verb for orderly arrangement and adorning. *With goodly stones and offerings* (*lithois kalois kai anathēmasin*). Instrumental case. Some of these stones in the substructure were enormous. "The

columns of the cloister or portico were monoliths of marble over forty feet high" (Plummer). Cf. Josephus, *War*, V. 5. The word *anathēma* (here only in the N.T.) is not to be confused with *anathema* from the same verb *anatithēmi*, but which came to mean a curse (Gal. 1:8; Acts 23:14). So *anathema* came to mean devoted in a bad sense, *anathēma* in a good sense. "Thus *knave*, lad, becomes a *rascal; villain*, a *farmer*, becomes a *scoundrel; cunning, skilful*, becomes *crafty*" (Vincent). These offerings in the temple were very numerous and costly (II Macc. 3:2–7) like the golden vine of Herod with branches as tall as a man (Josephus, *Ant.* XV. ii. 3).

6. *As for these things* (*tauta*). Accusative of general reference. *One stone upon another* (*lithos epi lithōi*). Stone upon stone (locative). Here both Mark 13:2 and Matt. 24:2 have *epi lithon* (accusative). Instead of *ouk aphethēsetai* (future passive) they both have *ou mē aphethēi* (double negative with aorist passive subjunctive). It was a shock to the disciples to hear this after the triumphal entry.

8. *That ye be not led astray* (*mē planēthēte*). First aorist passive subjunctive with *mē* (lest). This verb *planaō* occurs here only in Luke though often in the rest of the N.T. (as Matt. 24:4, 5, 11, 24, which see). Our word *planet* is from this word. *The time is at hand* (*ho kairos ēggiken*). Just as John the Baptist did of the kingdom (Matt. 3:2) and Jesus also (Mark 1:15). *Go ye not after them* (*mē poreuthēte opisō autōn*). First aorist passive subjunctive with *mē*. A needed warning today with all the false cries in the religious world.

9. *Be not terrified* (*mē ptoēthēte*). First aorist passive subjunctive with *mē* from *ptoeō* an old verb to terrify, from *ptoa*, terror. In the N.T. only here and Luke 24:37. *First* (*Prōton*). It is so easy to forget this and to insist that the end is "immediately" in spite of Christ's explicit denial here. See Matt. 24:4–42 and Mark 13:1–37 for discussion of details for Luke 21:8–36, the great eschatological discourse of Jesus

11. *Famines and pestilences* (*loimoi kai limoi*). Play on the two words pronounced just alike in the *Koiné* (itacism). *And terrors* (*phobēthra te*). The use of *te* . . . *te* in this verse groups the two kinds of woes. This rare word *phobēthra* is only here in the N.T. It is from *phobeō*, to frighten, and occurs only in the plural as here.

12. *But before all these things* (*pro de toutōn pantōn*). In Mark 13:8 = Matt. 24:8 these things are termed "the beginning of travail." That may be the idea here. Plummer insists that priority of time is the point, not magnitude. *Bringing you* (*apagomenous*). Present passive participle from *apagō*, an old verb to lead off or away. But here the participle is in the accusative plural, not the nominative like *paradidontes* (present active participle, delivering you up), agreeing with *humas* not expressed the object of *paradidontes*, "you being brought before or led off." "A technical term in Athenian legal language" (Bruce).

13. *It shall turn unto you* (*apobēsetai humin*). Future middle of *apobainō*. It will come off, turn out for you (dative of advantage). *For a testimony* (*eis marturion*). To their loyalty to Christ. Besides, "the blood of the martyrs is the seed of the church."

14. *Not to meditate beforehand* (*mē promeletāin*). The classical word for conning a speech beforehand. Mark 13:11 has *promerimnaō*, a later word which shows previous anxiety rather than previous preparation. *How to answer* (*apologēthēnai*). First aorist passive infinitive. It is the preparation for the speech of defence (apology) that Jesus here forbids, not the preparation of a sermon.

15. *Your adversaries* (*hoi antikeimenoi humin*). Those who stand against, line up face to face with (note *anti-*). *To withstand or to gainsay* (*antistēnai ē anteipein*). Two second aorist active infinitives with *anti-* in composition again. But these "antis" will go down before the power of Christ.

16. *Shall they cause to be put to death* (*thanatōsousin*).

Future active of *thanatoō*, to put to death or to make to die
(causative). Either makes sense here. Old and common
verb.

17. *Not a hair of your head shall perish (thrix ek tēs kephalēs
humōn ou mē apolētai).* Only in Luke. Second aorist middle
subjunctive of *apollumi* with *ou mē* (double negative). Jesus
has just said that some they will put to death. Hence it is
spiritual safety here promised such as Paul claimed about
death in Phil. 1:21.

19. *Ye shall win (ktēsesthe).* Future middle of *ktaomai*,
to acquire. They will win their souls even if death does
come.

20. *Compassed with armies (kukloumenēn hupo stratopedōn).* Present passive participle of *kukloō*, to circle, en-
circle, from *kuklos*, circle. Old verb, but only four times in
N.T. The point of this warning is the present tense, being
encircled. It will be too late after the city is surrounded.
It is objected by some that Jesus, not to say Luke, could
not have spoken (or written) these words before the Roman
armies came. One may ask why not, if such a thing as
predictive prophecy can exist and especially in the case of
the Lord Jesus. The word *stratopedōn (stratos,* army, *pedon,*
plain) is a military camp and then an army in camp. Old
word, but only here in the N.T. *Then know (tote gnōte).*
Second aorist active imperative of *ginōskō.* Christians did
flee from Jerusalem to Pella before it was too late as directed
in Luke 21:21 = Mark 13:14f. = Matt. 24:16f.

22. *That may be fulfilled (tou plēsthēnai).* Articular infinitive passive to express purpose with accusative of general reference. The O.T. has many such warnings (Hosea
9:7; Deut. 28:49–57, etc.).

24. *Edge of the sword (stomati machairēs).* Instrumental
case of *stomati* which means "mouth" literally (Gen. 34:26).
This verse like the close of verse 22 is only in Luke. Josephus
(*War,* VI. 9. 3) states that 1,100,000 Jews perished in the

destruction of Jerusalem and 97,000 were taken captive. Surely this is an exaggeration and yet the number must have been large. *Shall be led captive (aichmalōtisthēsontai).* Future passive of *aichmalōtizō* from *aichmē*, spear and *halōtos (haliskomai).* Here alone in the literal sense in the N.T. *Shall be trodden under foot (estai patoumenē).* Future passive periphrastic of *pateō*, to tread, old verb. *Until the times of the Gentiles be fulfilled (achri hou plērōthōsin kairoi ethnōn).* First aorist passive subjunctive with *achri hou* like *heōs hou.* What this means is not clear except that Paul in Rom. 11:25 shows that the punishment of the Jews has a limit. The same idiom appears there also with *achri hou* and the aorist subjunctive.

25. *Distress (sunochē).* From *sunechō.* In the N.T. only here and II Cor. 2:4. Anguish. *In perplexity (en aporiāi).* State of one who is *aporos*, who has lost his way (*a* privative and *poros*). Here only in the N.T. though an old and common word. *For the roaring of the sea (ēchous thalassēs).* Our word echo (Latin *echo*) is this word *ēchos*, a reverberating sound. Sense of rumour in Luke 4:37. *Billows (salou).* Old word *salos* for the swell of the sea. Here only in the N.T.

26. *Men fainting (apopsuchontōn anthrōpōn).* Genitive absolute of *apopsuchō*, to expire, to breathe off or out. Old word. Here only in N.T. *Expectation (prosdokias).* Old word from *prosdokaō*, to look for or towards. In the N.T. only here and Acts 12:11. *The world (tēi oikoumenēi).* Dative case, "the inhabited" (earth, *gēi*).

27. *And then shall they see (kai tote opsontai).* As much as to say that it will be not till then. Clearly the promise of the second coming of the Son of man in glory here (= Mark 13:26f. = Matt. 24:30f.) is pictured as not one certain of immediate realization. The time element is left purposely vague.

28. *Look up (anakupsate).* First aorist active imperative of *anakuptō*, to raise up. Here of the soul as in John 8:7, 10,

but in Luke 13:11 of the body. These the only N.T. examples of this common verb. *Redemption (apolutrōsis).* Act of redeeming from *apolutroō.* The final act at the second coming of Christ, a glorious hope.

29. *The fig tree, and all the trees (tēn sukēn kai panta ta dendra).* This parable of the fig-tree (= Mark 13:28–32 = Matt. 24:32–35) Luke applies to "all the trees." It is true about all of them, but the fig tree was very common in Palestine.

30. *Shoot forth (probalōsin).* Second aorist active subjunctive of *proballō,* common verb, but in the N.T. only here and Acts 19:33. *Summer (theros).* Not harvest, but summer. Old word, but in the N.T. only here (= Mark 13:28 = Matt. 24:32).

31. *Coming to pass (ginomena).* Present middle participle of *ginomai* and so descriptive of the process. *Nigh (eggus).* The consummation of the kingdom is here meant, not the beginning.

32. *This generation (hē genea hautē).* Naturally people then living. *Shall not pass away (ou mē parelthēi).* Second aorist active subjunctive of *parerchomai.* Strongest possible negative with *ou mē. Till all things be accomplished (heōs an panta genētai).* Second aorist middle subjunctive of *ginomai* with *heōs,* common idiom. The words give a great deal of trouble to critics. Some apply them to the whole discourse including the destruction of the temple and Jerusalem, the second coming and the end of the world. Some of these argue that Jesus was simply mistaken in his eschatology, some that he has not been properly reported in the Gospels. Others apply them only to the destruction of Jerusalem which did take place in A.D. 70 before that generation passed away. It must be said for this view that it is not easy in this great eschatological discourse to tell clearly when Jesus is discussing the destruction of Jerusalem and when the second coming. Plummer offers this solution:

"The reference, therefore, is to the destruction of Jerusalem regarded as the type of the end of the world."

33. *My words shall not pass away* (*hoi logoi mou ou mē pareleusontai*). Future middle indicative with *ou mē*, a bit stronger statement than the subjunctive. It is noteworthy that Jesus utters these words just after the difficult prediction in verse 32.

34. *Lest haply your hearts be overcharged* (*mē pote barēthōsin hai kardiai humōn*). First aorist passive subjunctive of *bareō*, an old verb to weigh down, depress, with *mē pote*. *With surfeiting* (*en krepalēi*). A rather late word, common in medical writers for the nausea that follows a debauch. Latin *crapula*, the giddiness caused by too much wine. Here only in the N.T. *Drunkenness* (*methēi*). From *methu* (wine). Old word but in the N.T. only here and Rom. 13:13; Gal. 5:21. *Cares of this life* (*merimnais biōtikais*). Anxieties of life. The adjective *biōtikos* is late and in the N.T. only here and I Cor. 6:3f. *Come on you* (*epistēi*). Second aorist active subjunctive of *ephistēmi*, ingressive aorist. Construed also with *mē pote*. *Suddenly* (*ephnidios*). Adjective in predicate agreeing with *hēmera* (day). *As a snare* (*hōs pagis*). Old word from *pēgnumi*, to make fast a net or trap. Paul uses it several times of the devil's snares for preachers (I Tim. 3:7; II Tim. 2:26).

36. *But watch ye* (*agrupneite de*). *Agrupneō* is a late verb to be sleepless (*a* privative and *hupnos*, sleep). Keep awake and be ready is the pith of Christ's warning. *That ye may prevail to escape* (*hina katischusēte ekphugein*). First aorist active subjunctive with *hina* of purpose. The verb *katischuō* means to have strength against (cf. Matt. 16:18). Common in later writers. *Ekphugein* is second aorist active infinitive, to escape out. *To stand before the Son of man* (*stathēnai emprosthen tou huiou tou anthrōpou*). That is the goal. There will be no dread of the Son then if one is ready. *Stathēnai* is first aorist passive infinitive of *histēmi*.

37. *Every day* (*tas hēmeras*). During the days, accusative of extent of time. *Every night* (*tas nuktas*). "During the nights," accusative of extent of time. *Lodged* (*ēulizeto*). Imperfect middle, was lodging, *aulizomai* from *aulē* (court).

38. *Came early* (*ōrthrizen*). Imperfect active of *orthrizō* from *orthros*, late form for *orthreuō*, to rise early. Only here in the N.T.

CHAPTER XXII

1. *The Passover* (*pascha*) Both names (unleavened bread and passover) are used here as in Mark 14:1. Strictly speaking the passover was Nisan 14 and the unleavened bread 15–21. This is the only place in the N.T. where the expression "the feast of unleavened bread" (common in LXX, Ex. 23: 15, etc.) occurs, for Mark 14:1 has just "the unleavened bread." Matt. 26:17 uses unleavened bread and passover interchangeably. *Drew nigh* (*ēggizen*). Imperfect active. Mark 14:1 and Matt. 26:2 mention "after two days" definitely.

2. *Sought* (*ezētoun*). Imperfect active of *zēteō*, were seeking, conative imperfect. *How they might put him to death* (*to pōs anelōsin auton*). Second aorist active deliberative subjunctive (retained in indirect question) of *anaireō*, to take up, to make away with, to slay. Common in Old Greek. Luke uses it so here and in 23:32 and eighteen times in the Acts, a favourite word with him. Note the accusative neuter singular article *to* with the whole clause, "as to the how, etc." *For they feared* (*ephobounto gar*). Imperfect middle describing the delay of the "how." The triumphal entry and the temple speeches of Jesus had revealed his tremendous power with the people, especially the crowds from Galilee at the feast. They were afraid to go on with their plan to kill him at the feast.

3. *Satan entered into Judas* (*eisēlthen eis Ioudan*). Ingressive aorist active indicative. Satan was now renewing his attack on Jesus suspended temporarily (Luke 4:13) "until a good chance." He had come back by the use of Simon Peter (Mark 8:33 = Matt. 16:23). The conflict went on and Jesus won ultimate victory (Luke 10:18). Now Satan

uses Judas and has success with him for Judas allowed him to come again and again (John 13:27). Judas evidently opened the door to his heart and let Satan in. Then Satan took charge and he became a devil as Jesus said (John 6:70). This surrender to Satan in no way relieves Judas of his moral responsibility.

4. *Went away* (*apelthōn*). Second aorist active participle of *aperchomai*. He went off under the impulse of Satan and after the indignation over the rebuke of Jesus at the feast in Simon's house (John 12:4–6). *Captains* (*stratēgois*). Leaders of the temple guards (Acts 4:1), the full title, "captains of the temple," occurs in verse 52. *How he might deliver him unto them* (*to pōs autois paradoi auton*). The same construction as in verse 2, the article *to* with the indirect question and deliberative subjunctive second aorist active (*paradoi*).

5. *Were glad* (*echarēsan*). Second aorist passive indicative of *chairō* as in Mark 14:11. Ingressive aorist, a natural exultation that one of the Twelve had offered to do this thing. *Covenanted* (*sunethento*). Second aorist indicative middle of *suntithēmi*. An old verb to put together and in the middle with one another. In the N.T. outside of John 9:22 only in Luke (here and Acts 23:20; 24:9). Luke only mentions "money" (*argurion*), but not "thirty pieces" (Matt. 26:15).

6. *Consented* (*exōmologēsen*). Old verb, but the ancients usually used the simple form for promise or consent rather than the compound. This is the only instance of this sense in the N.T. It is from *homologos* (*homos*, same, and *legō*, to say), to say the same thing with another and so agree. *Opportunity* (*eukarian*). From *eukairos* (*eu, kairos*), a good chance. Old word, but in the N.T. only here and parallel passage Matt. 26:16. *In the absence of the multitude* (*ater ochlou*). *Ater* is an old preposition, common in the poets, but rare in prose. Also in verse 35. It means "without," "apart from," like *chōris*. The point of Judas was just this. He would get Jesus into the hands of the Sanhedrin

during the feast in spite of the crowd. It was necessary to avoid tumult (Matt. 26:5) because of the popularity of Jesus.

7. *The day of unleavened bread came* (*ēlthen hē hēmera tōn azumōn*). The day itself came, not simply was drawing nigh (verse 1). *Must be sacrificed* (*edei thuesthai*). This was Nisan 14 which began at sunset. Luke is a Gentile and this fact must be borne in mind. The lamb must be slain by the head of the family (Ex. 12:6). The controversy about the day when Christ ate the last passover meal has already been discussed (Matt. 26:17 = Mark 14:12). The Synoptics clearly present this as a fact. Jesus was then crucified on Friday at the passover or Thursday (our time) at the regular hour 6 P.M. (beginning of Friday). The five passages in John (13:1f.; 13:27; 18:28; 19:14; 19:31) rightly interpreted teach the same thing as shown in my *Harmony of the Gospels for Students of the Life of Christ* (pp. 279–284).

8. *Peter and John* (*Petron kai Iōanēn*). Mark 14:13 has only "two" while Matt. 26:17 makes the disciples take the initiative. The word passover in this context is used either of the meal, the feast day, the whole period (including the unleavened bread). "Eat the passover" can refer to the meal as here or to the whole period of celebration (John 18:28).

9. *Where wilt thou that we make ready?* (*Pou theleis hetoimasōmen;*). Deliberative first aorist active subjunctive without *hina* after *theleis*, perhaps originally two separate questions.

10. *When you are entered* (*eiselthontōn humōn*). Genitive absolute. *Meet you* (*sunantēsei humin*). An old verb *sunantaō* (from *sun*, with, and *antaō*, to face, *anti*) with associative instrumental (*humin*). See on Mark 14:13 about the "man bearing a pitcher of water."

11. *Goodman of the house* (*oikodespotēi*). Master of the house as in Mark 14:14 and Matt. 10:25. A late word for the

earlier *despotēs oikou*. *I shall eat* (*phagō*). Second aorist
futuristic (or deliberative) subjunctive as in Mark 14:14.

12. *And he* (*k'akeinos*). *Kai* and *ekeinos* (*crasis*) where
Mark 14:15 has *kai autos*. Literally, And that one. See on
Mark for rest of the verse.

13. *He had said* (*eirēkei*). Past perfect active indicative
of *eipon* where Mark 14:16 has *eipen* (second aorist).

14. *Sat down* (*anepesen*). Reclined, fell back (or up).
Second aorist active of *anapiptō*.

15. *With desire I have desired* (*epithumiāi epethumēsa*).
A Hebraism common in the LXX. Associative instrumental
case of substantive and first aorist active indicative of same
like a cognate accusative. Peculiar to Luke is all this verse.
See this idiom in John 3:29; Acts 4:17. *Before I suffer* (*pro
tou me pathein*). Preposition *pro* with articular infinitive and
accusative of general reference, "before the suffering as to
me." *Pathein* is second aorist active infinitive of *paschō*.

16. *Until it be fulfilled* (*heōs hotou plērōthēi*). First aorist
passive subjunctive of *plēroō* with *heōs* (*hotou*), the usual
construction about the future. It seems like a Messianic
banquet that Jesus has in mind (cf. 14:15).

17. *He received a cup* (*dexamenos potērion*). This cup is a
diminutive of *potēr*. It seems that this is still one of the four
cups passed during the passover meal, though which one is
uncertain. It is apparently just before the formal introduction of the Lord's Supper, though he gave thanks here also
(*eucharistēsas*). It is from this verb *eucharisteō* (see also
verse 19) that our word Eucharist comes. It is a common
verb for giving thanks and was used also for "saying grace"
as we call it.

18. *The fruit of the vine* (*tou genēmatos tēs ampelou*). So
Mark 14:25 = Matt. 26:29 and not *oinos* though it was wine
undoubtedly. But the language allows anything that is
"the fruit of the vine." *Come* (*elthēi*). Second aorist active
subjunctive with *heōs* as in verse 16. Here it is the consum-

mation of the kingdom that Jesus has in mind, for the kingdom had already come.

19. *Which is given for you* (*to huper humōn didomenon*). Some MSS. omit these verses though probably genuine. The correct text in I Cor. 11:24 has "which is for you," not "which is broken for you." It is curious to find the word "broken" here preserved and justified so often, even by Easton in his commentary on Luke, p. 320. *In remembrance of me* (*eis tēn emēn anamnēsin*). Objective use of the possessive pronoun *emēn*, not the subjective. *This do* (*touto poieite*). Present active indicative, repetition, keep on doing this.

20. *After the supper* (*meta to deipnēsai*). Preposition *meta* and the accusative articular infinitive. The textual situation here is confusing, chiefly because of the two cups (verses 17 and 20). Some of the documents omit the latter part of verse 19 and all of verse 20. It is possible, of course, that this part crept into the text of Luke from I Cor. 11:24f. But, if this part is omitted, Luke would then have the order reversed, the cup before the bread. So there are difficulties whichever turn one takes here with Luke's text whether one cup or two cups. *The New Covenant* (*he kainē diathēkē*). See on Matt. 26:28 = Mark 14:24 for "covenant." Westcott and Hort reject "new" there, but accept it here and in I Cor. 11:25. See on Luke 5:38 for difference between *kainē* and *nea*. "The ratification of a covenant was commonly associated with the shedding of blood; and what was written in blood was believed to be indelible" (Plummer). *Poured out* (*ekchunnomenon*). Same word in Mark 14:24 = Matt. 26:28 translated "shed." Late form present passive participle of *ekchunnō* of *ekcheō*, to pour out.

21. *That betrayeth* (*tou paradidontos*). Present active participle, actually engaged in doing it. The hand of Judas was resting on the table at the moment. It should be noted that Luke narrates the institution of the Lord's Supper before

the exposure of Judas as the traitor while Mark and Matthew reverse this order.

22. *As it hath been determined* (*kata to hōrismenon*). Perfect passive participle of *horizō*, to limit or define, mark off the border, our "horizon." But this fact does not absolve Judas of his guilt as the "woe" here makes plain.

23. *Which of them it was* (*to tis ara eiē ex autōn*). Note the article *to* with the indirect question as in verses 2 and 4. The optative *eiē* here is changed from the present active indicative *estin*, though it was not always done, for see *dokei* in verse 24 where the present indicative is retained. They all had their hands on the table. Whose hand was it?

24. *Contention* (*philoneikia*). An old word from *philoneikos*, fond of strife, eagerness to contend. Only here in the N.T. *Greatest* (*meizōn*). Common use of the comparative as superlative.

25. *Have lordship over* (*kurieuousin*). From *kurios*. Common verb, to lord it over. *Benefactors* (*euergetai*). From *eu* and *ergon*. Doer of good. Old word. Here only in the N.T. Latin Benefactor is exact equivalent.

26. *Become* (*ginesthō*). Present middle imperative of *ginomai*. Act so. True greatness is in service, not in rank.

27. *But I* (*Egō de*). Jesus dares to cite his own conduct, though their leader, to prove his point and to put a stop to their jealous contention for the chief place at this very feast, a wrangling that kept up till Jesus had to arise and give them the object lesson of humility by washing their feet (John 13:1–20).

28. *In my temptations* (*en tois peirasmois mou*). Probably "trials" is better here as in James 1:2 though temptations clearly in James 1:13ff. This is the tragedy of the situation when Jesus is facing the Cross with the traitor at the table and the rest chiefly concerned about their own primacy and dignity.

29. *And I appoint unto you* (*kăgō diatithēmai humin*).

They had on the whole been loyal and so Jesus passes on to them (*diathēmai* verb from which *diathēkē* comes).

30. *And ye shall sit* (*kathēsesthe*). But Westcott and Hort read in the text *kathēsthe* (present middle subjunctive with *hina*). The picture seems to be that given in Matt. 19:28 when Jesus replied to Peter's inquiry. It is not clear how literally this imagery is to be taken. But there is the promise of honour for the loyal among these in the end.

31. *Asked to have you* (*exēitēsato*). First aorist indirect middle indicative of *exaiteō*, an old verb to beg something of one and (middle) for oneself. Only here in the N.T. The verb is used either in the good or the bad sense, but it does not mean here "obtained by asking" as margin in Revised Version has it. *That he might sift you* (*tou siniasai*). Genitive articular infinitive of purpose. First aorist active infinitive of *siniazō*, to shake a sieve, to sift, from *sinion*, a winnowing fan. Later word. Here only in the N.T.

32. *That thy faith fail not* (*hina mē eklipēi he pistis mou*). Second aorist active subjunctive of purpose with *hina* after *edeēthēn* (*I prayed*) of *ekleipō*, old verb. Our word *eclipse* is this word. Evidently Jesus could not keep Satan from attacking Peter. He had already captured Judas. Did he not repeatedly attack Jesus? But he could and did pray for Peter's faith and his praying won in the end, though Peter stumbled and fell. *And do thou* (*kai su*). The words single out Peter sharply. *Once thou hast turned again* (*pote epistrepsas*). First aorist active participle of *epistrephō*, common verb to turn to, to return. But the use of this word implied that Peter would fall though he would come back and "strengthen thy brethren."

33. *To prison and to death* (*eis phulakēn kai eis thanaton*). Evidently Peter was not flattered by the need of Christ's earnest prayers for his welfare and loyalty. Hence this loud boast.

34. *Until thou shalt thrice deny that thou knowest me* (*heōs*

tris me aparnēsēi eidenai). "Thrice" is in all four Gospels here for they all give this warning to Peter (Mark 14:30 = Matt. 26:34 = Luke 22:34 = John 18:38). Peter will even deny knowing Jesus (*eidenai*).

35. *Without purse* (*ater ballantiou*). Money bag or purse. Old word, but in the N.T. only in Luke (10:4; 12:33; 22: 35ff.). *Wallet* (*pēras*). See on Matt. 10:10. *Lacked ye anything* (*mē tinos husterēsate;*). Answer No expected (*outhenos* below). Ablative case after *hustereō*.

36. *Buy a sword* (*agorasatō machairan*). This is for defence clearly. The reference is to the special mission in Galilee (Luke 9:1–6 = Mark 6:6–13 = Matt. 9:35–11:1). They are to expect persecution and bitter hostility (John 15:18–21). Jesus does not mean that his disciples are to repel force by force, but that they are to be ready to defend his cause against attack. Changed conditions bring changed needs. This language can be misunderstood as it was then.

38. *Lord, behold, here are two swords* (*kurie idou machairai hōde duo*). They took his words literally. And before this very night is over Peter will use one of these very swords to try to cut off the head of Malchus only to be sternly rebuked by Jesus (Mark 14:47 = Matt. 26:51f. = Luke 22:50f. = John 18:10f.). Then Jesus will say: "For all that take the sword shall perish with the sword" (Matt. 26:52). Clearly Jesus did not mean his language even about the sword to be pressed too literally. So he said: "It is enough" (*Hikanon estin*). It is with sad irony and sorrow that Jesus thus dismisses the subject. They were in no humour now to understand the various sides of this complicated problem. Every preacher and teacher understands this mood, not of impatience, but of closing the subject for the present.

39. *As his custom was* (*kata to ethos*). According to the custom (of him). It was because Judas knew the habit of Jesus of going to Gethsemane at night that he undertook

to betray him without waiting for the crowd to go home
after the feast.

40. *At the place* (*epi tou topou*).   The place of secret prayer
which was dear to Jesus.   *Pray that ye enter not into temptation* (*proseuchesthe mē eiselthein eis peirasmon*).   "Keep on
praying not to enter (ingressive aorist infinitive, not even
once) into temptation."   It is real "temptation" here, not
just "trial."   Jesus knew the power of temptation and the
need of prayer.   These words throw a light on the meaning
of his language in Matt. 6:13.   Jesus repeats this warning
in verse 46.

41. *About a stone's throw* (*hōsei lithou bolēn*).   Accusative
of extent of space.   Luke does not tell of leaving eight disciples by the entrance to Gethsemane nor about taking Peter,
James, and John further in with him.   *Kneeled down* (*theis ta
gonata*).   Second aorist active participle from *tithēmi*.   Mark
14:35 says "fell on the ground" and Matt. 26:39 "fell on
his face."   All could be true at different moments.   *Prayed*
(*proseucheto*).   Imperfect middle, was praying, kept on praying.

42. *If thou be willing* (*ei boulei*).   This condition is in the
first petition at the start.   *Be done* (*ginesthō*).   Present middle imperative, keep on being done, the Father's will.

43. *An angel* (*aggelos*).   The angels visited Jesus at the
close of the three temptations at the beginning of his
ministry (Matt. 4:11).   Here the angel comes during the
conflict.

44. *In an agony* (*en agōniāi*).   It was conflict, contest
from *agōn*.   An old word, but only here in the N.T.   Satan
pressed Jesus harder than ever before.   *As it were great drops
of blood* (*hōsei thromboi haimatos*).   Thick, clotted blood.
An old word (*thromboi*) common in medical works, but here
only in the N.T.   This passage (verses 43 and 44) is absent
from some ancient documents.   Aristotle speaks of a bloody
sweat as does Theophrastus.

45. *Sleeping for sorrow* (*koimōmenous apo tēs lupēs*). Luke does not tell of the three turnings of Jesus to the trusted three for human sympathy.

46. *Why sleep ye?* (*Ti katheudete;*). This reproach Luke gives, but not the almost bitter details in Mark 14:37–42 = Matt. 26:40–46).

47. *Went before them* (*proērcheto*). Imperfect middle. Judas was leading the band for he knew the place well (John 18:2).

48. *With a kiss* (*philēmati*). Instrumental case. Jesus challenges the act of Judas openly and calls it betrayal, but it did not stop him.

49. *What would follow* (*to esomenon*). Article and the future middle participle of *eimi*, to be. *Shall we smite with a sword?* (*ei pataxomen en machairēi;*). Note *ei* in a direct question like the Hebrew. Luke alone gives this question. Instrumental use of *en*. They had the two swords already mentioned (22:38).

50. *His right ear* (*to ous autou to dexion*). Mark 14:47 and Matt. 26:51 do not mention "right," but Luke the Physician does. John 18:10 follows Luke in this item and also adds the names of Peter and of Malchus since probably both were dead by that time and Peter would not be involved in trouble.

51. *Suffer us thus far* (*eāte heōs toutou*). Present active imperative of *eāō*, to allow. But the meaning is not clear. If addressed to Peter and the other disciples it means that they are to suffer this much of violence against Jesus. This is probably the idea. If it is addressed to the crowd, it means that they are to excuse Peter for his rash act. *He touched his ear and healed him* (*hapsamenos tou otiou iasato auton*). Whether Jesus picked up the piece of the ear and put it back is not said. He could have healed the wound without that. This miracle of surgery is given alone by Luke.

52. *As against a robber?* (*hōs epi leistēn;*). They were treating Jesus as if he were a bandit like Barabbas.

53. *But this is your hour* (*all' hautē estin humōn hē hōra*). So Jesus surrenders. The moral value of his atoning sacrifice on the Cross consists in the voluntariness of his death. He makes it clear that they have taken undue advantage of him in this hour of secret prayer and had failed to seize him in public in the temple. But "the power of darkness" (*hē exousia tou skotous*), had its turn. A better day will come. The might, authority of darkness.

54. *Into the high priest's house* (*eis tēn oikian tou archiereōs*). Luke alone mentions "the house." Though it is implied in Mark 14:53 = Matt. 26:57. *Followed* (*ēkolouthei*). Imperfect, was following, as Matt. 26:58 and John 18:15. Curiously Mark 14:54 has the aorist.

55. *When they had kindled a fire* (*periapsantōn pur*). Genitive absolute, first aorist active participle of *periaptō*, an old verb, but here only in the N.T. Kindle around, make a good fire that blazes all over. It was April and cool at night. The servants made the fire. *And had sat down together* (*kai sunkathisantōn*). Genitive absolute again. Note *sun-* (together), all had taken seats around the fire. *Peter sat in the midst of them* (*ekathēto ho Petros mesos autōn*). Imperfect tense, he was sitting, and note *mesos*, nominative predicate adjective with the genitive, like John 1:26, good Greek idiom.

56. *In the light* (*pros to phōs*). Facing (*pros*) the light, for the fire gave light as well as heat. Mark 14:65 has "warming himself in the light," John (18:18, 25) "warming himself." *Looking steadfastly* (*atenisasa*). Favourite word in Luke (4:20, etc.) for gazing steadily at one. *This man also* (*kai houtos*). As if pointing to Peter and talking about him. The other Gospels (Mark 14:67 = Matt. 26:69 = John 18:25) make a direct address to Peter. Both could be true, as she turned to Peter.

57. *I know him not (ouk oida auton)*. Just as Jesus had predicted that he would do (Luke 22:34).

58. *After a little while another (meta brachu heteros)*. Matt. 26:71 makes it after Peter had gone out into the porch and mentions a maid as speaking as does Mark 14:69, while here the "other" *(heteros)* is a man (masculine gender). It is almost impossible to co-ordinate the three denials in the four accounts unless we conceive of several joining in when one led off. This time Peter's denial is very blunt, "I am not."

59. *After the space of about one hour (diastasēs hōsei hōras mias)*. Genitive absolute with second aorist active participle feminine singular of *diistēmi*. This classical verb in the N.T. is used only by Luke (22:59; 24:51; Acts 27:28). It means standing in two or apart, about an hour intervening. *Confidently affirmed (diischurizeto)*. Imperfect middle, he kept affirming strongly. An old verb *(dia, ischurizomai)*, to make oneself strong, to make emphatic declaration. In the N.T. only here and Acts 12:15. *For he is a Galilean (kai gar Galilaios estin)*. Matt. 26:73 makes it plain that it was his speech that gave him away, which see.

60. *I know not what thou sayest (ouk oida ho legeis)*. Each denial tangles Peter more and more. *While he yet spake (eti lalountos autou)*. Genitive absolute. Peter could hear the crowing all right.

61. *The Lord turned (strapheis ho kurios)*. Second aorist passive participle of *strephō*, coming verb. Graphic picture drawn by Luke alone. *Looked upon Peter (eneblepsen tōi Petrōi)*. Ingressive aorist active indicative of *enblepō*, an old and vivid verb, to glance at. *Remembered (hupemnēsthē)*. First aorist passive indicative of *hupomimnēskō*, common verb to remind one of something *(hupo* giving a suggestion or hint). The cock crowing and the look brought swiftly back to Peter's mind the prophecy of Jesus and his sad denials. The mystery is how he had forgotten that warning.

62. *And he went out and wept bitterly (kai exelthōn exō*

eklausen pikrōs). A few old Latin documents omit this verse which is genuine in Matt. 26:75. It may be an insertion here from there, but the evidence for the rejection is too slight. It is the ingressive aorist (*eklausen*), he burst into tears. "Bitter" is a common expression for tears in all languages and in all hearts.

63. *That held* (*hoi sunechontes*). See on 8:45; 19:43 for this verb *sunechō*. Here alone in the N.T. for holding a prisoner (holding together). The servants or soldiers, not the Sanhedrin. *Mocked* (*enepaizon*). Imperfect active, were mocking, inchoative, began to mock, to play like boys. *And beat him* (*derontes*). Present active participle of *derō*, to flay, tan, or hide. Literally, "beating."

64. *Blindfolded* (*perikalupsantes*). First aorist active participle of *perikaluptō*, old verb, to put a veil around. In the N.T. only here and Mark 14:65. See Mark 14:65 and Matt. 26:67f. for further discussion.

65. *Many other things* (*hetera polla*). These are just samples.

66. *As soon as it was day* (*hōs egeneto hēmera*). Mark 15:1 (= Matt. 27:1) has "morning." *The assembly of the people* (*to presbuterion tou laou*). The technical word for "the eldership" (from *presbuteros*, an old man or elder) or group of the elders composing the Sanhedrin. The word occurs in the LXX for the Sanhedrin. In the N.T. occurs only here and Acts 22:5 of the Sanhedrin. In I Tim. 4:14 Paul uses it of the elders in a church (or churches). The Sanhedrin was composed of the elders and scribes and chief priests (Mark 15:1) and all three groups are at this meeting. Luke's language (both chief priests and scribes, *te . . . kai*) seems to apply the word *presbuterion* to the whole Sanhedrin. Sadducees (chief priests) and Pharisees (scribes) were nearly equally represented. *Into their council* (*eis to sunedrion autōn*). The place of the gathering is not given, but Jesus was led into the council chamber.

67. *If thou art the Christ* (*Ei su ei ho Christos*). The Messiah, they mean. The condition is the first class, assuming it to be true. *If I tell you* (*Ean humin eipō*). Condition of the third class, undetermined, but with likelihood of being determined. This is the second appearance of Jesus before the Sanhedrin merely mentioned by Mark 15:1 and Matt. 27:1 who give in detail the first appearance and trial. Luke merely gives this so-called ratification meeting after daybreak to give the appearance of legality to their vote of condemnation already taken (Mark 14:64 = Matt. 26:66). *Ye will not believe* (*ou mē pisteusēte*). Double negative with the aorist subjunctive, strongest possible negative. So as to verse 68.

69. *The Son of man* (*ho huios tou anthrōpou*). Jesus really answers their demand about "the Messiah" by asserting that he is "the Son of man" and they so understand him. He makes claims of equality with God also which they take up.

70. *Art thou the Son of God?* (*Su oun ei ho huios tou theou;*). Note how these three epithets are used as practical equivalents. They ask about "the Messiah." Jesus affirms that he is the Son of Man and will sit at the right hand of the power of God. They take this to be a claim to be the Son of God (both humanity and deity). Jesus accepts the challenge and admits that he claims to be all three (Messiah, the Son of man, the Son of God). *Ye say* (*Humeis legete*). Just a Greek idiom for "Yes" (compare "I am" in Mark 14:62 with "Thou has said" in Matt. 26:64).

71. *For we ourselves have heard* (*autoi gar ēkousamen*). They were right if Jesus is not what he claimed to be. They were eternally wrong for he is the Christ, the Son of man, the Son of God. They made their choice and must face Christ as Judge.

CHAPTER XXIII

1. *The whole company* (*hapan to plēthos*). All but Nicodemus and Joseph of Arimathea who were probably not invited to this meeting.

2. *Began to accuse* (*ērxanto katēgorein*). They went at it and kept it up. Luke mentions three, but neither of them includes their real reason nor do they mention their own condemnation of Jesus. They had indulged their hatred in doing it, but they no longer have the power of life and death. Hence they say nothing to Pilate of that. *We found* (*heuramen*). Second aorist active indicative with first aorist vowel *a*. Probably they mean that they had caught Jesus in the act of doing these things (*in flagrante delicto*) rather than discovery by formal trial. *Perverting our nation* (*diastrephonta to ethnos hēmōn*). Present active participle of *diastrephō*, old verb to turn this way and that, distort, disturb. In the N.T. only here and Acts 13:10. The Sanhedrin imply that the great popularity of Jesus was seditious. *Forbidding to give tribute to Caesar*, (*kōluonta phorous kaisari didonai*). Note object infinitive *didonai* after the participle *kōluonta*. Literally, hindering giving tribute to Caesar. This was a flat untruth. Their bright young students had tried desperately to get Jesus to say this very thing, but they had failed utterly (Luke 20:25). *Saying that he himself is Christ a king* (*legonta hauton Christon basilea einai*). Note the indirect discourse here after the participle *legonta* with the accusative (*hauton* where *auton* could have been used), and the infinitive. This charge is true, but not in the sense meant by them. Jesus did claim to be the Christ and the king of the kingdom of God. But the Sanhedrin wanted Pilate to think that he set himself up as a rival to Caesar.

Pilate would understand little from the word "Christ," but "King" was a different matter. He was compelled to take notice of this charge else he himself would be accused to Caesar of winking at such a claim by Jesus.

3. *Thou sayest (su legeis).* A real affirmative as in 22:70. The Gospels all give Pilate's question about Jesus asking of the Jews in precisely the same words (Mark 15:2; Matt. 27:11; Luke 23:3; John 18:33).

4. *The multitude (tous ochlous).* The first mention of them. It is now after daybreak. The procession of the Sanhedrin would draw a crowd (Plummer) and some may have come to ask for the release of a prisoner (Mark 15:8). There was need of haste if the condemnation went through before friends of Jesus came. *I find no fault (ouden heuriskō aition).* In the N.T. Luke alone uses this old adjective *aitios* (Luke 23:4, 14, 22; Acts 19:40) except Heb. 5:9. It means one who is the author, the cause of or responsible for anything. Luke does not give the explanation of this sudden decision of Pilate that Jesus is innocent. Evidently he held a careful examination before he delivered his judgment on the case. That conversation is given in John 18:33–38. Pilate took Jesus inside the palace from the upper gallery (verse 33) and then came out and rendered his decision to the Sanhedrin (verse 38) who would not go into the palace of Pilate (John 18:28).

5. *But they were the more urgent (hoi de epischuon).* Imperfect active of *epischuō*, to give added (*epi*) strength (*ischuō*). And they kept insisting. Evidently Pilate had taken the thing too lightly. *He stirred up the people (anaseiei ton laon).* This compound is rare, though old (Thucydides), to shake up (back and forth). This is a more vigorous repetition of the first charge (verse 2, "perverting our nation"). *Beginning from Galilee (arxamenos apo tēs Galilaias).* These very words occur in the address of Peter to the group in the house of Cornelius (Acts 10:37). The idiomatic use of

arxamenos appears also in Acts 1:22. Galilee (Grote) **was** the mother of seditious men (see Josephus).

6. *A Galilean* (*Galilaios*). If so, here was a way out for Herod without going back on his own decision.

7. *When he knew* (*epignous*). Second aorist active participle from *epiginōskō*, having gained full (*epi*, added knowledge). *Of Herod's jurisdiction* (*ek tēs exousias Hērōidou*). Herod was naturally jealous of any encroachment by Pilate, the Roman Procurator of Judea. So here was a chance to respect the prerogative (*exousia*) of Herod and get rid of this troublesome case also. *Sent him up* (*anepempsen*). First aorist active indicative of *anapempō*. This common verb is used of sending back as in verse 11 or of sending up to a higher court as of Paul to Caesar (Acts 25:21). *Who himself also was* (*onta kai auton*). Being also himself in Jerusalem. Present active participle of *eimi*.

8. *Was exceeding glad* (*echarē lian*). Second aorist passive indicative of *chairō*, ingressive aorist, became glad. *Of a long time* (*ex hikanōn chronōn*). For this idiom see 8:27; 20:9; Acts 8:11). *He hoped* (*ēlpizen*). Imperfect active. He was still hoping. He had long ago gotten over his fright that Jesus was John the Baptist come to life again (9:7-9). *Done* (*ginomenon*). Present middle participle. He wanted to see a miracle happening like a stunt of a sleight-of-hand performer.

9. *He questioned* (*epērōtā*). Imperfect active, kept on questioning. *In many words* (*en logois hikanois*). Same use of *hikanos* as in verse 8.

10. *Stood* (*histēkeisan*). Second perfect active intransitive of *histēmi* with sense of imperfect. They stood by while Herod quizzed Jesus and when he refused to answer, they broke loose with their accusations like a pack of hounds with full voice (*eutonōs*, adverb from adjective *eutonos*, from *eu*, well, and *teinō*, to stretch, well tuned). Old word, but in the N.T. only here and Acts 18:28.

11. *Set him at nought (exouthenēsas).* First aorist active participle from *exoutheneō*, to count as nothing, to treat with utter contempt, as zero. *Arraying him in gorgeous apparel (peribalōn esthēta lampran).* Second aorist active participle of *periballō*, to fling around one. *Lampran* is brilliant, shining as in James 2:2, so different from the modest dress of the Master. This was part of the shame.

12. *For before they were at enmity between themselves (proüpērchon gar en echthrāi ontes pros heautous).* A periphrastic imperfect of the double compound *proüperchō*, an old verb, to exist (*huparchō*) previously (*pro-*), here alone in the N.T., with *ontes* (participle of *eimi*) added.

13. *Called together (sunkalesamenos).* First aorist middle participle (to himself). Pilate included "the people" in the hope that Jesus might have some friends among them.

14. *As one that perverteth the people (hōs apostrephonta ton laon).* Pilate here condenses the three charges in verse 2 into one (Plummer). He uses a more common compound of *strephō* here, *apostrephō*, to turn away from, to seduce, to mislead, whereas *diastrephō* in verse 2 has more the notion of disturbing (turning this way and that). Note the use of *hōs* with the particle, the alleged reason. Pilate understands the charge against Jesus to be that he is a revolutionary agitator and a dangerous rival to Caesar, treason in plain words. *Having examined him before you (enōpion hūmōn anakrinas).* Right before your eyes I have given him a careful examination (*ana*) up and down, *krinō*, to judge, sift. Old and common verb in the general sense and in the forensic sense as here and which Luke alone has in the N.T. (Luke 23:14; 4:9; 12:19; 28:18; Acts 24:8) except I Cor. 9:3. *Whereof (hōn).* Attraction of the relative *ha* to the case (genitive) of the unexpressed antecedent *toutōn*.

15. *No nor yet (all' oude).* But not even. *Hath been done by him (estin pepragmenon autōi).* Periphrastic perfect passive indicative of *prassō*, common verb, to do. The case of *autōi* can be regarded as either the dative or the instrumental (Robertson, *Grammar*, pp. 534, 542).

16. *Chastise* (*paideusas*). First aorist active participle of *paideuō*, to train a child (*pais*), and then, as a part of the training, punishment. Our English word chasten is from the Latin *castus*, pure, chaste, and means to purify (cf. Heb. 12: 6f.). Perhaps Pilate may have split a hair over the word as Wycliff puts it: "I shall deliver him amended." But, if Jesus was innocent, Pilate had no doubt to "chastise" him to satisfy a mob. Verse 17 is omitted by Westcott and Hort as from Mark 15:6 = Matt. 27:15.

18. *All together* (*panplēthei*). An adverb from the adjective *panplēthēs*, all together. Used by Dio Cassius. Only here in the N.T. *Away* (*aire*). Present active imperative, Take him on away and keep him away as in Acts 21:36; 22:22, of Paul. But *release* (*apoluson*) is first aorist active imperative, do it now and at once.

19. *Insurrection* (*stasin*). An old word for sedition, standing off, the very charge made against Jesus (and untrue). If Jesus had raised insurrection against Caesar, these accusers would have rallied to his standard. *And for murder* (*kai phonon*). They cared nought for this. In fact, the murderer was counted a hero like bandits and gangsters today with some sentimentalists. *Was cast* (*ēn blētheis*). Periphrastic aorist passive indicative of *ballō*, a quite unusual form.

21. *But they shouted* (*hoi de epephōnoun*). Imperfect active of *epiphōneō*, to call to. Old verb and a verb pertinent here. They kept on yelling. *Crucify, crucify* (*staurou, staurou*). Present active imperative. Go on with the crucifixion. Mark 15:13 has *staurōson* (first aorist active imperative), do it now and be done with it. No doubt some shouted one form, some another.

22. *Why, what evil?* (*Ti gar kakon;*). Note this use of *gar* (explanatory and argumentative combined).

23. *But they were instant* (*hoi de epekeinto*). Imperfect middle of *epikeimai*, an old verb for the rush and swirl of a tempest. *With loud voices* (*phōnais megalais*). Instrumental case. Poor Pilate was overwhelmed by this tornado. *Prevailed* (*katischuon*). Imperfect active of *katischuō* (see Matt. 16:18; Luke 21:36). The tempest Pilate had invited (23:13).

24. *Gave sentence* (*epekrinen*). Pronounced the final sentence. The usual verb for the final decision. Only here in the N.T.

25. *Whom they asked for* (*hon ēitounto*). Imperfect middle, for whom they had been asking for themselves. Luke repeats that Barabbas was in prison "for insurrection and murder." *To their will* (*tōi thelēmati autōn*). This is mob law by the judge who surrenders his own power and justice to the clamour of the crowd.

26. *They laid hold* (*epilabomenoi*). Second aorist middle participle of the common verb *epilambanō*. The soldiers had no scruples about taking hold of any one of themselves (middle voice). Mark 15:21 and Luke 27:32 use the technical word for this process *aggareuō*, which see for discussion and also about Cyrene. *Laid on him* (*epethēkan*). K first aorist of *epitithēmi*. *To bear it* (*pherein*). Present infinitive, to go on bearing.

27. *Followed* (*ēkolouthei*). Imperfect active, was following. Verses 27 to 32 are peculiar to Luke. *Bewailed* (*ekoptonto*). Imperfect middle of *koptō*, to cut, smite, old and common verb. Direct middle, they were smiting themselves on the breast. "In the Gospels there is no instance of a woman being hostile to Christ" (Plummer). Luke's Gospel is appropriately called the Gospel of Womanhood (1:39–56; 2:36–38; 7:11–15; 37–50; 8:1–3; 10:38–42; 11:27; 13:11–16). *Lamented* (*ethrēnoun*). Imperfect active of *thrēneō*, old verb from *threomai*, to cry aloud, lament.

28. *Turning* (*strapheis*). Luke is fond of this second aorist passive participle of *strephō* (7:9, 44, 55; 10:23). If he had

been still carrying the Cross, he could not have made this dramatic gesture. *Weep not* (*mē klaiete*). Present active imperative with *mē*, Stop weeping.

29. *Blessed* (*makariai*). A beatitude to the barren, the opposite of the hopes of Jewish mothers. Childless women are commiserated (1:25, 36). *To the hills* (*tois bounois*). A Cyrenaic word. In the N.T. only here and 3:5. Quotation from Hosea 10:8.

31. *In the green tree* (*en hugrōi xulōi*). Green wood is hard to burn and so is used for the innocent. *In the dry* (*en tōi xērōi*). Dry wood kindles easily and is a symbol for the guilty. This common proverb has various applications. Here the point is that if they can put Jesus to death, being who he is, what will happen to Jerusalem when its day of judgment comes? *What shall be done* (*ti genētai*). Deliberative subjunctive.

32. *Were led* (*ēgonto*). Imperfect passive of *agō*, were being led. *Malefactors* (*kakourgoi*). Evil (*kakon*), doers (work, *ergon*). Old word, but in the N.T. only in this passage (32, 33, 39) and II Tim. 2:9. Luke does not call them "robbers" like Mark 15:27 = Matt. 27:38, 44. *To be put to death* (*anairethēnai*). First aorist passive infinitive of *anaireō*, old verb, to take up, to take away, to kill.

33. *The skull* (*to kranion*). Probably because it looked like a skull. See on Matt. 27:33 =Mark 15:22. *There they crucified him* (*ekei estaurōsan*). There between the two robbers and on the very cross on which Barabbas, the leader of the robber band, was to have been crucified. *One* (*hon men*), *the other* (*hon de*). Common idiom of contrast with this old demonstrative *hos* and *men* and *de*.

34. *Father forgive them* (*Pater, aphes autois*). Second aorist active imperative of *aphiēmi*, with dative case. Some of the oldest and best documents do not contain this verse, and yet, while it is not certain that it is a part of Luke's Gospel, it is certain that Jesus spoke these words, for they are utterly

unlike any one else. Jesus evidently is praying for the Roman soldiers, who were only obeying, but not for the Sanhedrin. *Cast lots* (*ebalon klēron*). Second aorist active indicative of *ballō*. See Mark 15:24; Matt. 27:35. John 19:23f.
shows how the lot was cast for the seamless garment, the
four soldiers dividing the other garments.

35. *The people stood beholding* (*histēkei*). Past perfect
active of *histēmi*, intransitive and like imperfect. A graphic
picture of the dazed multitude, some of whom may have been
in the Triumphal Entry on Sunday morning. *Scoffed*
(*exemuktērizon*). Imperfect active, perhaps inchoative,
began to turn up (out, *ex*) at the dying Christ. The language
comes from Psalm 22:7. *The Christ of God* (*ho Christos tou
theou*). He had claimed to be just this (22:67, 70). The
sarcastic sneer (he saved others; let him save others, for himself he cannot save) is in Mark 15:31; Matt. 27:42. Luke
alone gives the contemptuous use of *houtos* (this fellow) and
the fling in "the elect" (*ho eklektos*). These rulers were
having their day at last.

36. *Mocked* (*enepaixan*). Even the soldiers yielded to the
spell and acted like boys in their jeers. Aorist tense here and
different verb also from that used of the rulers. They were
not so bitter and persistent.

37. *If* (*ei*). Condition of the first class as is text in verse
35 used by the rulers. The soldiers pick out "the king of the
Jews" as the point of their sneer, the point on which Jesus
was condemned. But both soldiers and rulers fail to understand that Jesus could not save himself if he was to save
others.

38. *A superscription* (*epigraphē*). Mark 15:26 has "the
superscription of his accusation" Matt. 27:37, "his accusation," John 19:19 "a title." But they all refer to the charge
written at the top on the cross giving, as was the custom,
the accusation on which the criminal was condemned, with
his name and residence. Put all the reports together and we

have: This is Jesus of Nazareth the King of the Jews. This full title appeared in Latin for law, in Aramaic for the Jews, in Greek for everybody (John 19:20).

39. *Railed* (*eblasphēmei*). Imperfect active, implying that he kept it up. His question formally calls for an affirma-- tive answer (*ouchi*), but the ridicule is in his own answer: "Save thyself and us." It was on a level with an effort to break prison. Luke alone gives this incident (39–43), though Mark 15:32 and Matt 27:44 allude to it.

40. *Rebuking* (*epitimōn*). From what Mark and Matthew say both robbers sneered at Jesus at first, but this one came to himself and turned on his fellow robber in a rage. *Dost thou not even fear God?* (*Oude phobēi ton theon;*). *Oude* here goes with the verb. *Phobēi* (second person singular present indicative middle of *phobeomai*. Both of you will soon appear before God. Jesus has nothing to answer for and you have added this to your other sins.

41. *Nothing amiss* (*ouden atopon*). Nothing out of place (*a* privative, *topos*, place). Old word, three times in the N.T. (Luke 23:44; Acts 28:6; II Thess. 3:2). This can only mean that this robber accepts the claims of Jesus to be true. He is dying for claiming to be Messiah, as he is.

42. *In thy kingdom* (*eis tēn basileian sou*, text of Westcott and Hort or *en tei basileiāi sou*, margin). Probably no difference in sense is to be found, for *eis* and *en* are essentially the same preposition. He refers to the Messianic rule of Jesus and begs that Jesus will remember him. It is not clear whether he hopes for immediate blessing or only at the judgment.

43. *Today shalt thou be with me in Paradise* (*Sēmeron met' emou esēi en tōi paradeisōi*). However crude may have been the robber's Messianic ideas Jesus clears the path for him. He promises him immediate and conscious fellowship after death with Christ in Paradise which is a Persian word and is used here not for any supposed intermediate state, but the

very bliss of heaven itself. This Persian word was used for an enclosed park or pleasure ground (so Xenophon). The word occurs in two other passages in the N.T. (II Cor. 12:4; Rev. 2:7), in both of which the reference is plainly to heaven. Some Jews did use the word for the abode of the pious dead till the resurrection, interpreting "Abraham's bosom" (Luke 16:22f.) in this sense also. But the evidence for such an intermediate state is too weak to warrant belief in it.

45. *The sun's light failing* (*tou hēliou ekleipontos*). Genitive absolute of the present active participle of *ekleipō*, an old verb, to leave out, omit, pass by, to fail, to die. The word was used also of the eclipse of the sun or moon. But this was impossible at this time because the moon was full at the passover. Hence many documents change this correct text to "the sun was darkened" (*eskotisthē ho hēlios*) to obviate the difficulty about the technical eclipse. But the sun can be darkened in other ways. In a London fog at noon the street lights are often turned on. The Revised Version translates it correctly, "the sun's light failing." Leave the darkness unexplained. *In the midst* (*meson*). In the middle. Mark 15:38 and Matt. 27:51 have "in two" (*eis duo*).

46. *Father* (*Pater*). Jesus dies with the words of Psalm 31:5 on his lips. *Gave up the ghost* (*exepneusen*). First aorist active indicative of *ekpneō*, to breathe out, to expire, old word, but in the N.T. only here and Mark 15:37, 39. There is no special reason for retaining "ghost" in the English as both Matt. 27:50 (yielded up his spirit, *aphēken to pneuma*) and John 19:30 (gave up his spirit, *paredōken to pneuma*) use *pneuma* which is the root of *ekpneō*, the verb in Mark and Luke.

47. *Glorified* (*edoxazen*). Imperfect active. Began to glorify (inchoative) or kept on glorifying.

48. *Certainly* (*ontōs*). Really, old adverb from the participle *ōn* from *eimi*, to be. Used also in 24:34 of the resurrection of Jesus. *A righteous man* (*dikaios*). Mark 15:39

(Matt. 27:54) which see, represents the centurion as saying *theou huios* (God's Son) which may mean to him little more than "righteous man." *That came together (sunparagenomenoi)*. Double compound (*sun*, together, *para*, along), that came along together. *To this sight (epi tēn theōrian tautēn)*. This spectacle (*theōrian* from *theōreō*, verse 35). *Returned (hupestrephon)*. Imperfect active of *hupostrephō*. See them slowly wending their way back to the city from this Tragedy of the Ages which they had witnessed in awe.

49. *Stood afar off (histēkeisan apo makrothen)*. Same verb as in verse 35. Melancholy picture of the inner circle of the acquaintances of Jesus and the faithful band of women from Galilee. *Seeing these things (horōsai tauta)*. And helpless either to prevent them or to understand them. They could only stand and look with blinded eyes.

51. *He had not consented to their counsel and deed (houtos ouk ēn sunkatatetheimenos tēi boulēi kai tēi praxei autōn)*. This parenthesis is given by Luke alone and explains that, though a councillor (*bouleutēs*, Mark 5:43) he had not agreed to the vote of the Sanhedrin. It is fairly certain that both Joseph and Nicodemus were suspected of sympathy with Jesus and so were not invited to the trial of Jesus. *Was looking for (prosedecheto)*. Imperfect middle. Mark 15:43 has the periphrastic imperfect (*ēn prosdechomenos*).

52. *Asked for (ēitēsato)*. First aorist middle (indirect) indicative as in Mark 15:43 = Matt. 27:58. The middle voice shows that Joseph of Arimathea asked the body of Jesus as a personal favour.

53. *Took it down (kathelōn)*. Second aorist active participle of *kathaireō* as in Mark 15:46. *Wrapped (enetulixen)*, as in Matt. 27:59 where Mark 15:46 has *eneilēsen* (wound), which see. John 19:40 has "bound" (*edēsan*). See Matt. and Mark also for the linen cloth (*sindoni*). *Hewn in stone (laxeutōi)*. From *laxeuō* (*las*, a stone, *xeō*, to polish). In the LXX and here only in the N.T. Nowhere else so far as

known. See the usual Greek verb *latomeō* in Mark 15:46 = Matt. 27:60. *Where never man had yet lain (hou ouk ēn oudeis oupō keimenos)*. Triple negative and periphrastic past perfect passive in sense (*keimai*), though periphrastic imperfect passive in form. Same item in John 19:40 who uses *ēn tetheimenos* (periphrastic past perfect passive in form).

54. *The day of the Preparation (hēmera paraskeuēs)*. The technical Jewish phrase for the day before the sabbath for which see discussion on Matt. 27:62. *Drew on (epephōsken)*. Imperfect active, began to dawn or give light. However, it was sundown, not sunrise when the Jewish sabbath (twenty-four-hour day) began. The confusion is to us, not to the Jews or the readers of the Greek New Testament. Luke is not speaking of the twelve-hour day which began with sunrise, but the twenty-four-hour day which began with sunset.

55. *Had come with him (ēsan sunelēluthuiai)*. Periphrastic past perfect active of *sunerchomai*. *Followed after (katakolouthēsasai)*. Aorist active participle of *katakoloutheō*, an old verb, but in the N.T. only here and Acts 16:17. It is possible that they followed after Joseph and Nicodemus so that they "beheld the tomb," (*etheasanto to mnēmeion*), and also "how his body was laid" (*hōs etethē to sōma autou*). First aorist passive indicative of *tithēmi*. They may in fact, have witnessed the silent burial from a distance. The Syriac Sinaitic and the Syriac Curetonian give it thus: "and the women, who came with Him from Galilee went to the sepulchre in their footsteps, and saw the body when they had brought it in there." At any rate the women saw "that" and "how" the body of Jesus was laid in this new tomb of Joseph in the rocks.

56. *On the sabbath they rested (to sabbaton hēsuchasan)*. They returned and prepared spices before the sabbath began. Then they rested all during the sabbath (accusative of extent of time, *to sabbaton*).

CHAPTER XXIV

1. *At early dawn* (*orthrou batheos*). Genitive of time. Literally, at deep dawn. The adjective *bathus* (deep) was often used of time. This very idiom occurs in Aristophanes, Plato, et cetera. John 20:1 adds "while it was yet dark." That is, when they started, for the sun was risen when they arrived (Mark 16:2). *Which they had prepared* (*ha hētoimasan*). Mark 16:1 notes that they bought other spices after the sabbath was over besides those which they already had (Luke 23:56).

2. *Rolled away* (*apokekulismenon*). Perfect passive participle of *apokuliō*, late verb and in the N.T. only in this context (Mark 16:3; Matt. 28:2) while John 20:1 has *ērmenon* (taken away).

3. *Of the Lord Jesus* (*tou kuriou Iēsou*). The Western family of documents does not have these words and Westcott and Hort bracket them as Western non-interpolations. There are numerous instances of this shorter Western text in this chapter. For a discussion of the subject see my *Introduction to the Textual Criticism of the New Testament*, pp. 225–237. This precise combination (the Lord Jesus) is common in the Acts, but nowhere else in the Gospels.

4. *While they were perplexed thereabout* (*en tōi aporeisthai autas peri toutou*). Luke's common Hebraistic idiom, *en* with the articular infinitive (present passive *aporeisthai* from *aporeō*, to lose one's way) and the accusative of general reference. *Two men* (*andres duo*). Men, not women. Mark 16:5 speaks of a young man (*neaniskon*) while Matt. 28:5 has "an angel." We need not try to reconcile these varying accounts which agree in the main thing. The angel looked like a man and some remembered two. In verse 23 Cleopas and

his companion call them "angels." *Stood by* (*epestēsan*).
Second aorist active indicative of *ephistēmi*. This common
verb usually means to step up suddenly, to burst upon one.
In dazzling apparel (*en esthēti astraptousēi*). This is the correct text. This common simplex verb occurs only twice in
the N.T., here and Luke 17:24 (the Transfiguration). It has
the same root as *astrapē* (lightning). The "men" had the
garments of "angels."

5. *As they were affrighted* (*emphobōn genomenōn autōn*).
Genitive absolute with second aorist middle of *ginomai*, to
become. Hence, *when they became affrighted*. They had
utterly forgotten the prediction of Jesus that he would rise
on the third day.

6. *He is not here, but is risen* (*ouk estin hōde, alla ēgerthē*).
Another Western non-interpolation according to Westcott
and Hort. The words are genuine at any rate in Mark 16:6;
Matt. 28:7. *The third day rise again* (*tēi tritēi hēmerāi anastēnai*). See 9:22; 18:32, 33 where Jesus plainly foretold this
fact. And yet they had forgotten it, for it ran counter to all
their ideas and hopes.

9. *From the tomb* (*apo tou mnēmeiou*). Some documents
omit these words. This word for tomb is like our "memorial" from *mimnēskō*, to remind. *Told* (*apēggeilan*). It
was a wonderful proclamation. Luke does not separate the
story of Mary Magdalene from that of the other women as
John does (20:2–18).

11. *As idle talk* (*hōs lēros*). Old word for nonsense, only
here in the N.T. Medical writers used it for the wild talk
of those in delirium or hysteria. *Disbelieved* (*ēpistoun*). Imperfect active of *apisteō*, old verb from *apistos*, without confidence or faith in. They kept on distrusting the story of the
women.

12. This entire verse is a Western non-interpolation.
This incident is given in complete form in John 18:2–10
and most of the words in this verse are there also. It is of

a piece with many items in this chapter about which it is not easy to reach a final conclusion. *Stooping and looking in (parakupsas)*. First aorist active participle of *parakuptō*, to stoop besides and peer into. Old verb used also in John 20:5, 11; James 1:25; I Pet. 1:12. *By themselves (mona)*. Without the body. *To his home (pros hauton)*. Literally, "to himself."

13. *Were going (ēsan poreuomenoi)*. Periphrastic imperfect middle of *poreuomai*. *Sixty stadia (stadious hexēkonta)*. About seven miles.

14. *They communed (hōmiloun)*. Imperfect active of *homileō*, old and common verb (from *homilos*, in company with). In the N.T. only here (and verse 15) and Acts 20:11; 24:26. Our word homiletics is derived from this word for preaching was at first largely conversational in style and not declamatory.

15. *While they communed and questioned together (en tōi homilein autous kai sunzētein)*. Same idiom as in verse 14, which see. Note *sunzētein;* each questioned the other. *Jesus himself (autos Iēsous)*. In actual person. *Went with them (suneporeueto autois)*. Imperfect middle, was going along with them.

16. *Were holden that they should not know him (ekratounto tou mē epignōnai auton)*. Imperfect passive of *krateō*, continued being held, with the ablative case of the articular infinitive, "from recognizing him," from knowing him fully (*epi-gnōnai*, ingressive aorist of *epiginōsko*). The *mē* is a redundant negative after the negative idea in *ekratounto*.

17. *That you have with another (hous antiballete pros allēlous)*. *Anti-ballō* is an old verb and means to throw in turn, back and forth like a ball, from one to another, a beautiful picture of conversation as a game of words. Only here in the N.T. *They stood still (estathēsan)*. First aorist passive of *histēmi*, intransitive. They stopped. *Looking sad (skuthrōpoi)*. This is the correct text. It is an old adjective from

skuthros, gloomy and *ops,* countenance. Only here in the N.T.

18. *Dost thou alone sojourn?* (*su monos paroikeis;*). *Monos* is predicate adjective. "Hast thou been dwelling alone (all by thyself)?" *And not know?* (*kai ouk egnōs;*). Second aorist active indicative and difficult to put into English as the aorist often is. The verb *paroikeō* means to dwell beside one, then as a stranger like *paroikoi* (Eph. 2:19). In Jerusalem everybody was talking about Jesus.

21. *But we hoped* (*hēmeis de ēlpizomen*). Imperfect active, we were hoping. Note emphasis in *hēmeis* (we). *Redeem* (*lutrousthai*). From the bondage of Rome, no doubt. *Yea and beside all this* (*alla ge kai sun pāsin toutois*). Particles pile up to express their emotions. *Yea* (*alla* here affirmative, as in verse 22, not adversative) at least (*ge*) also (*kai*) together with all these things (*sun pāsin toutois*). Like Pelion on Ossa with them in their perplexity. *Now the third day* (*tritēn tautēn hēmeran agei*). A difficult idiom for the English. "One is keeping this a third day." And he is still dead and we are still without hope.

22. *Amazed us* (*exestēsan hēmas*). First aorist active (transitive) indicative with accusative *hēmas* of *existēmi.* The second aorist active is intransitive. *Early* (*orthrinai*). A poetic and late form for *orthrios.* In the N.T. only here and Rev. 24:22. Predicate adjective agreeing with the women.

23. *Had seen* (*heōrakenai*). Perfect active infinitive in indirect assertion after *legousai.* Same construction for *zēin* after *legousin.* But all this was too indirect and uncertain (women and angels) for Cleopas and his companion.

25. *Foolish men* (*anoētoi*). Literally without sense (*nous*), not understanding. Common word. *Slow of heart* (*bradeis tēi kardiāi*). Slow in heart (locative case). Old word for one dull, slow to comprehend or to act. *All that* (*pāsin hois*). Relative attracted from the accusative *ha* to the

case of the antecedent *pāsin* (dative). They could only understand part of the prophecies, not all.

26. *Behooved it not? (ouchi edei;).* Was it not necessary? The very things about the death of Jesus that disturbed them so were the strongest proof that he was the Messiah of the Old Testament.

27. *Interpreted (diērmēneusen).* First aorist active (constative aorist) indicative of *diermēneuō* (Margin has the imperfect *diērmēneuen*), intensive compound *(dia)* of *hermēneuō*, the old verb to interpret from *hermēneus*, interpreter, and that from *Hermēs*, the messenger of the gods as the people of Lystra took Paul to be (Acts 14:12). But what wonderful exegesis the two disciples were now hearing! *Concerning himself (peri heauton).* Jesus found himself in the Old Testament, a thing that some modern scholars do not seem able to do.

28. *Made as though (prosepoiēsato).* First aorist active middle (Some MSS. have *prosepoieito* imperfect) indicative of *prospoieō*, old verb to conform oneself to, to pretend. Only here in the N.T. Of course he would have gone on if the disciples had not urged him to stay.

29. *Constrained (parebiasanto).* Strong verb *parabiazomai*, to compel by use of force (Polybius and LXX). In the N.T. only here and Acts 16:15. It was here compulsion of courteous words. *Is far spent (kekliken).* Perfect active indicative of *klinō*. The day "has turned" toward setting.

30. *When he had sat down (en tōi kataklithēnai auton).* Luke's common idiom as in verses 4 and 15. Note first aorist passive infinitive (on the reclining as to him). *Gave (epedidou).* Imperfect, inchoative idea, began to give to them, in contrast with the preceding aorist (punctiliar) participles.

31. *Were opened (diēnoichthēsan).* Ingressive first aorist passive indicative of *dianoigō*. *Knew (epegnōsan).* Effective first aorist active indicative fully recognized him. Same word in verse 16. *Vanished (aphantos egeneto).* Became

invisible or unmanifested. *Aphantos* from *a* privative and *phainomai*, to appear. Old word, only here in the N.T.

32. *Was not our heart burning?* (*Ouchi hē kardia hemōn kaiomenē ēn;*). Periphrastic imperfect middle. *Spake* (*elalei*). Imperfect active, was speaking. This common verb *laleō* is onomatopoetic, to utter a sound, *la-la* and was used of birds, children chattering, and then for conversation, for preaching, for any public speech. *Opened* (*diēnoigen*). Imperfect active indicative of the same verb used of the eyes in verse 31.

33. *That very hour* (*autēi tēi hōrāi*). Locative case and common Lukan idiom, at the hour itself. They could not wait. *Gathered* (*ēthroismenous*). Perfect passive participle of *athroizō*, old verb from *athroos* (copulative *a* and *throos*, crowd). Only here in the N.T.

34. *Saying* (*legontas*). Accusative present active participle agreeing with "the eleven and those with them" in verse 33. *Indeed* (*ontōs*). Really, because "he has appeared to Simon" (*ōpthē Simōni*). First aorist passive indicative of *horaō*. This is the crucial evidence that turned the scales with the disciples and explains "indeed." Paul also mentions it (I Cor. 15:5).

35. *Rehearsed* (*exēgounto*). Imperfect middle indicative of *exēgeomai*, verb to lead out, to rehearse. Our word exegesis comes from this verb. Their story was now confirmatory, not revolutionary. The women were right then after all. *Of them* (*autois*). To them, dative case. They did not recognize Jesus in his exegesis, but did in the breaking of bread. One is reminded of that saying in the *Logia of Jesus:* "Raise the stone and there thou shalt find me, cleave the wood and there am I."

36. *He himself stood* (*autos estē*). He himself stepped and stood. Some documents do not have "Peace be unto you."

37. *Terrified* (*ptoēthentes*). First aorist passive participle of *ptoeō*, old verb and in the N.T. only here and Luke 21:9

which see. *Affrighted* (*emphoboi genomenoi*). Late adjective from *en* and *phobos* (fear). Both these terms of fear are strong. *Supposed* (*edokoun*). Imperfect active of *dokeō*, kept on thinking so.

38. *Why are ye troubled?* (*ti tetaragmenoi este;*). Periphrastic perfect passive indicative of *tarassō*, old verb, to agitate, to stir up, to get excited.

39. *Myself* (*autos*). Jesus is patient with his proof. They were convinced before he came into the room, but that psychological shock had unnerved them all. *Handle* (*psēlaphēsate*). This very word is used in I John 1:1 as proof of the actual human body of Jesus. It is an old verb for touching with the hand. *Flesh and bones* (*sarka kai ostea*). At least this proves that he is not just a ghost and that Jesus had a real human body against the Docetic Gnostics who denied it. But clearly we are not to understand that our resurrection bodies will have "flesh and bones." Jesus was in a transition state and had not yet been glorified. The mystery remains unsolved, but it was proof to the disciples of the identity of the Risen Christ with Jesus of Nazareth.

40. Another Weston non-interpolation according to Westcott and Hort. It is genuine in John 20:20.

41. *Disbelieved for joy* (*apistountōn autōn apo tēs charas*). Genitive absolute and a quite understandable attitude. They were slowly reconvinced, but it was after all too good to be true. *Anything to eat* (*brōsimon*). Only here in the N.T., though an old word from *bibrōskō*, to eat.

42. *A piece of broiled fish* (*ichthuos optou meros*). *Optos* is a verbal from *optaō*, to cook, to roast, to broil. Common word, but only here in the N.T. The best old documents omit "and a honeycomb" (*kai apo melissiou kēriou*).

44. *While I was yet with you* (*eti ōn sun humin*). Literally, *Being yet with you*. The participle *ōn* takes the time of the principal verb.

45. *Opened he their mind* (*diēnoixen autōn ton noun*). The

same verb as that in verses 31 and 32 about the eyes and the Scriptures. Jesus had all these years been trying to open their minds that they might understand the Scriptures about the Messiah and now at last he makes one more effort in the light of the Cross and the Resurrection. They can now see better the will and way of God, but they will still need the power of the Holy Spirit before they will fully know the mind of Christ.

46. *It is written* (*gegraptai*). Perfect passive indicative of *graphō*, to write, the usual phrase for quoting Scripture. Jesus now finds in the Old Testament his suffering, his resurrection, and the preaching of repentance and forgiveness of sins to all nations. Note the infinitives *pathein, anastēnai, kēruchthēnai*.

47. *Beginning* (*arxamenoi*). Aorist middle participle of *archō*, but the nominative plural with no syntactical connection (an anacoluthon).

49. *Until ye be clothed* (*heōs hou endusēsthe*). First aorist middle subjunctive of *enduō* or *endunō*. It is an old verb for putting on a garment. It is here the indirect middle, put on yourselves power from on high as a garment. They are to wait till this experience comes to them. This is "the promise of the Father." It is an old metaphor in Homer, Aristophanes, Plutarch, and Paul uses it often.

50. *Over against Bethany* (*heōs pros Bēthanian*). That is on Olivet. On this blessed spot near where he had delivered the great Eschatological Discourse he could see Bethany and Jerusalem.

51. *He parted from them* (*diestē ap' autōn*). Second aorist active (intransitive) indicative of *diistēmi*. He stood apart (*dia*) and he was gone. Some manuscripts do not have the words "and was carried into heaven." But we know that Jesus was taken up into heaven on a cloud (Acts 1:9).

52. *Worshipped him* (*proskunēsantes auton*). Here again we have one of Westcott and Hort's Western non-interpola-

tions that may be genuine or not. *With great joy (meta charas megalēs).* Now that the Ascension has come they are no longer in despair. Joy becomes the note of victory as it is today. No other note can win victories for Christ. The bells rang in heaven to greet the return of Jesus there, but he set the carillon of joy to ringing on earth in human hearts in all lands and for all time.